Reading the Bible
as a Postexilic Biblical Author Read

"Dr. Huu-Thien's study of the Chronicler's interpretative method—and connecting this to post-colonial and dalit readings of scripture—is a clear and fascinating study. His book is of value not only to Asian readers, exposing flaws in both post-colonial and dalit readings, but also for Western readers who will benefit significantly from this study and its approach. I highly commend this book."

—**Paul Barker**, bishop, Anglican Diocese of Melbourne

"Huu-Thien brings a bold and innovative perspective to biblical studies, challenging conventional deconstructionist, postcolonial, and historical-critical interpretations. Through meticulous textual analysis and a deep understanding of the Asian context, he offers a refreshing approach that bridges scholarship and cultural relevance. This book not only critiques established frameworks but also provides new insights, making it an essential read for those seeking a deeper and more contextualized understanding of the biblical narrative."

—**Riad A. Kassis**, International Director, Langham Partnership International

"In this fine study, Dr. Huu-Thien explores perennial hermeneutical questions involving the interplay between the meaning of biblical texts and their relevance to readers. Through comparing and contrasting the interpretive approaches of the Chronicler with contemporary Asian contextual and postcolonial readings, Dr. Huu-Thien presents a compelling model of holistic interpretation that combines faithful exegesis and relevant contemporary application. I heartily recommend this academically insightful and pastorally applicable work."

—**C. Y. Timothy Kao**, affiliate faculty, Singapore Bible College

"This book does something fresh: it brings the hermeneutical moves of the Chronicler into conversation with various recent Asian reading approaches. It provides a thoughtful entrée into Asian contextual readings while evaluating them in light of how the Chronicler reads Scripture. Huu-Thien is even-handed as he engages with interpreters across cultures, time, and traditions. I commend it to anyone open to the critical questions surrounding contextual readings of the Bible."

—**Daniel Owens**, pastor of discipleship, New Covenant Church, Naperville, Illinois

"How should Scripture interpret Scripture? This principle of hermeneutics is often given lip service without due attention to actual texts. But in this volume, Dr. Huu-Thien not only traces the contours of the Chronicler's appropriation of other Old Testament materials, but he also develops a striking analogy between postexilic reading in Judah and postcolonial reading in Asia. Here is a sophisticated demonstration of how 1–2 Chronicles models the posture of faithful resistance for Asian Christians today, both in 'what it meant' and 'what it means.'"

—**Jerry Hwang**, associate professor of theology, Trinity Christian College

"How do we read the Bible from the contexts of Asia? What are the different ways of interpreting it? In this book by Dr. Huu-Thien we are provided with different approaches to the text. But more than this, he shows us how even in the text of the Bible itself, we already have a model of what it means to read the text contextually. This will be a valuable textbook for those who want to read the Bible in the Asian context."

—**Federico G. Villanueva**, regional commissioning editor for Asia, Langham Publishing

Reading the Bible *as a* Postexilic Biblical Author Read

The Chronicler's Reading of Biblical Sources—
A Model for Postcolonial Reading
and Asian Contextual Reading of the Bible

T. N. HUU-THIEN

WIPF & STOCK · Eugene, Oregon

READING THE BIBLE AS A POSTEXILIC BIBLICAL AUTHOR READ
The Chronicler's Reading of Biblical Sources—A Model for Postcolonial Reading and Asian Contextual Reading of the Bible

Copyright © 2025 T. N. Huu-Thien All rights reserved. Except for brief quotations in critical publications or reviews, no part of this book may be reproduced in any manner without prior written permission from the publisher. Write: Permissions, Wipf and Stock Publishers, 199 W. 8th Ave., Suite 3, Eugene, OR 97401.

Wipf & Stock
An Imprint of Wipf and Stock Publishers
199 W. 8th Ave., Suite 3
Eugene, OR 97401

www.wipfandstock.com

PAPERBACK ISBN: 979-8-3852-3602-2
HARDCOVER ISBN: 979-8-3852-3603-9
EBOOK ISBN: 979-8-3852-3604-6

VERSION NUMBER 01/29/25

The research on the book of Chronicles and its biblical sources is based on the *Biblia Hebraica Stuttgartensia* (BHS). To help readers conveniently understand biblical verses in Hebrew, the English version of the Bible, the New Revised Standard Version (NRSV), is placed parallel to the Hebrew verses (BHS) in the tables.

Unless otherwise noted, English Scripture quotations are from New Revised Standard Version Bible, copyright © 1989 National Council of the Churches of Christ in the United States of America. Used by permission. All rights reserved worldwide.

To Lan-Khue,
Thien-Duc, and Thien-Hoai

Contents

List of Tables | ix
Preface | xi
Acknowledgments | xiii

1 Introduction | 1
2 The Chronicler's General Methodology with Biblical Sources | 20
3 Asian Contextual Reading and Postcolonial Reading of the Bible | 50
4 Comparing the Chronicler's Reading and Postcolonial Biblical Reading | 65
5 Comparing the Chronicler's Reading and the Asian Contextual Reading | 112
6 Concluding Chapter | 148

Bibliography | 159

List of Tables

Table 1. Textual Differences Between Psalm 132:8–10 and 2 Chronicles 6:41–42 | 41

Table 2. The Chronicler's Reading of 2 Kings 23:29–30a | 91

Table 3. The Chronicler's Reading of 2 Kings 18:13—19:37 | 97

Table 4. The Chronicler's Reading of 2 Kings 21:1–18 | 99

Table 5. The Chronicler's Reading of 2 Kings 24:18–20 | 103

Table 6. The Chronicler's Reading of 2 Kings 22:1—23:30 | 106

Table 7. The Chronicler's Reading of 2 Samuel 6:1–19 | 123

Table 8. The Chronicler's Reading of 2 Samuel 10:1–2 | 127

Table 9. The Chronicler's Reading of 2 Samuel 7:14–15 | 130

Table 10. The Chronicler's Reading of 2 Samuel 5:21 | 132

Table 11. The Chronicler's Reading of 2 Samuel 8:18 | 132

Table 12. The Chronicler's Reading of 1 Kings 8:34 | 134

Table 13. The Chronicler's Reading of Psalm 132:10 | 135

Table 14. The Chronicler's Reading of 1 Kings 15:9–24 | 136

Table 15. Parallels Between 2 Chronicles 33:1–9 and 2 Kings 21:1–9 | 139

Table 16. The Chronicler's Reading of 1 Samuel 31:10 | 142

Table 17. The Chronicler's Reading of 2 Samuel 7:1–11 | 143

Table 18. Summary of the Chronicler's Reading and the Two Modern Biblical Readings | 148

Preface

SCHOLARS OBSERVE THAT OVER the past two hundred years, biblical interpretation in the West has traditionally focused on studying mainly what the text meant. For Western biblical scholars, the study of what the Bible means to readers today falls within the realm of theological studies rather than biblical studies. In contrast, Asian biblical interpretation is holistic, studying both what the text meant and what the text means. This research aims to present a biblical model for Asian biblical hermeneutics. Interestingly, the present study finds that long before any modern biblical reading approaches emerged, the Chronicler, as demonstrated in the book of Chronicles, read his biblical sources in ways similar to Asian biblical reading.

A detailed comparison is made between the Chronicler's reading and two common approaches to Asian biblical reading: the Asian contextual reading (with Dalit biblical reading selected for comparison) and the postcolonial reading, which has been employed in Asia as well as worldwide. This study demonstrates that the Chronicler's reading and the Asian biblical readings are similar in how the biblical texts are read, both for what the text meant to its first readers and for what the text means to contemporary readers. To achieve this twofold aim of reading, the Chronicler's reading and the two approaches of Asian biblical interpretation share several interpretative principles, such as seeking parallel themes and situations between biblical contexts and the contemporary contexts of readers, the abstraction ladder, biblical theology, and the fusion of the two horizons. In other words, Asian biblical reading finds a similar reading model in the Bible through the Chronicles.

Asian biblical interpreters, however, sometimes adopt ways of reading the Bible that are not faithful to what the text meant, such as deconstruction

(Dalit biblical interpreters) and ignoring of the world of the Bible (postcolonial biblical readers). This is the main difference between the Chronicler's reading and the two reading approaches. Moreover, the Asian reading approaches are continuations of Western reading approaches in using historical-critical and literary approaches, while the Chronicler's reading does not use them.

The present investigation proposes a reading model in which Asian readers are called to distinguish between the foundational criterion and the purpose of reading. Interpreting the Bible faithfully according to what the text meant is foundational to subsequent contextualization and relevant application. Reading the Bible with relevance to Asian readers' contexts is the second aspect of the twofold aim of interpretation, and the content of such concerns for relevance is variable according to the diverse contexts and interests of contemporary readers. Asian readers may employ historical-critical and literary approaches to meet the foundational criterion and then use the shared interpretative principles mentioned above to achieve their purposes of reading. This proposed reading model synthesizes the strengths of the Chronicler's reading and the two reading approaches to achieve the twofold aim of biblical interpretation.

Acknowledgments

I HAVE BEEN ABLE to complete this doctoral research only by God's grace and mercy. I am deeply grateful to the Lord for leading me through this journey of research. I would like to express my deep gratitude to the following individuals whom God has used to help me through this journey.

- Rev. Dr. Chen-Yuan Timothy Kao, my primary supervisor, for wholeheartedly instructing me from the beginning to the end of my dissertation writing.
- Rev. Dr. Federico G. Villanueva, my additional supervisor, for advising me on sections of Asian biblical reading. Dr. Federico has also provided me with pastoral care via the Langham community throughout the journey.
- Dr. Janet C. Harris, for encouraging and giving me partial support that enabled me to begin this journey.
- Dr. J. Mark Ritchie, for assistance in editing my English writing for my dissertation.
- Dr. Riad A. Kassis and Langham leaders, who have given me financial support needed to complete this research (from my second year to the end of this journey).
- The three external examiners whose criticisms have helped to consolidate my dissertation.
- Last but not least, my wife, Lan-Khue, and my children, Thien-Duc and Thien-Hoai, who have sacrificed so much so I could spend the time needed for research and writing. Without my wife's encouragement and excellent care of our children, I would not have been able to finish this work.

1

Introduction

THE TWOFOLD GOAL OF evangelical biblical interpretation is both to study what a biblical text meant to its first readers and what it means to readers today. Modern Western interpretation, however, tends to focus on the former concern, neglecting the latter.[1] Krister Stendahl indicates that there is a tension in studying the Bible for both what the text meant and what the text means. This tension derives from the competitive nature of the differing methods of studying the Bible, which can be broadly designated as descriptive (i.e., biblical studies seeking to determine what the texts meant) and prescriptive (i.e., theological and philosophical disciplines aiming to discern theological messages and present them with relevance to present-day readers). Our challenge is to formulate an integrated reading approach that helps readers to grasp both what the biblical texts meant in their original contexts and what the texts mean in readers' contexts.[2] For Asian biblical interpreters, it is unsatisfying to focus on what the text meant while neglecting what it means today because Asian biblical interpretation is holistic.[3] D. A. Carson discerns two kinds of readings of the Bible. The first lets the readers' contexts determine the meaning of the Bible. The second lets the Bible be in control and attempts to address the Bible's meaning

1. Vanhoozer, *Theological Interpretation*, 18.
2. Stendahl, "Biblical Theology," 421–22.
3. Villanueva, "Challenge of Asian Biblical Interpretation," 12–13.

in terms of its relevance to a certain context.⁴ Balancing these two aspects of the goal in biblical interpretation is a challenge because some interpretive approaches emphasize the former while others focus on the latter. The Chronicler⁵ appropriates many earlier biblical sources for the new context in the postexilic period, as demonstrated in the book of Chronicles. To what extent does the book of Chronicles offer a model that integrates both concerns in interpretation? This is the main aim of our present study.

An Overview of Western Biblical Studies

For a long time, modern biblical interpreters in the West have focused primarily on the original historical meaning as the goal of interpretation. Kevin Vanhoozer indicates that, for the past two hundred years, biblical studies in the West has aimed to reconstruct the world of the Bible.⁶ Modern approaches of biblical interpretation, widely taught at universities, theological seminaries, and Bible colleges in the West, have focused on investigating what the text meant by employing historical-critical methods (e.g., source criticism, form criticism, redaction criticism, grammatical historical methods) and literary approaches. Modern Western biblical scholarship has largely avoided addressing contemporary issues and questions of modern readers.⁷

In recent decades, biblical scholars in the West have attempted to address this lack. For example, the general editor of the NIV Application Commentary series affirms that most Bible commentaries interpret the biblical text in terms of its original meaning in its ancient historical world, while the few commentaries that include some applications are more like sermons and devotional works. The NIV Application Commentary series studies both the original meaning of the text and contemporary issues of readers to find a bridge to connect the biblical world and the reader's world. The interpreters of this series employ biblical theology to discover timeless principles from a biblical passage and compare similar situations between the Bible and the reader's world for application. They state that they help readers to bring the

---

4. Carson, "Church and Mission," 220.

5. Biblical scholars use the term "the Chronicler" to refer to the author or final editor of the book of Chronicles.

6. Vanhoozer, *Theological Interpretation*, 18.

7. Dietrich and Luz, *Bible in a World Context*, ix–x.

Introduction

original message of a biblical passage into the reader's modern context.[8] Similarly, Vanhoozer and others advocate theological interpretation of the Bible. Practitioners of this approach research what the text (in its final form) meant to its first readers, investigate what the text meant to church communities throughout church history (reception history), and finally use biblical theology to discern theological themes significant to readers today.[9] Theological interpretation of the Bible is presented in two commentary series: the Brazos Theological Commentary on the Bible and the Eerdmans Two Horizons biblical commentary series.[10] Amos Yong rightly criticizes Western approaches to the Bible that view what the Bible means to readers today only as a secondary issue of application that relies solely on what the text meant to its first audience. This reading does not really deal with questions and concerns that readers face in their daily lives.[11]

Besides approaches that focus on what biblical texts meant to their first readers, some approaches focus on what the text means to readers today such as those found in devotional reading and reader-response criticism. Unlike historical-critical approaches and literary approaches, which study what the text meant, reader-response approaches focus mainly on presenting what the text means to readers. Edgar V. McKnight states that reader-response criticism lets the reader play "a role in the 'production' or 'creation' of meaning and significance."[12] Scholars distinguish "meaning," which refers to an author's intention or what a text meant, and "significance," which refers to what the text means to varied readers.[13] Readers employing this kind of approach focus on finding what the Bible means to their community and interests. For devotional reading, DeSilva indicates that ordinary Christians often use a devotional approach to the Bible to find what the text means to readers. Many devotional readers are not concerned with academic methods that focus on the biblical text's original meaning, as they believe that they only need the Holy Spirit to help them read the Bible in a manner that is meaningful to them.[14]

---

8. Arnold, *1 and 2 Samuel*, 9–12; Garland, *Mark*, 7–10.
9. Vanhoozer, *Theological Interpretation*, 20–24.
10. Fowl, *Theological Interpretation*, ix–x.
11. Yong, *Future of Evangelical Theology*, 108–10.
12. McKnight, "Reader-Response Criticism," 230.
13. Osborne, *Hermeneutical Spiral*, 93; Hwang, "Authorial Intent," 21.
14. DeSilva, *Introduction*, xix.

In summary, academic biblical studies focus solely on what the texts meant. In contrast, devotional reading and reader-response approaches emphasize what the text means today. The latter belong to the first category as classified by Carson, while the attempts of Western interpreters, such as the authors of the NIV Application Commentary series and the practitioners of theological interpretation of the Bible, belong to the second category.

An Overview of Asian Biblical Studies

Unlike Western biblical interpretation, approaches of Asian biblical interpretation that have emerged in recent decades usually study the Bible both for what the text meant and for what the text means. Asian interpretative approaches to the Bible are holistic, not separating "what the text meant from what it means. The two may be distinct, but they are closely linked."[15] Lee also affirms that Asian biblical interpretation incorporates "exegeting and perceiving the messages of the Bible."[16] The literature review of Asian biblical interpretation below will present in detail Asian reading approaches to the Bible that have been commonly employed in biblical commentaries and scholarly essays.

Not only do modern approaches to Asian biblical reading study the Bible for the twofold goal, but so does an ancient Asian biblical reading, namely, the Chronicler's reading. Long before the emergence of modern methods of biblical interpretation, the book of Chronicles had already demonstrated a biblical reading approach that aimed to grasp both what the text meant and what it means to the Chronicler's postexilic community. The Chronicler and his audience were ancient Jews in the postexilic period (geographically, they were in ancient Asia). Originally a sacred text for Jews in the postexilic period, the book of Chronicles contains many texts that are parallel to passages found in other biblical books, such as Genesis, Exodus, Numbers, Joshua, 1–2 Samuel, 1–2 Kings, Ruth, Psalms, Ezra, and Nehemiah.[17] Chronicles is a rare instance of a book of the Bible for which its biblical

---

15. Villanueva, "Challenge," 12–13.
16. Lee, "Asian Biblical Interpretation," 70.
17. E.g., 1 Chr 1:1–4 // Gen 5:3–32; 10:1; 1 Chr 1:5–23 // Gen 10:2–4, 6–8, 13–18a, 22–29; 1 Chr 16:8–36 // Ps 105:1–15; Ps 96:1–13; Ps 106:1, 47–48; 1 Chr 2:9–17 // Ruth 4:19–22; 1 Chr 4:28–33 // Josh 19:2–8; 1 Chr 6:1–4, 7 // Exod 6:16–24; 1 Chr 9:3–17a // Neh 11:4–19a; 1 Chr 10:1–12 // 1 Sam 31; 1 Chr 11:1–9 // 2 Sam 5:1–3, 6–10; 2 Chr 1:6–13 // 1 Kgs 3:4–15; 2 Chr 7:11–22 // 2 Kgs 9:1–9; 2 Chr 36:22, 23 // Ezra 1:1–3a; and so on. Most parts of Chronicles (1 Chr 10–2 Chr 36) are parallel to Samuel–Kings.

Introduction

sources are extant.[18] Biblical scholars generally agree that the Chronicler used existing materials to actualize the messages of those biblical materials in ways relevant to the Chronicler's postexilic audience.[19]

In other words, unlike Western biblical studies in the modern age, which usually separates "what the text meant" from "what the text means," the book of Chronicles, a product of ancient Asian biblical interpretation, illustrates a holistic approach. Studying the Bible for both what the text meant and what the text means make biblical reading meaningful and applicable to modern readers.

Gap in Scholarship and Research Questions

Vanhoozer interestingly opines, "To be distracted by what is 'behind' or 'before' the text, however, is to miss its message; such non-theological biblical criticism is like music criticism by the deaf and art criticism by the blind."[20] Yong likewise emphasizes that biblical readers need an approach to study both the world of the Bible and "to read the Bible as if it really mattered to their lives."[21] Such an integrated approach is necessary to achieve the twofold goal of being (1) faithful to what the text meant and (2) relevant in terms of what the text means. This present work attempts to formulate interpretative principles based on a careful examination of the Chronicler's reading and Asian biblical interpretive approaches. There are many investigations of the Chronicler's use of biblical materials. But there exist no studies comparing the Chronicler's reading of biblical materials to modern approaches of Asian biblical reading. This present research is the first comparative study between the Chronicler's reading and Asian biblical reading. Our comparative study will seek to discover whether and how the Chronicler's reading and Asian biblical reading integrate two aspects of the goal of biblical interpretation. This comparative study presents a comparison between the Chronicler's reading and Asian biblical reading approaches to identify hermeneutical principles that will enable contemporary Asian interpreters to achieve the twofold aim of biblical interpretation.

Moreover, this present work will investigate how Asian biblical reading in modern times is similar to and different from the Chronicler's

---

18. Kalimi, *Reshaping of Ancient Israelite History*, 1.
19. Details of this statement will be discussed in chapter 2.
20. Vanhoozer, *Theological Interpretation*, 20.
21. Yong, *Future of Evangelical Theology*, 110.

reading in the ancient Asian context. This research will help us identify any connection between ancient Asian reading, as demonstrated through the book of Chronicles, and contemporary Asian biblical reading. This will discern to what extent Asian biblical reading finds a precedent in the Bible through the book of Chronicles.

Definitions

People who read the Bible are both ordinary readers and scholars trained to interpret it. Part of this study considers how scholars use reading approaches to interpret the Bible and convey their interpretations to ordinary readers. Since this study addresses different kinds of readers and issues related to biblical hermeneutics, some terms need to be defined for clarity.

The term *reader(s)* in this study refers to general readers, both ordinary readers and scholars. The term *commentator(s)* and *interpreter(s)* refer to scholar(s) trained to interpret the Bible.

Biblical theology is an interpretative approach that reader(s) often use in biblical reading. Yet scholars define biblical theology differently because they hold different views of the canon, the relationship between the Old Testament and the New Testament, the nature of revelation, major themes, and so on.[22] For example, Klink and Lockett summarize five types of biblical theology: biblical theology as historical description of ideas through the Bible, biblical theology as history of redemption portrayed in the Bible, biblical theology as worldview story through the Bible, biblical theology as canonical approach, and biblical theology as theological construction of ideas/themes through the Bible.[23] Generally, any study of concepts, ideas, or thoughts based on the Bible may be termed "biblical theology."[24] For this study, *biblical theology*, as used by Asian biblical interpreters, traces or elaborates on an idea or theme through the various passages of Scripture.

Contextualization is a term used to describe the task of discovering what the text means to readers today.[25] This book uses the phrase *relevant contextualization* or *relevant interpretation* to indicate that interpreters read biblical passages faithfully to what the texts meant and then actualize the biblical sources so that their contemporary readers perceive their relevance.

22. Carson, "Biblical Theology," 39.
23. Klink and Lockett, *Understanding Biblical Theology*, 20–25.
24. Carson, "Biblical Theology," 35.
25. Osborne, *Hermeneutical Spiral*, 21–22.

Introduction

Literature Review

The Chronicler's Reading

This present work is the first comparative study between the Chronicler's reading and Asian biblical reading, so there is no similar study in the past for a literature review. There are, however, numerous studies of the Chronicler's use of biblical sources. Chapter 2 will review and evaluate varied views of the origins of the Chronicler's biblical sources and different opinions concerning the Chronicler's general methodology in working with his biblical sources. Through this review, chapter 2 will argue that the Chronicler's reading of his biblical sources is generally similar to Asian biblical reading.

Asian Biblical Interpretation

Within the last several decades, Asian biblical interpretation has emerged and is developing rapidly. Although the term "Asia" is broad, two reading approaches that have been most often used by Asians and demonstrated in many publications are the Asian contextual reading of the Bible and the postcolonial biblical reading.

The Postcolonial Biblical Reading

The postcolonial approach employs decolonizing interpretation of the Bible with a focus on the perspectives of the colonized and marginalized.[26] While practitioners of this reading approach come from all over the world, R. S. Sugirtharajah, the leading scholar of postcolonial reading, is an Asian. He argues that many biblical narratives were written in different colonial contexts, namely, the Egyptian, Assyrian, Persian, Hellenistic, and Roman.[27] Moreover, he observes that Western approaches to biblical interpretation, which have emerged in the colonial era and existed for several hundred years, have tended to ignore colonial perspectives embedded in the biblical texts. Postcolonial biblical interpretation examines such perspectives of the colonized inherent in the biblical texts, and then rereads biblical texts through postcolonial lenses, e.g., those of nationalism, multiculturalism,

---

26. Lee, "Asian Biblical Interpretation," 68–69; Kuan, "Asian Biblical Interpretation," 74.
27. Sugirtharajah, "Postcolonial Biblical Interpretation," 67.

plurality, the diaspora, and refugees.[28] Besides numerous studies of Sugirtharajah using this approach,[29] Bible commentary series that employ postcolonial reading to interpret the whole Bible have been published.[30] Chapter 3 will discuss this reading approach in detail, including the reason for its emergence, its methodology, and the differences between this approach and other Asian biblical reading approaches. Chapter 4 will compare the postcolonial reading with the Chronicler's reading.

The Asian Contextual Reading

The Asian contextual approach uses reader's contextual issues (e.g., feminist issues, realities and struggles of poor and oppressed people [*Minjung*],[31] concerns of the outcasts [e.g., Dalit and Indian tribal people], topics of social justice, liberation, etc.) as keys to read the Bible.[32] The Asian reader's contextual issues vary depending on the different nations, cultures, traditions, and economic and political concerns being brought into conversation with the Bible, but the principles of this reading approach are the same. Practitioners of this approach read the Bible through the lens of their contextual issues.

For example, *Minjung* biblical interpretation, an approach of the Asian contextual reading originating from Korea, reads biblical texts through the experiences of poor and oppressed people. This approach directly reads the exploited, oppressed, and powerless Hebrews and Jews in the Old and New Testament in terms of the *Minjung* people.[33] For instance, Cyris Moon, expounding the word "cry" in Exod 3:7–8, states that "It usually describes the cry of the helpless *Minjung* calling for help in the

---

28. Sugirtharajah, *Asian Biblical Hermeneutics*, 17–19; Sugirtharajah, "Postcolonial Biblical Interpretation," 67.

29. Among Sugirtharajah's works: "Bible and Its Asian Readers"; "Introduction"; "From Orientalist to Post-Colonial"; *Postcolonial Bible*; *Bible and the Third World*; *Postcolonial Reconfigurations*; *Bible and Empire*; *Postcolonial Biblical Reader*; *Exploring Postcolonial Biblical Criticism*; *Bible and Asia*.

30. Boer, *Postcolonialism and the Hebrew Bible*; Gossai, *Postcolonial Commentary*; Segovia and Sugirtharajah, *Postcolonial Commentary*.

31. *Minjung* literally means "people" in Korean, but Korean people use this term to refer to exploited and poor people.

32. Lee, "Asian Biblical Interpretation," 68; Pagolu, "Reading the Bible," 6.

33. Moon, "Culture in the Bible," 182–84.

face of oppression and injustice. . . . God is concerned with a specific oppressed *Minjung* called 'the Hebrews.'"[34]

Another example of the Asian contextual model is the *Burakumin* reading approach. *Burakumin* refers to those Japanese people who suffer discrimination because they are tribal people or because they perform the most menial and unsanitary tasks in society. Scholars have identified this approach as belonging to the contextual model.[35] For example, reading the story of the conversion of Cornelius in Acts 10, the *Burakumin* identify themselves with Cornelius, a gentile, who experienced discrimination in Jewish society. But his faith in Jesus Christ makes Cornelius a worthy member of the church. Just as Peter's attitude toward gentiles was transformed after seeing a vision and encountering Cornelius, who had faith in Jesus Christ, so the *Burakumin* hope that Japanese society will also be transformed when encountering *Burakumin* who have faith in Jesus Christ.[36]

Inductive Bible study with contextual application is another instance of the Asian contextual model. Taimaya Ragui points out that inductive Bible study has been employed by ordinary Christians to deepen their personal spiritual life.[37] This approach includes steps such as reading the Bible in its final form, understanding biblical messages through the genre and structure of the biblical text, and asking questions to find out how the biblical theology of these texts addresses the reader's contemporary context.[38]

Feminist biblical reading also belongs to the Asian contextual model. For example, while reading John 4:5–30, an interpreter notes that some Indian women may have had experiences similar to that of the Samaritan woman in terms of taking water from a public place. Jesus can save and liberate outcast woman like the Samaritan woman through his living water. He gives outcast women a new identity in the community of Christ, the church, just as he transformed the Samaritan woman into a missionary.[39] In another biblical passage (1 Sam 25), Aruna Gnanadason reads the story of Abigail through the lens of a third-world woman. She argues that just as Abigail performed brave actions to stop David from committing violence

---

34. Moon, "Culture in the Bible," 183–84.
35. Lee, "Asian Biblical Interpretation," 69; Sugirtharajah, *Bible and Asia*, 200.
36. Sugirtharajah, *Bible and Asia*, 201.
37. Ragui, "Mapping Hermeneutical Trends," 53.
38. Ragui, "Mapping Hermeneutical Trends," 54.
39. Premnath, "Biblical Interpretation in India," 8.

and consequently "converted" David, so also Indian women must try to resist all kinds of oppression and even stop violence.[40]

Concerning tribal biblical reading, K. Lallawmzuala indicates that practitioners of this approach read the Bible to find biblical messages that address the contextual issues of tribal people, such as the "socio-economic, political and cultural realities" of tribes. He adds that tribal biblical interpretation is a subcategory of liberation hermeneutics because the liberation approach reads the Bible to find biblical messages for the poor and oppressed, to whom tribal people usually belong.[41]

Dalit biblical reading is another approach to Asian contextual reading. It is practiced mainly by Dalit Christians in India. For example, a Dalit reader interprets Mark 7:24–31 through the lens of Dalit women who are poor and excluded from society due to gender and caste discrimination. The Syrophoenician woman, who like a Dalit woman was a social outsider, received Jesus' miracle. This story brings hope to Dalit women as they read that Jesus came to break the boundaries of society, and thus people like Dalits would be "accepted as living human beings" in Christianity.[42]

In Southeast Asia, Alle G. Hoekema describes a contextual reading of Gen 1–11 from an Indonesian perspective. This reading combines three approaches: the historical-critical approach, narrative criticism, and reader-response, with the last being a dialogue between the biblical narrative and Indonesian ideology.[43] For example, reading Gen 6:18, this study engages in a dialogue with a similar Indonesian myth. Just as the Indonesian myth implies that the sins of creation against God caused divine punishment, so the cause of God's destruction in Gen 6:7 is humanity's sins against God rather than humanity's offenses against one another. This reading specifically uses an Indonesian perspective to interpret the biblical story.[44]

Recently, Lim C. M. Stephen has proposed a contextual reading for Singaporeans to read the Bible through the lens of multicentric perspectives, namely, Western, Asian, and Singaporean standpoints. Since the Singaporean context is a junction of multiple cultures and identities, Lim's proposed reading approach aims to engage many voices, including the

---

40. Gnanadason, "We Dare to Be Pregnant," 67–68.
41. Lallawmzuala, "Issues in Biblical Interpretation," 13.
42. Nelavala, "Smart Syrophoenician Woman," 65, 67, 69.
43. Hoekema, "Genesis 1–11," 220, 222.
44. Hoekema, "Genesis 1–11," 227.

marginalized in Singapore.[45] For example, Lim reads Dan 1 through the Western lens, the Confucian lens, and the Malay Muslim lens. Regarding the Western lens, Lim refers to many Western commentators to show that Daniel's abstinence from the food of the Babylonian king demonstrates his piety by refraining from defiled gentile food. Moreover, the abstinence from food shows Daniel's resistance to participation in the exploitative system of the empire since the food on the king's table is the outcome of the exploitation of people.[46] Regarding the Confucian lens, Lim reads the narrative through this lens because Confucian thought has had an important influence on the formation of the Singaporean state. Confucius advocated gentle resistance against legitimate kings instead of open rebellion and left many writings helpful for maintaining governmental order through generations. Similarly, Daniel's abstinence from the food of the king while embracing Babylonian education and identity (new Babylonian names) indicates a gentle resistance and an attempt to build a better governmental order.[47] Regarding the Malay Muslims, they always observe their religious practices in daily life and those religious observances keep Malay Muslim communities from assimilation into foreign cultures. Similarly, the abstinence of Daniel and his friends from the food of the king is an observance of religious practices in daily life. This is the way Daniel and his friends could show their Jewish identity in Babylon.[48] In short, Lim reads the Bible through the lens of Singaporean contextual issues, which include Western, Confucian, and Malay Muslim perspectives.

The Asian intertextual (or crosstextual) reading is another approach to Asian contextual reading of the Bible. Since the primary feature of Asian biblical hermeneutics is to read the Bible in an Asian context, Archie Lee, a prominent practitioner of this reading approach with hundreds of related studies,[49] argues that this context is not only in terms of time and space, but also of Asian texts. He states, "Asian context contains multiple texts and is itself a text."[50] Practitioners of the Asian intertextual approach read a

---

45. Lim, *Contextual Biblical Hermeneutics*, 22.

46. Lim, *Contextual Biblical Hermeneutics*, 108–10.

47. Lim, *Contextual Biblical Hermeneutics*, 111–14.

48. Lim, *Contextual Biblical Hermeneutics*, 114–15, 120–21.

49. Brenner-Idan, Lee, and Yee, *Genesis*; Brenner-Idan and Yee, *Joshua and Judges*; Brenner-Idan and Lee, *Samuel, Kings and Chronicles*; Brenner-Idan, Yee, and Lee, *Five Scrolls*.

50. Lee, "Cross-Textual Hermeneutics," 190–91.

biblical text together with a chosen Asian religious text in a certain form for mutual illumination and supplementation.[51] For example, George Soares-Prabhu has made an intertextual study of Matt 28:16–20 and a Buddhist text (Mahavagga 1:10—11:1) concerning similar missionary commands in Christianity and Buddhism.[52] He uses literary analysis and form criticism to read Matt 28:16–20 in the context of the book of Matthew and to read the Buddhist text to demonstrate that the two texts are similar in their form and tripartite structure, but that their content is different.[53] He states that historical-critical criticism is necessary, but "it must not go on to become the sole or dominant method of an Asian exegesis."[54] Soares-Prabhu demonstrates that the two mission commands in Matthew 28:16–20 and Mahavagga 1:10—11:1 are similar in terms of literary form but different in terms of religious traditions. He states that the difference in religious traditions between the two mission commands shows that the Buddhist text helps readers recognize gaps in the mission command of Matthew. Matthew's command focuses on Christology and neglects the welfare of missioner and missioned. The Buddhist texts help to fill in the gaps.[55]

Asian people living outside Asia also employ the Asian contextual reading to interpret the Bible. Roy Sano indicates that for the past fifty years Asian American biblical readers have employed redaction criticism and canonical criticism through the lens of liberation in terms of ethnic and gender perspectives to identify their Asian identity in a foreign community. For example, they read Ruth as the symbol of a foreigner (like an Asian in America) divinely supported by God for immigration and integration into the new community.[56] They also read Ruth as God's sign for mixed marriage between Asian people and people of other races.[57] Those readings belong to the contextual reading.

Khiok-Khng Yeo, a Malaysian Chinese American, has proposed a crosscultural hermeneutics that falls under the Asian contextual reading. Yeo states that he employs the crosscultural approach to read the Bible in a Chinese context. Yeo argues that crosscultural reading was initiated by

---

51. Lee, "Asian Biblical Interpretation," 68; Pagolu, "Reading the Bible," 6–7.
52. Soares-Prabhu, "Two Mission Commands," 274–75.
53. Soares-Prabhu, "Two Mission Commands," 276–78.
54. Soares-Prabhu, "Two Mission Commands," 273.
55. Soares-Prabhu, "Two Mission Commands," 278–82.
56. Sano, "Shifts in Reading the Bible," 105–7.
57. Sano, "Shifts in Reading the Bible," 114–16.

Introduction

the apostle Paul.[58] This approach belongs to the contextual reading, for, as Yeo states, "To do a cross-cultural reading of biblical texts is also to let the biblical text respond to the particular context of the reader"[59] and "a cross-cultural reading is also a contextual reading."[60] Yeo's crosscultural hermeneutics comprises three steps with the following reading approaches: historical-critical, literary-rhetorical, and intertextual studies. To figure out Paul's rhetorical practice, Yeo begins with historical-critical approaches to understand how Paul's discourse conveyed God's truth to his original audience's contextual issues.[61] Next, through the literary-rhetorical approach, Yeo argues that the meaning of a text is an interpretation of a dialogue between the text's author and the reader. He writes, "The authority of interpretation does not reside in the frozen text or in the first writer but is to be found in the interactive process of [reading] the text, involving both the writer and the reader, which I have previously called 'rhetorical interaction.'"[62] From this, Yeo suggests engaging in an intertextual interpretation to read a biblical text from the reader's Chinese context.[63] For instance, to understand the concept of trust or faith in a Pauline epistle from the Chinese context, Yeo proposes a comparative study of the concept of trust/faith in Galatians and the Confucian concept of trust in the Analects.[64] Nevertheless, Western approaches should first be used to avoid eisegesis of biblical texts and to discern Paul's message to his original audience, and then, as a second step, comparative textual studies are to be done to obtain greater mutual understanding.[65] Obviously, Yeo's crosscultural reading belongs to the contextual reading.

Among reading approaches of the Asian contextual model, Dalit biblical reading has been used to interpret the whole Bible and is demonstrated through the Dalit Bible Commentary series.[66] In terms of publications, while other reading approaches of the Asian contextual reading interpret several biblical passages, the Dalit Bible Commentary series demonstrates

---

58. Yeo, *What Has Jerusalem*, 1.
59. Yeo, *What Has Jerusalem*, 4.
60. Yeo, *What Has Jerusalem*, 309.
61. Yeo, *What Has Jerusalem*, 16.
62. Yeo, "Culture and Intersubjectivity," 86.
63. Yeo, *What Has Jerusalem*, 2.
64. Yeo, "On Confucian Xin," 27.
65. Yeo, *What Has Jerusalem*, 2–3, 309–10.
66. John and Massey, *One Volume*; Massey, *One Volume*.

the Asian contextual reading adequately through the interpretation of the whole Bible. Thus, this present study selects Dalit biblical reading as a representative of the Asian contextual reading to compare with the Chronicler's reading. Chapter 3 will discuss Dalit biblical interpretation in detail.

Conclusion

Although Asian reading approaches may include more than the ones mentioned above, these two Asian reading models have been widely employed and demonstrated in many publications. Besides the aforementioned Bible commentaries, the two Asian reading approaches have been demonstrated in many other publications such as the *Global Bible Commentary*,[67] *Voices from the Margin: Interpreting the Bible in the Third World*,[68] *Ways of Being, Ways of Reading: Asian American Biblical Interpretation*,[69] *T&T Clark Handbook of Asian American Biblical Hermeneutics*,[70] *Reading Romans with Eastern Eyes*,[71] *Twin Cultures Separated by Centuries: An Indian Reading of 1 Corinthians*,[72] the one volume South Asia Biblical Commentary,[73] the Asia Bible Commentary series,[74] and so on.

---

67. Patte, *Global Bible Commentary*, xxi. This commentary is very short. It mainly introduces interpreters' contexts and reading approaches to study what biblical texts mean to interpreters' communities. Biblical scholars from all continents in the world have been invited to write the Global Bible Commentary in order to demonstrate what biblical texts mean in interpreters' contexts. Asian interpreters of the commentary use the reading approaches as mentioned above. For example, Melanchthon uses the Dalit reading approach from an Indian feminist perspective to interpret the Song of Songs (Melanchthon, "Song of Songs," 180–85), while Swarup uses the Asian contextual reading through the lens of Dalits and Indians to interpret Zechariah (Swarup, "Zechariah," 318–24). The postcolonial biblical reading is used by Sugirtharajah to interpret Matt 5–7 (Sugirtharajah, "Matthew 5–7," 361–68), by Kinukawa to interpret Mark (Kinukawa, "Mark," 367–78), by Wong to interpret Esther (see Wong, "Esther," 135–40), by Prior to interpret Ecclesiastes (Prior, "Ecclesiastes," 175–79), and by Ho to interpret Micah (Ho, "Micah," 295–300). Archie Lee uses crosstextual reading to interpret Lamentations (Lee, "Lamentations," 226–35).

68. Sugirtharajah, *Voices from the Margin*.
69. Foskett and Kuan, *Ways of Being*.
70. Kim and Yang, *T&T Clark Handbook*.
71. Wu, *Reading Romans*.
72. Spurgeon, *Twin Cultures*.
73. Wintle, *South Asia Bible Commentary*.
74. Spurgeon, *Romans*; Villanueva, *Psalms 1–72*.

Introduction

In summary, there are no comparative studies between the two common Asian models of biblical reading and the Chronicler's reading. Chapter 2 will review past studies of the Chronicler's use of biblical sources. Chapter 3 will review in detail the contexts, reasons, purposes, and basic features of the two Asian models of biblical reading. Chapters 2 and 3 provide a background for chapters 4 and 5, which present the comparative studies of the Chronicler's reading and the two Asian models of biblical interpretation.

Scope of the Study

The focus of this present study is a comparative study of the Chronicler's reading and the two Asian models of biblical reading. Due to space limitations, this book does not provide further discussion on Western approaches to reading the Bible.

Moreover, while the present work focuses on Asian biblical readings, this study does not suppose that Asian biblical interpretation comprises only the two mentioned reading approaches. Asia is a broad and complex geographical region, so Asian reading approaches may include more than the two mentioned approaches. This study has chosen these two reading approaches as test cases because they are the best represented in the literature. Other reading approaches which have been proposed by Asian scholars are either not widely used or are not widely demonstrated via publications. For instance, Moonjang Lee proposes postcritical reading (or a "hermeneutical bilingualism"), which combines Western biblical reading methods and other reading methods from Asian religious traditions (e.g., the Neo-Confucian approach [meditation to perceive knowledge] and the Zen Buddhist approach [enlightenment through intuition to see the nature of things]) for Asian biblical interpretation. The purpose of postcritical reading is to overcome the limitations of Western reading methods and to help Asian Bible readers awaken and transform themselves.[75] However, Lee's postcritical reading has not been widely employed and demonstrated through publications. Therefore, this present study selects the two Asian models of biblical reading because those reading models have been widely practiced and are demonstrated through biblical commentary series and numerous articles and essays.

---

75. Lee, "Post Critical Reading," 276–77, 283.

The Chronicler's reading belongs to the fields of inner-biblical interpretation,[76] and the biblical interpretation of early Judaism in the Second Temple era. This present work, however, limits its study to the Chronicler's reading only because the work of the Chronicler, namely, the books of 1 and 2 Chronicles, is authoritative for Christian communities. This present study aims to present a biblical model for reading demonstrated clearly in the Bible through the book of Chronicles.

For the Chronicler's reading of sources, there is a general consensus among scholars that the Chronicler employed two types of sources: biblical sources and other sources (nonbiblical or extrabiblical).[77] The focus of this present study is on biblical sources, not the other sources. Moreover, the Chronicler selects certain passages in his *Vorlagen* (textual sources), the Deuteronomistic History's version.[78] Scholars suggest various reasons why the Chronicler does not include some other passages in his *Vorlagen* (e.g., Samuel–Kings). For example, the Chronicler does not present the account of David and Bathsheba (2 Sam 11:2—12:25) nor Solomon's sins (1 Kgs 11:1–40) because the Chronicler wants to highlight the positive aspects of David and Solomon and to uphold them as ideal kings.[79] We cannot study the Chronicler's interpretative principles demonstrated in a passage which the Chronicler does not present. To examine the Chronicler's interpretative principles of reading the Bible, this present work focuses on biblical passages which the Chronicler actually includes.

Research Methodology

This present work employs philosophical hermeneutics, inner-biblical interpretation, and comparative studies to find answers to the research questions.

Philosophical Hermeneutics

This present study examines Asian approaches to biblical reading. This task belongs to the field of philosophical hermeneutics, which, strictly speaking, is not a particular method of biblical interpretation. Rather, "philosophical

---

76. For more details of this field, see Zakovitch, "Inner-Biblical Interpretation," 27–63; Menn, "Inner-Biblical Exegesis," 55–79.

77. Duke, "Recent Research," 23–27.

78. Chapter 2 will discuss the Chronicler's sources.

79. Klein and Krüger, *1 Chronicles*, 44.

hermeneutics seeks to describe what happens when we interpret, with or without our noticing."[80] In other words, our study aims to elucidate and then evaluate the philosophies of interpretation underlying Asian reading approaches, as well as the interpretative principles and methodologies that the two Asian reading models have employed to achieve the twofold aim of biblical interpretation.

Inner-biblical Interpretation

Regarding the examination of the Chronicler's use and reading of biblical sources, this task belongs to the field of inner-biblical interpretation, which studies exegesis and interpretation appearing within the Bible itself.[81] This task assists us in discovering how the Chronicler interprets and shapes his sources (e.g., Samuel–Kings, Psalms) as found in the final form of his work to serve his audience in the postexilic time. We will thus use the Hebrew Bible published as *Biblia Hebraica Stuttgartensia* to investigate the Chronicler's reading.

Comparative Studies

This book will then compare the two Asian models of biblical reading to the Chronicler's reading to discover to what extent each model interprets the Bible faithfully to what it meant to its first readers and appropriately for what it means to the Asian contexts. The comparative studies will present similarities and differences between the Chronicler's reading and each of the two models of Asian biblical interpretation.

Finally, this book will propose interpretative principles to help readers study the Bible both faithfully in terms of what it meant to its first readers and with relevance in terms of what it means to readers today.

Structure of the Book

The next chapter will review and examine the general methodology of the Chronicler in working with his biblical sources. Chapter 3 will review the two modern reading approaches of biblical interpretation: postcolonial and

80. Westphal, "Philosophical/Theological Response," 160.
81. Zakovitch, "Inner-Biblical Interpretation," 27.

Asian contextual readings. Chapters 4 and 5 will compare these modern reading approaches with the Chronicler's reading to answer the following questions: To what extent does the Chronicler read the existing texts in the voice of his postexilic colonized audience, similar to practitioners of postcolonial reading? To what extent does the Chronicler bring postexilic contextual issues to read the biblical materials, akin to the Asian contextual reading? These chapters aim to demonstrate how and to what extent these hermeneutical approaches can produce readings that are faithful to what biblical texts meant and, at the same time, relevant to Asian readers in their present contexts.

Based on our investigation, the concluding chapter will synthesize the findings and provide suggestions for interpreting the Bible based on the Chronicler's reading to achieve the dual aim of faithfulness to what the Bible meant to its first readers and relevance to present readers' Asian contexts.

Thesis Statement

In this study, Asian biblical reading finds a biblical counterpart in the Chronicler's reading as demonstrated in the book of Chronicles. This finding will be illustrated through similarities between the Chronicler's reading and the two Asian reading models. However, this study also identifies differences among them.

The Chronicler's reading and the two Asian reading models are similar in terms of reading the Bible for both what the text meant and what the text means. They share several reading principles, such as seeking parallel themes and situations between biblical contexts and contemporary contexts of readers, the so-called abstraction ladder, biblical theology, and fusion of the two horizons.

Besides similarities, there are also differences between the Chronicler's reading and those Asian reading approaches. Evidence shown in this book demonstrates that while the Chronicler's reading is generally faithful to his biblical sources, some Asian reading approaches are not. Dalit biblical interpreters have been encouraged to use deconstruction in reading the Bible. This practice makes Dalit biblical reading subvert and negate what the Bible meant. Consequently, Dalit biblical interpretation is not faithful to what the text meant while using deconstruction. Practitioners of postcolonial biblical reading study the world behind biblical texts and the world in front of biblical texts, but they often ignore the world of biblical

Introduction

texts (genre, structure, and literary perspectives of the text). This omission makes the postcolonial biblical reading unfaithful to what the Bible meant. Moreover, the two Asian reading models are appropriations of Western reading approaches in using historical-critical and literary approaches, while the Chronicler's reading obviously does not use these modern Western approaches.

To achieve a biblical reading that is consistently faithful to what the text meant and relevant to Asian readers' contexts, this present work proposes a reading model in which Asian readers need to differentiate between a foundational criterion of reading and the purposes of reading. Reading the Bible faithfully to discern what the text meant is the necessary and foundational criterion. Applying the Bible appropriately to address the Asian readers' various contexts is the practical purpose of reading. The actual forms of such practical application will vary according to the different Asian readers' diverse contexts and interests. Asian interpreters may employ historical-critical and literary approaches to meet the foundational criterion and then use the shared interpretative principles mentioned above to achieve their specific purposes of reading. When Asian readers fulfill the foundational criterion and also achieve their various applicable purposes, they thereby achieve the twofold aim of biblical interpretation. Such a successful synthesis approach will embody the strengths of the Chronicler's reading and of the two Asian reading models.

2

The Chronicler's General Methodology with Biblical Sources

To STUDY THE CHRONICLER'S work with biblical sources, it is necessary to understand the Chronicler's postexilic context, the nature of the Chronicler's sources, and how the Chronicler generally used them. There are many parallel texts between the book of Chronicles and other biblical books. For example, the list of names in 1 Chr 1–9 parallels Genesis, Exodus, Numbers, Joshua, and so on.[1] In fact, most parts of Chronicles (1 Chr 10–2 Chr 36) parallel Samuel–Kings. Given these parallels, one justifiably wonders whether the Chronicler used those biblical texts as sources. Put another way, the questions are whether the Chronicler's *Vorlagen* (textual sources) included the aforementioned texts as represented by the Masoretic Text (hereafter MT) and whether the Chronicler used other sources. A further related question is how the Chronicler handled the texts. This first chapter will examine these questions. Additionally, this chapter will explore to what extent the Chronicler's general method is similar to Asian biblical interpretation, specifically in terms of reading for both what the text meant and what the text means to their respective contemporary readers. To begin, we must first investigate the date of the composition of Chronicles and the

---

1. For more details about all the parallel texts between Chronicles and other biblical sources, see Curtis and Madsen, *Books of Chronicles*, 17–19; Klein and Krüger, *1 Chronicles*, 32–38.

overall context of the Chronicler's community, as this will pave the way for discussing the Chronicler's general methodology.

The Date of Chronicles

There is no consensus among scholars on a specific date for Chronicles. Scholars have suggested various dates, ranging from 538 BCE to 150 BCE.[2] The earliest year, 538 BCE, is based on 2 Chr 36:20–23 referring to the time of King Cyrus of Persia, and the proposed year 150 BCE is based on Eupolemus's use of Chronicles and Sirach's quotation from Chronicles (Sir 47:8–10).[3] One thing all scholars agree on is that Chronicles was composed in the postexilic period. Since there is no additional available data to further narrow the proposed time frame for Chronicles' composition, we also hold the view that Chronicles was composed in the postexilic period and some time before 150 BCE when the historian Eupolemus used Chronicles. With its historical period as a backdrop, chapters 4 and 5 will demonstrate how the Chronicler used and read his sources to serve his postexilic community.

An Overall Context of the Chronicler's Postexilic Community

Let us now explore in more detail the postexilic context of the Chronicler. The Chronicler worked in an area called Yehud. This was the area of the former southern kingdom that included Jerusalem and its vicinity, to which the exiled Jews returned. Other biblical books were also composed in this location during this period (e.g., Ezra-Nehemiah, Haggai, and Zechariah).[4] The postexilic community's political situation was one of colonial subjugation by the Persian empire (538–332 BCE) and subsequently by the Greek empire (332–63 BCE). The Chronicler's postexilic community lived in a time of conflicts between powerful forces. During the reign of the Persian empire, the Egyptians often fought against the Persian rulers. The Egyptians eventually defeated the Persians and gained temporary

---

2. Klein and Krüger, *1 Chronicles*, 13; For more detail about the debate on the date of Chronicles, see Duke, "Recent Research," 16–20.

3. Klein and Krüger, *1 Chronicles*, 13; Duke, "Recent Research," 16; Thompson, *1, 2 Chronicles*, 32.

4. Hoglund, "Material Culture," 15.

independence from 404 BCE to 343 BCE.[5] During the Greek empire, after the death of Alexander the Great in 323 BCE, there were continuous wars between the Ptolemaic dynasty, which was based in Egypt and controlled the area of Palestine, and the Seleucid dynasty, which was based in Syria and ruled Mesopotamia and the surrounding areas.[6] Living in the midst of such struggles among powerful factions instilled in the Chronicler's community a deep sense of risk and discomfort. These circumstances naturally motivated the Chronicler to interpret and appropriate the biblical texts to seek consolation and a solution from the Lord of Israel (hereafter YHWH), to wish for deliverance from foreign dominion, and even to hope for the restoration of Davidic reign.

The Chronicler's *Vorlage* and the Parallel MT Samuel–Kings

There are two main views on the relationship between the parallel texts in Chronicles (1 Chr 10—2 Chr 36) and Samuel–Kings. A few scholars, such as Graeme Auld and Raymond Person, argue that the Chronicler and the authors of Samuel–Kings both used a common source, one that is no longer extant. The majority of scholars, however, hold that the Chronicler utilized, as his main source, a text similar to the MT Samuel–Kings.[7]

The "Common Source" View

Graeme Auld, a leading advocate of the "common source" position, builds his case on the hypothetical grounds that Samuel–Kings might not have been written earlier than Chronicles.[8] Auld's position has been supported by Raymond Person, who leans on the work of Young, Rezetko, and Ehrensvärd,[9] concerning the variety of linguistic features in Samuel–Kings

---

5. Perdue and Carter, *Israel and Empire*, 121–23.

6. Perdue and Carter, *Israel and Empire*, 137–38; VanderKam, *Introduction to Early Judaism*, 12, 16.

7. E.g., among current scholars, Steven L. McKenzie, Ralph W. Klein, Thomas Krüger, William M. Schniedewind, Gary Knoppers, Edward L. Curtis, A. A. Madsen, Mark Shipp, H. G. M. Williamson, Sarah Japhet, Issac Kalimi, Zipora Talshir, Mark Boda, J. A. Thompson, Roddy Braun, Raymond Dillard, and Pancratius C. Beentjes.

8. Auld, *Kings Without Privilege*, 4, 9–10.

9. Young, Rezetko, and Ehrensvärd, *Linguistic Dating*; Rezetko, "Dating Biblical

and Chronicles (a mixture of Standard [or early] Biblical Hebrew and Late Biblical Hebrew). Person opposes the view that Samuel–Kings is a preexilic or exilic work in contrast with Chronicles, which is a postexilic work. From this, Person concludes that linguistically Samuel–Kings and Chronicles are almost identical and share a common source.[10] Auld performs a comparative study of Samuel–Kings and Chronicles to reconstruct a common source containing the parallel passages.[11] Auld argues that textual differences between Samuel–Kings and Chronicles are not included in the common source. The differences between them are due to the Chronicler's more faithful adaptation of the common source to paint an idealized portrait of the kings of Judah, whereas the author of Samuel–Kings adds more information to portray the kings in a more nuanced way, as he does, for example, in the narrative on Solomon.[12]

Raymond Person has drawn from Auld's thesis to propose that Samuel–Kings and Chronicles derive from a shared source. Person agrees with Auld's hypothesis that the shared source begins with the narrative of Saul's death because this narrative is the first parallel between Samuel–Kings and Chronicles.[13] Person differs from Auld's view, however, by arguing that this shared source was not a single text, but rather "a family of texts" of an early version of Samuel–Kings in the exilic period (though, in Person's view, this shared source is not the *Vorlage* of the extant Samuel–Kings).[14] For Person, the Deuteronomistic History (hereafter DH) and Chronicles were two historiographical works produced in the postexilic era by two scribal schools (the Deuteronomistic school and the Chronistic school) within the same broader tradition in the oral culture of ancient Israel.[15] Then, relying on David M. Carr's theory concerning how ancient written texts were created from oral transmission, and on an "interview of the Serbo-Croatian oral poet Mujo Kukuruzovic,"[16] Person argues that the variations between Sam-

---

Hebrew," 215–50; Rezetko, "'Late' Common Nouns," 379–418.

10. Person, *Deuteronomic History*, 23–26, 37–39.

11. Following Auld, Craig Y. S. Ho, a student of Auld, uses textual analysis of 1 Sam 31:1–13 and 1 Chr 10:1–12 as a case study to argue that the source of Chronicles is not the parallel passages in Samuel. See Ho, "Conjectures and Refutations," 82–106.

12. Auld, *Kings Without Privilege*, 39–41, 148.

13. Person, *Deuteronomic History*, 91; Auld, *Kings Without Privilege*, 42; Auld, *Life in Kings*, 16n72.

14. Person, *Deuteronomic History*, 126, 166.

15. Person, *Deuteronomic History*, 47, 163–70.

16. Person, *Deuteronomic History*, 48.

uel–Kings and Chronicles may be due to the trend of expansion through memorial repetition of the common source in the oral culture of ancient Israel, rather than resulting from significant theological differences, because the two scribal schools worked within the same broader tradition.[17]

Chronicles' Dependence on Samuel–Kings and Other Parallel Biblical Passages

In contrast, the majority of scholars hold the position that the Chronicler's sources are similar to the parallel MT Samuel–Kings passages. The main argument for this view is as follows. If Chronicles did not rely on Samuel–Kings and if Chronicles' first readers were not already familiar with Samuel–Kings, then most of Chronicles would not have made sense to them. For example, after the long genealogies (1 Chr 1–9), the first story in Chronicles is that of Saul's death (1 Chr 10:1–12 // 1 Sam 31:1–13). Chronicles adds the comment that Saul died for his unfaithfulness and for inquiring of a medium (1 Chr 10:13). There are no other narratives about Saul in Chronicles. Thus, if Chronicles' first readers were not familiar with 1 Sam 13–15 (accounts of Saul's unfaithfulness to YHWH) and 1 Sam 28 (the account of Saul consulting a medium), and if Chronicles did not rely on these passages, Chronicles' evaluation of Saul's death (1 Chr 10:13–14) would not have made sense to its original audience.[18] Another example concerns the account of Ahijah's oracle. Both Kings and Chronicles tell of the fulfillment of God's oracle through Ahijah (2 Chr 10:15 // 1 Kgs 12:15), but only Kings contains the content of the oracle (1 Kgs 11:29–40). Second Chronicles 10:15 only makes sense if Chronicles' first readers were already familiar with the content of the oracle as recorded in Kings.[19] Thus, it is reasonable to accept Chronicles' dependence on the books of Kings. Numerous other examples demonstrating that the Chronicler depended on passages in Samuel–Kings have been presented by Klein and Krüger.[20]

---

17. Person, *Deuteronomic History*, 128–29. In a recent article, Person observes that some scholars use the case study of Serbo-Croatian epic in the nineteenth century to argue for the hypothesis that the Greek Homeric epics derived from oral traditions. From that hypothesis, he argues for the oral traditions of 2 Sam 7 and 1 Chr 17. See Person, "Problem of 'Literary Unity,'" 217–38.

18. Knoppers, *I Chronicles 1–9*, 67; Klein and Krüger, *1 Chronicles*, 31–37.

19. Dillard, *2 Chronicles*, 87.

20. See details Klein and Krüger, *1 Chronicles*, 31–37; also Knoppers, *I Chronicles 1–9*, 67.

The Chronicler's General Methodology with Biblical Sources

Weaknesses of the "Common Source" View

We now proceed to demonstrate why the "common source" view is neither convincing nor widely accepted among scholars. McKenzie responds to Auld's arguments and presents much evidence to argue that it is unreasonable to conclude that the Chronicler does not rely on Samuel–Kings.[21] Auld's rejoinder does succeed. For example, since the first parallel between Samuel–Kings and Chronicles is the account of Saul's death (1 Chr 10 // 1 Sam 31), McKenzie contends that it is unreasonable that the common source should abruptly begin with the death of Saul. He argues that the Chronicler could have relied on 1 Samuel 28, because the Chronicler added the reasons for Saul's death (1 Chr 10:13–14) to the narrative in 1 Samuel 28.[22] Auld replies that the Chronicler might have known the story of Saul consulting the female medium "by ear or by repute."[23] Even so, Auld still admits that further study is needed because he could not answer all of McKenzie's challenges.[24] For another example, McKenzie shows that while both Kings and Chronicles tell of the fulfillment of God's oracle through Ahijah (2 Chr 10:15 // 1 Kgs 12:15), only Kings contains the content of the oracle (1 Kgs 11:29–40). From this, McKenzie questions the reasonableness of the view that the Chronicler (as well as the Chronicler's contemporary readers) did not know this oracle.[25] Auld concedes that it is difficult to provide a clear answer to this argument and again admits that this requires further investigation.[26]

In a recent study, Auld analyzes the textual development of the DH and Chronicles and attempts to reconstruct a sample of the shared text behind the DH and Chronicles. However, he still cannot explain the matter of Saul's death narrative as mentioned above. He presents an answer similar to his previous one along with a quote from Raymond Person. Auld writes, "I agree with Ray Person that Chr may allude to stories already being told orally but not yet in the written tradition shared with Sam."[27] Regarding Person's arguments, Sandra Richter comments that "Person's

---

21. McKenzie, "Chronicler as Redactor," 81–87.
22. McKenzie, "Chronicler as Redactor," 81.
23. Auld, "What Was the Main Source," 93.
24. Auld, "What Was the Main Source," 97.
25. McKenzie, "Chronicler as Redactor," 83.
26. Auld, "What Was the Main Source," 97.
27. Auld, *Life in Kings*, 108.

assumptions and conclusions in these chapters outweigh his data, and the reader is left with the impression that his reconstruction is too speculative, and the proposed model simply not quantifiable."[28] Scholars have identified weaknesses in Person's arguments as follows. Although there are mixed linguistic features of Standard Biblical Hebrew (hereafter SBH) and Late Biblical Hebrew (hereafter LBH) in both the DH and Chronicles, Person does not adequately spell out the predominance of SBH found in the DH over the LBH used in Chronicles.[29] Moreover, Person argues for shared texts in oral form (transmitted orally) without other evidence except for the written forms of the DH and Chronicles, and he does not deal with literary features (e.g., chiastic structures) displayed in numerous texts in the DH and Chronicles.[30] Benjamin Johnson warns that Person's reconstruction of the oral context of the DH and Chronicles based on the modern analogy of Serbo-Croatian oral poetry should be treated with caution, because the validity of drawing conclusions about the hypothetical context in ancient times based on modern oral poetry is highly dubious.[31]

Since the "common source" view is not compelling, most scholarly works relating to Chronicles in recent decades have advocated the view that Chronicles depended on Samuel–Kings. For example, having examined the two views on the relationship between Samuel–Kings and Chronicles, Andrew Taehang Ohm presents evidence to support the dependence view and concludes that this hypothesis is more probable. For instance, 2 Chr 22:7–10 records Jehu's revolt, but Chronicles does not tell the whole story or all the reasons for it (as stated in 2 Kgs 9–10). Ohm argues that Chronicles depends on 2 Kgs 9–10 and adds "of the house of Judah" in 2 Chr 22:10 to emphasize the legitimacy of the bloodline of Judah.[32]

In her study of the narratives of Hezekiah in Chronicles, Kings, Isaiah, and Jeremiah, Amber Warhurst has also reviewed the relationship between Chronicles and other biblical books. She states that "it is reasonable to

---

28. Richter, review of *Deuteronomic History* (by Person), 422.

29. Williams, review of *Deuteronomic History* (by Person), 316.

30. Williams, review of *Deuteronomic History* (by Person), 316.

31. Johnson, review of *Deuteronomic History* (by Person), 138.

32. Taehang Ohm, "Two Faces of Manasseh," 152; Ohm also critiques Craig Y. S. Ho's argument by pointing out that it is deficient and subjective in terms of the textual critical analysis of 1 Sam 31:13 // 1 Chr 10:12, and that Ho's argument also does not fit the Chronicler's ideology of idealizing the kings of Judah. Ohm concludes that Auld's theory "is still sketchy rather than being a profound textual argument." See Taehang Ohm, "Two Faces of Manasseh," 149–50, 160.

The Chronicler's General Methodology with Biblical Sources

conclude that Chronicles was composed through direct reliance on Samuel–Kings."[33] Beside the aforementioned main argument of the dependence view, Warhurst adds two other arguments: the chronological order and the order of the regnal reports of the Judean kings in Chronicles is the same as that in Samuel–Kings. In addition, Chronicles refers to all the same sources as Samuel–Kings.[34]

In the course of his study on the tribe of Benjamin in the DH and Chronicles, Benjamin D. Giffone argues that the Chronicler omits negative features of the tribe of Benjamin from the DH to portray a positive relationship between the tribes of Benjamin and Judah in order to obtain Benjamin's support for the Jerusalem cult.[35] To argue for this, Giffone seeks to reconstruct the sociopolitical context of Yehud in the Chronicler's time (assumed to be the late Persian period) and to demonstrate that the tribe of Benjamin was thriving, whereas the Jerusalem cult was impoverished and lacked support from others.[36]

Daniel E. Kim, who has studied the concept of rest in Mesopotamian literature and the Hebrew Bible, also argues that the Chronicler relies on Samuel–Kings. For example, although 2 Sam 7:1, 11 are parallel to 1 Chr 17:1, 10, the phrases concerning "rest" in 2 Sam 7:1 and 11 are absent in 1 Chr 17:1 and 10. Kim believes that 2 Sam 7:1 and 11 are original. His reasoning is that these two statements of rest are the theological center of the DH since the whole of the DH was structured on this ideological center of David's rest in the past (2 Sam 7:1) and in the future (2 Sam 7:11).[37] Kim then argues that the Chronicler intentionally omits the dual rest statements from 2 Sam 7:1 and 11 so that 1 Chr 17 emphasizes the selection of David's son to build the temple.[38]

More recent is the study by Sheila Tuller Keiter exploring the portrait of King Solomon in the Hebrew Bible and later Jewish literature (classical rabbinic and major medieval literature). For the Solomon narrative in Chronicles, Keiter follows the majority view by citing studies (e.g., William Schniedewind and Pancratius C. Beentjes) that argue the Chronicler

---

33. Warhurst, "Merging and Diverging," 15.
34. Warhurst, "Merging and Diverging," 12.
35. Giffone, "Sit at My Right Hand," 55.
36. Giffone, "Sit at My Right Han," iii.
37. Kim, "From Rest to Rest," 124.
38. Kim, "From Rest to Rest," 153–54.

employs the account of Solomon in Kings.[39] According to Keiter, the Chronicler alters the Solomon narrative in Kings to portray Solomon as a spiritual figure by focusing on Solomon's building of the temple and his overall success, and then by ending the Solomon narrative with him reigning in peace and wealth.[40]

Conclusion

Based on all of the above, we find that the leading scholars of the "common source" view have not been able to prove their hypothesis. Auld cannot answer why the putative shared source suddenly starts with the narrative of Saul's death. His most recent study basically quotes Raymond Person's argument for oral traditions. Yet Person's own argument takes as its starting point Auld's own thesis and the study of modern Serbo-Croatian poetic oral transmission. Consequently, these arguments of the "common source" view are circular and not as convincing as the "dependence" view. Therefore, the majority of scholars rightly hold to the "dependence" view. This present study takes the majority opinion and posits that the parallel texts in Chronicles are due to the Chronicler's use and reading of existing biblical materials (i.e., primarily the DH).

The Chronicler's *Vorlage* and the Parallel MT Psalms

Besides the DH, there are psalms in Chronicles that are parallel to MT Psalms (e.g., the composite psalm in 1 Chr 16:8–36 // Ps 105:1–15; Ps 96:1–13; Ps 106:1, 47–48 and 2 Chr 6:41–42 // Ps 132:8–10). Since psalms were orally circulated among Israelites in ancient times and then put in writing in the Second Temple period, as evidenced in the Qumran scrolls, almost the same period as the date of Chronicles, this section will briefly investigate the origins of these psalms in Chronicles and argue that the parallel MT Pss 105:1–15; 96:1–13; 106:1, 47–48; and 132:8–10 are the *Vorlagen* of Chronicles.

---

39. Keiter, "Jewish Understanding," 74–77.
40. Keiter, "Jewish Understanding," 78–81.

The Composite Psalm in 1 Chronicles 16:8–36

The composite psalm in 1 Chr 16:8–36 is introduced in verse 7: בַּיּוֹם הַהוּא אָז נָתַן דָּוִיד בָּרֹאשׁ לְהֹדוֹת לַיהוָה בְּיַד־אָסָף וְאֶחָיו ("Then on that day David gave the singing of praise to YHWH into the hand of Asaph and his brothers"). Yet this verse does not identify the author of the psalm. Based on the parallels between the three parts of the psalm and the three MT Psalms (1 Chr 16:8–22 // Ps 105:1–15; 1 Chr 16:23–33 // Ps 96:1–13; 1 Chr 16:34–36 // Ps 106:1, 47–48), scholars have proposed different views concerning the authorship of the composite psalm and the relationships between the parallel texts.

The Psalm (1 Chr 16:8–36) as the *Vorlage* of Psalms 96, 105, and 106

Carl Friedrich Keil and Franz Delitzsch propose that the entire psalm in 1 Chr 16:8–36 was composed by David around 1000 BCE for use on the occasion of the ark transfer. They suggest that since Asaph and his brothers were tasked to sing praises to YHWH, and since David initiated the liturgical psalmody, it should be concluded that David was the composer of this psalm and that the Chronicler had just inserted the psalm into 1 Chr 16.[41] This view is based on the title Παραλειπόμενα of the Septuagint (hereafter LXX) Chronicles ("what was passed over"). These two scholars believe that this Greek title indicates that Chronicles contains much historical information that is not found in other books of the Old Testament.[42] Regarding the parallels between MT 1 Chr 16:8–36 and the three MT Pss 105:1–15; 96:1–1, 3; and 106:1, 47–48, Keil and Delitzsch argue that poets in the postexilic period used the composite psalm in 1 Chr 16:8–36 to compose Psalms 96, 105, and 106.[43] For the textual differences between the composite psalm in 1 Chr 16:8–36 and the parallel psalms, the two scholars believe that the textual differences are due to editing by the author of the Psalter. For instance, regarding בְּמִקְדָּשׁוֹ ("in his sanctuary," Ps 96:6) and בִּמְקֹמוֹ ("in his place," 1 Chr 16:27), they state that the historical circumstances of 1 Chr 16:8–36 were in David's time when the temple did not yet exist; thus, it is logical that 1 Chr 16:27 used the term "in his place." Meanwhile, they think the poet of Ps 96

---

41. Keil and Delitzsch, *1 and 2 Kings*, 209–10, 218.
42. Keil and Delitzsch, *1 and 2 Kings*, 9–10.
43. Keil and Delitzsch, *1 and 2 Kings*, 216–18.

lived in the postexilic era, after the temple had been built, so he changed "in his place" to "in his sanctuary."[44]

This view is not compelling for the following reasons. First, scholars generally agree that the LXX title Παραλειπόμενα (lit., "what was passed over" or "what was omitted") does not refer to the literary nature of Chronicles, as it contains many textual parallels between Chronicles and other biblical books. If the title reflects the nature of Chronicles, there should not be many repetitions between Chronicles and other biblical books.[45] Second, scholars who hold that the Chronicler composed the psalm in 1 Chr 16:8–36 from the three Pss 96, 105, 106 could argue in reverse that the textual differences between 1 Chr 16:27 (בִּמְקֹמוֹ, "in his place") and Ps 96:6 (בְּמִקְדָּשׁוֹ, "in his sanctuary") is due to the Chronicler's intentional change. They propose that the Chronicler made this intentional change to fit the narrative setting of 1 Chr 13–16 when the temple had not yet been built.[46] Indeed, although Keil and Delitzsch argue for Davidic authorship of the hymn in 1 Chr 16:8–36, they also admit the possibility that the Chronicler made the composite psalm (1 Chr 16:8–36) by drawing upon the three Pss 105:1–15; 96; and 106:1, 47–48. They state that they could not disprove the alternative view that the Chronicler combined the three psalms to produce the song sung at the event of the ark transfer.[47] For the textual differences between 1 Chr 16:8–36 and the three Pss 105:1–15; 96; and 106:1, 47–18, the two scholars also concede that they cannot ascertain whether the composite psalm (1 Chr 16:8–36) is the original or the three Pss 105:1–15; 96; and 106:1, 47–48 are the originals.[48]

In contrast to Keil and Delitzsch, Gerald Wilson argues for the dependence of Ps 106 on the psalm in 1 Chr 16, though he does not make any claims regarding the authorship of the composite psalm in 1 Chr 16. He states that Ps 106:47–48 was composed from 1 Chr 16:35–36.[49] Wilson rejects the view that the parallels between 1 Chr 16:8–36 and the three MT Pss 105; 96; 106:1, 47–48 are proof that the MT Psalter was already shaped

---

44. Keil and Delitzsch, *1 and 2 Kings*, 217.

45. Johnstone, *Chronicles and Exodus*, 67; Japhet, *From the Rivers of Babylon*, 320.

46. Butler, "Forgotten Passage," 142–50; Grol, "1 Chronicles 16," 110.

47. Keil and Delitzsch, *1 and 2 Kings*, 212.

48. Keil and Delitzsch stated, "If we compare the text of our hymn with the text of these psalms, the divergences are of such sort that we cannot decide with certainty which of the two texts is the original." Keil and Delitzsch, *1 and 2 Kings*, 215.

49. Wilson, *Editing of the Hebrew Psalter*, 185.

The Chronicler's General Methodology with Biblical Sources

into five books during the Chronicler's time (i.e., fourth century BCE). To build his case, Wilson compares the doxologies which conclude books 1–4 of the MT Psalter (Pss 41:14, 72:19, 89:53, and 106:48) and observes that they are similar except for the phrase וְאָמַר כָּל־הָעָם אָמֵן ("let all the people say amen," Ps 106:48). This phrase, which bears a narrative tone, appears in 1 Chr 16:36.[50] Wilson states that, since this phrase has no parallel in the other psalmic doxologies, it is evidence for the dependence of Ps 106 on 1 Chr 16.[51]

Based on Wilson's argument that Ps 106 depended on 1 Chr 16, George Brooke further argues that all the textual differences between Pss 105, 106, and 1 Chr 16 are due to the changes made by the authors of Pss 105 and 106. For example, while the MT 1 Chr 16:13 is parallel to the MT Ps 105:6, they differ in that the name "Abraham" (Ps 105:6) replaces "Israel" (1 Chr 16:13). Brooke argues that the name "Abraham" is important in Ps 105 because it occurs three times in the psalm. Also, the name "Israel" usually accompanies the name "Jacob" (1 Chr 16:13) rather than "Abraham." Thus, Brooke believes that the author of Ps 105 deliberately changed the name "Israel" from the parent text of 1 Chr 16:13 to "Abraham" in Ps 105:6.[52]

Yet Wilson's argument fails to convince us for several reasons. First, Wilson argues that Ps 106:47–48 is based on 1 Chr 16:35–36 because of the parallelism of the two texts, but he does not argue or present any evidence for Ps 105:1–15 (// 1 Chr 16:8–22) and Ps 96:1–13 (// 1 Chr 16:23–34). Second, a comparison of the four doxologies in the MT Psalter (Pss 41:14, 72:19, 89:53, and 106:48) shows that there are many textual differences between these four verses,[53] not only in the phrase "let all the people say amen" in MT Ps 106:48, as Wilson claims. Moreover, Wilson does not explain why the phrase "let all the people say," which appears both in MT Ps 106:48 and MT 1 Chr 16:36, is the evidence for the dependence of Ps 106 on 1 Chr 16, and not vice versa. Furthermore, Emanuel Tov explains that the division of

---

50. Wilson, *Editing of the Hebrew Psalter*, 183–84.
51. Wilson, *Editing of the Hebrew Psalter*, 185.
52. Brooke, "Psalms 105 and 106," 274–75, 279–80.
53. Klein and Krüger, *1 Chronicles*, 366. For instance:
   וּבָרוּךְ שֵׁם כְּבוֹדוֹ לְעוֹלָם וְיִמָּלֵא כְבוֹדוֹ אֶת־כֹּל הָאָרֶץ אָמֵן וְאָמֵן ("Blessed be the name of his glory forever; may his glory fill the whole earth. Amen and Amen" [Ps 72:19]).
   בָּרוּךְ יְהוָה לְעוֹלָם אָמֵן וְאָמֵן ("Blessed be YHWH forever. Amen and Amen" [Ps 89:53]).
   בָּרוּךְ־יְהוָה אֱלֹהֵי יִשְׂרָאֵל מִן־הָעוֹלָם וְעַד הָעוֹלָם וְאָמַר כָּל־הָעָם אָמֵן הַלְלוּ־יָהּ ("Blessed be YHWH, the God of Israel, from everlasting to everlasting. And let all the people say, 'Amen.' Praise Yah!" [Ps 106:48]).

texts into verses was orally transmitted when the scribes wrote the Qumran scrolls. Subsequently, the Masoretes used the *silluq* accent to signify the division of texts that was orally transmitted. As for the parallel passages, the sign for the division of texts is different. Tov comments,

> Note, however, that there are differences between parallel passages within MT (see Sperber*), since sometimes one-and-a-half verses in one book form one verse in another one. For example, Gen 25:14–15a form only one verse in 1 Chr 1:30 and Ps 96:8–9a likewise form only one verse in 1 Chr 16:29.[54]

Comparing MT Gen 25:14–15a with MT 1 Chr 1:30, we observe that Gen 25:14–15a is obviously the parent text of Chronicles, not vice versa. There is a *silluq* following the last word of MT 1 Chr 1:30. This *silluq* indicates that Gen 25:14 and Gen 25:15a were combined in 1 Chr 1:30. Similarly, in the case of MT Ps 96:8–9a // MT 1 Chr 16:29, MT 1 Chr 16:29 has a *silluq* following the last word (קׇדֶשׁ). This *silluq* suggests that 1 Chr 16:29 was formed by the combination of Ps 96:8 and Ps 96:9a. In other words, this *silluq* indicates that this combination was orally transmitted from Qumran. Since Chronicles was composed and redacted during the Second Temple period, to which the Qumran community also belonged, Tov's argument undermines Wilson's view. According to the tradition of textual division during this period, it is apparent that the composite psalm in 1 Chr 16 is derived from Ps 96, not vice versa.

If Wilson's argument is not compelling, then Brooke's argument certainly cannot stand. Berlin points out that even Brooke himself admits that "the result of this study is somewhat insecure, given that in part it is based on an argument from silence."[55] For one thing, Brooke's argument about the change from Abraham (Ps 105:6) to Israel (1 Chr 16:13) could be used in reverse: Ps 105:1–15 could, arguably, be the parent text, and then the Chronicler changes "Abraham" to "Israel" to make the content fit Chronicles' theme of "Israel" and also to form a synonymous parallelism of Israel and Jacob.[56]

In opposition to the view that the composite psalm (1 Chr 16:8–36) is the *Vorlage* of Pss 105, 96, and 106, the positions presented below argue that 1 Chr 16:8–36 is derived from the three psalms.

---

54. Tov, *Textual Criticism*, 52.
55. Berlin, "Psalms," 21; Brooke, "Psalms 105 and 106," 290.
56. Williamson, *Israel*, 62–64.

The Chronicler's General Methodology with Biblical Sources

Parallel MT Psalms 96, 105, and 106 as the *Vorlagen* of 1 Chronicles 16:8–36

There are three views on the composite psalm (1 Chr 16:8–36) deriving from Psalms 105, 96, and 106, suggested by scholars as follows.

DAVID AS THE AUTHOR OF THE COMPOSITE PSALM IN 1 CHRONICLES 16:8–36

Barton Payne argues that David authored the composite psalm (as appears in 1 Chr 16:8–36) for the occasion of the ark transfer by reemploying portions of the three Pss 105, 96, and 106. Then the Chronicler, who was Ezra, inserted this psalm into 1 Chr 16. Payne cites 2 Chr 29:30, which says that the Levites sang the words of David and Asaph. Payne infers that 2 Chr 29:30 might refer to the composite psalm in 1 Chr 16:8–36.[57] Payne also assumes that even if the Chronicler had put a psalm in David's mouth, this psalm's authorship has to be Davidic because Chronicles was inspired by the Holy Spirit and became a part of the Scriptures.[58] Payne's argument is unpersuasive for the following reasons. Although 2 Chr 29:30 says that King Hezekiah asked the Levites to sing the words of David and Asaph (וַיֹּאמֶר יְחִזְקִיָּהוּ הַמֶּלֶךְ וְהַשָּׂרִים לַלְוִיִּם לְהַלֵּל לַיהוָה בְּדִבְרֵי דָוִיד וְאָסָף), there is no evidence that Hezekiah meant that the psalm in 1 Chr 16:8–36 was sung at the event in 2 Chr 29. Moreover, Payne's argument for Davidic authorship of the composite psalm, based on the assumption that the words of the Chronicler were inspired by the Holy Spirit to ascribe the psalm to David, is not an argument but a faith assertion. Moreover, along that line of reasoning, since the whole of Chronicles was inspired by the Holy Spirit and accepted as Scripture, could not the Chronicler himself have had divine authority to compose the new psalm in 1 Chr 16:8–36? Therefore, the view that David as the author of the composite psalm (1 Chr 16:8–36) is not compelling.

A LATER REDACTOR AS THE AUTHOR OF THE COMPOSITE PSALM IN 1 CHRONICLES 16:8–36

A few scholars, such as Martin Noth and James A. Loader, postulate that the composite psalm was adapted from Pss 105, 96, and 106, and was inserted

---

57. Payne, "1 and 2 Chronicles," 310.
58. Payne, "1 and 2 Chronicles," 390.

into Chronicles by a later redactor. Noth assumes that lists of names in Chronicles are later insertions because the lists interrupt the coherence of the self-contained narratives which the Chronicler had available before him as sources.[59] From this, he argues that 1 Chr 16:5–38 were later insertions because verses 5–6 and 37–38 contain lists of Levites with their duties. As for the composite psalm (1 Chr 16:7–36) in between these lists, Noth proposes that the psalm was inserted even later than these lists because the psalm interrupts the lists.[60] Moreover, Loader argues that 1 Chr 16:4 and 39 were originally consecutively conjoined as a unit by the Chronicler on the basis of the connection between the verbal form in 1 Chr 16:4 (וַיִּתֵּן) and the direct object marker at the beginning of 1 Chr 16:39 (וְאֵת צָדוֹק). First Chronicles 15:18 and 16:38 indicate that the duty of Obed-edom and Jeiel was to be gatekeepers, whereas 1 Chr 16:5–6 indicates that their duty was to be musicians.[61] Based on the above, some scholars conclude that the lists are the work of a later redactor rather than the Chronicler himself.[62]

Yet this view is not supported by recent scholars for the following reasons. First, ancient Near Eastern and Greek literature show that lists of names or genealogies and narrative texts both could be employed by the original author rather than requiring a later redactor, and thus the composite psalm in 1 Chr 16:8–36 and its surrounding lists of names could very well be the work of the Chronicler himself.[63] Second, Peter B. Dirksen observes that both 1 Chr 16:4 and 1 Chr 16:6 describe the activities before the ark in Jerusalem. If 1 Chr 16:4 is considered original material of the Chronicler, then 1 Chr 16:6 should be also. On this basis, Dirksen concludes that the list of names in 1 Chr 16:5–6 is also the original work of the Chronicler.[64] Third, to argue that 1 Chr 16:5–6 is a secondary interpolation because of the different duties of Obed-edom and Jeiel (1 Chr 15:18; 16:38 and 1 Chr 15:21; 16:5), and from that to conclude that the composite psalm is also a secondary interpolation, is not a necessary line of reasoning based on hard evidence. The reason is that the Chronicler uses repetition of one or

---

59. Noth, *Chronicler's History*, 31–33.
60. Noth, *Chronicler's History*, 35.
61. Loader, "Redaction and Function," 69.
62. Braun, *1 Chronicles*, 187–88; Noth, *Chronicler's History*, 35, 150.
63. Knoppers, *I Chronicles 10–29*, 655; Knoppers, *I Chronicles 1–9*, 245–64. Knoppers studies ancient Mediterranean materials from Persian and Hellenistic times to show that an ancient Mesopotamian or a Greek writer may use genealogies, poems, and narratives together.
64. Dirksen, *1 Chronicles*, 219, 222.

more phrases to signal that material is being inserted by him in between the repeated verses or phrases (for example, 1 Chr 5:1–3; 11:10–11; 12:20–23; 2 Chr 1:6; 3:3; 6:12–14; 12:2–9; 21:20—22:2; and so on).[65] In the same way, the Chronicler repeats the list of names (1 Chr 16:5–7 and 37–38), with the modification of the duties of the two persons, to signify that the composite psalm (1 Chr 16:8–36) is inserted in between the repeated lists.[66] In light of all this, Noth and Loader's arguments for a later redactor based on the repeated lists of names fail to persuade.

Their arguments can only demonstrate that the composite psalm has been inserted into an extant work. They fail to prove whether it was composed by the Chronicler or by a later redactor. Whether the Chronicler interpolated the composite psalm, or a later redactor inserted it, is a matter of debate. The latter view involves additional assumptions and is therefore more complicated. James Watts suggests that according to the principle of Occam's razor, the former view is simpler and therefore more probable.[67] Thus, most recent scholars who have worked on this topic support the view that the Chronicler himself inserted the composite psalm, which he had created by integrating lines from Pss 105, 96, and 106 as they are now reflected in the MT.

THE CHRONICLER AS THE AUTHOR OF THE COMPOSITE PSALM IN 1 CHRONICLES 16:8–36

The position that the Chronicler is the author of the composite psalm in 1 Chr 16:8–36 is based on the following observations. The first concerns the parallels between 1 Chr 16:8–36 and Pss 105, 96, and 106.[68] Besides the parallel texts in 1 Chr 16:8–36 and the three psalms, there are numerous other parallels between Chronicles and other biblical books, such as 1 Sam 31 // 1 Chr 10, 1 Sam 28–30 // 1 Chr 12, and so on.[69] Based on these parallels, many scholars argue that the Chronicler is using these older biblical books as textual sources to compose his literary work. These scholars conclude

---

65. Butler, "Forgotten Passage," 146–47; Kalimi, *Reshaping of Ancient Israelite History*, 276–82, 292–94; Williamson, *1 and 2 Chronicles*, 121–22.

66. Butler, "Forgotten Passage," 146; Boda, *1–2 Chronicles*, 148; Williamson, *1 and 2 Chronicles*, 121–22; Johnstone, *1 Chronicles*, 191.

67. Watts, *Psalm and Story*, 164.

68. Japhet, *I and II Chronicles*, 312; Knoppers, *I Chronicles 10–29*, 636–40.

69. See more detail of sources of Chronicles at Klein and Krüger, *1 Chronicles*, 32–37.

that the Chronicler is consistent in his literary adaptation: if elsewhere the Chronicler has used texts from older biblical books to compose Chronicles, it is likely that he is also using Pss 105, 96, and 106 to compose the psalm in 1 Chr 16.[70] Moreover, the method of composing a new psalm by adapting from several existing psalms emerged before and was practiced during the Qumran era (for example, Ps 108 was conjoined from Pss 57 and 60). Japhet cites this phenomenon as support for the view that the composite psalm in 1 Chr 16 was composed from the three existing psalms.[71]

The second observation is that the contents of Pss 105:1–15; 96:1–13; and 106:1, 47–48, which form the composite psalm, harmonize with the surrounding narrative context of Chronicles in several ways. Mark Shipp proposes that the Chronicler introduces the three duties of some Levites before the ark in 1 Chr 16:4 (remembrance, giving thanks, and praising YHWH) and then structures the composite psalm (sung before the ark) to relate to these three duties in the following way. The texts of the three psalms (105:1–15; 96:1–13; and 106:1, 47–48) are structured in the composite psalm into four sections relating to the duties mentioned in 1 Chr 16:4: the Introduction (Ps 105:1–7 // 1 Chr 16:8–14) includes all the three duties (1 Chr 16:8, 10, 12 // Ps 105:1, 3, 5); the Remember section (Ps 105:8–15 // 1 Chr 16:15–22) relates to the duty of remembrance (1 Chr 16:15 // Ps 105:8); the Praise section (Ps 96:1–13 // 1 Chr 16:23–33) to the duty of praise (1 Chr 16:25 // Ps 96:4); and the Give-Thanks section (Ps 106:1, 47–48 // 1 Chr 16:34–36) to the duty of thanksgiving (1 Chr 16:34, 35 // Ps 106:1, 47).[72] Moreover, James Watts highlights the semantic links between the three source psalms and its surrounding context in Chronicles such as צוה, "command" (Ps 105:8 [// 1 Chr 16:15] with 1 Chr 15:15 and 16:40), בְּרִית, "covenant" (Ps 105:8 [// 1 Chr 16:15, 17] with 1 Chr 15:25, 26, 28, 29 and 16:6, 37), and military terms (Ps 96:7–8 [// 1 Chr 16:28–29] with 1 Chr 18:2, 6; Ps 106:47 [// 1 Chr 16:35] with 1 Chr 11:1, 14; 13:2; 18:6, 13).[73] To these, Kleinig adds תָּמִיד, "continually" (Ps 105:4 [// 1 Chr 16:11] with 1 Chr 16:6, 37, and 40).[74] Furthermore, Williamson discerns

---

70. Japhet, *I and II Chronicles*, 16; Thompson, *1, 2 Chronicles*, 23; Klein and Krüger, *1 Chronicles*, 32–37. Many other scholars such as Steven McKenzie, Isaac Kalimi, Trent Butler, Andrew Hill, Eugene H. Merrill, H. G. M. Williamson, Raymond B. Dillard, Roddy Braun, Paul D. Hanson, Kenneth G. Hoglund, and Ehud Ben Zvi hold the same view.

71. Japhet, *I and II Chronicles*, 312.

72. Shipp, "'Remember His Covenant Forever,'" 34–37.

73. Watts, *Psalm and Story*, 158–59.

74. Kleinig, *Lord's Song*, 136. Kleinig also quotes the works of Watts, *Psalm and Story*;

parallel themes between the psalm in 1 Chr 16:8–36 and David's prayer of thanksgiving in 1 Chr 29:10–19, such as Israel's patriarchs as sojourners (Ps 105:12–13 [// 1 Chr 16:19–20] and 1 Chr 29:15), praise of YHWH's kingship (Ps 96:1–13 [// 1 Chr 16:23–33] and 1 Chr 29:11–12), and the petitions for the conditions of a permanent dynasty placed at the end of both the composite psalm and David's prayer (Ps 106:47 [// 1 Chr 16:35] and 1 Chr 29:18–19). On these grounds, Williamson argues that the Chronicler places the composite psalm in 1 Chr 16 to form a framework for the entire unit of 1 Chr 17–29 via these common themes.[75]

The third observation that points to the Chronicler's editing pertains to the textual differences between the psalm in 1 Chr 16 and Pss 105, 96, and 106. For example, the textual differences between 1 Chr 16:29 (פָּנָיו, "before him") and Ps 96:8 (חַצְרוֹתָיו, "to his courts") can be ascribed to an intentional change by the Chronicler to fit the narrative setting of 1 Chr 13–16 when the temple had not yet been built.[76] The same is seen in the textual differences between 1 Chr 16:27 (בִּמְקֹמוֹ, "in his place") and Ps 96:6 (בְּמִקְדָּשׁוֹ, "in his sanctuary").[77] Another example is the textual difference between 1 Chr 16:13 (יִשְׂרָאֵל, "Israel") and Ps 105:6 (אַבְרָהָם, "Abraham"). The change from "Abraham" to "Israel" can be attributed to the Chronicler's deliberate editing to imply that the message of this psalm is a timeless principle for all true Israel, including the Chronicler's readers.[78]

In addition, as noted in the evaluation above, Tov argues that the evidence of the *silluq* in MT 1 Chr 16:29 suggests that the Qumran community recognized that the composite psalm (1 Chr 16:8–36) derived from Ps 96 and not vice versa.[79] It stands to reason that the composite psalm in Chronicles is composed by adapting from Pss 105, 96, and 106.

Conclusion

In short, the view that the Chronicler is the author of the composite psalm in 1 Chr 16:8–36 is most plausible because it is supported by the parallels between Chronicles and other biblical books, as well as 1 Chr 16:8–36

---

and Shipp, "'Remember His Covenant Forever.'"

75. Williamson, *1 and 2 Chronicles*, 185–86; DeVries, *1 and 2 Chronicles*, 149.
76. Klein and Krüger, *1 Chronicles*, 366–67; Grol, "1 Chronicles 16," 110.
77. Grol, "1 Chronicles 16," 110; Klein and Krüger, *1 Chronicles*, 366–67.
78. Braun, *1 Chronicles*, 192; Wallace, "What Chronicles Has to Say," 288.
79. Tov, *Textual Criticism*, 49–52.

paralleling Pss 105, 96, and 106. The Chronicler is consistent in his literary method: as he has used other biblical sources, so he also adapts Pss 105, 96, and 106 to construct the composite psalm. Moreover, this view is convincing because it explains how Pss 105:1–15; 96:1–13; and 106:1:47–48 (which comprise the composite psalm) harmonize with the surrounding context of Chronicles via semantic links and textual changes. This position also demonstrates that the textual differences between the composite psalm in 1 Chr 16 and its parent texts of MT Pss 105, 96, and 106 are due to the Chronicler's editing. Finally, this view is supported by linguistic features of the composite psalm and the three source psalms, as well as the *silluq* tradition tracing back to the Qumran community shown in the *silluq* evidence.

The Psalm in 2 Chronicles 6:41–42

Another psalmic text in Chronicles that parallels the Psalter is 2 Chr 6:41–42 (// MT Ps 132:8–10). Psalms 132:8–10 is found at the end of Solomon's prayer in 2 Chr 6. The words of Solomon's prayer at the dedication of the temple are narrated in both 1 Kgs 8:23–53 and 2 Chr 6:14–42, with similarities in the first part (1 Kgs 8:23–49 // 2 Chr 6:14–39) and differences at the end of the prayer (2 Chr 6:41–42 parallels Ps 132:8–10 instead of the end of Solomon's prayer in 1 Kgs 8:50–53). From these similarities and differences, scholars have proposed different views on the origin of the psalm in 2 Chr 6:41–42. Scholarly hypotheses on this are not as diverse as those on 1 Chr 16. Major differences mainly involve authorship and the relationship between the psalm in 2 Chr 6:41–42 and MT Ps 132:8–10. Two views argue that 2 Chr 6:41–42 is the work of King Solomon. Most scholars hold the third view that the Chronicler incorporated the MT Ps 132:8–10 into 2 Chr 6.

2 Chronicles 6:41–42 as Solomon's Words and Not Related to Psalm 132:8–10

Keil and Delitzsch argue that 2 Chr 6:41–42 is authentically Solomon's prayer, rather than a later insertion of Ps 132:8–10, because the content is relevant to the event of the temple's dedication in Solomon's time (that Solomon prayed to invite God's ark to arise and rest in the temple). Moreover, Solomon's prayer in 2 Chr 6:41–42 is relevant to the following verses (2 Chr

The Chronicler's General Methodology with Biblical Sources

7:1–3) in which God answered his prayer.[80] Being consistent with their assumption that the Chronicler used noncanonical sources (not books such as Samuel, Kings, or the Psalter), Keil and Delitzsch state that we cannot determine whether 2 Chr 6:41–42 draws on Ps 132:8–10 or vice versa.[81] The weakness of Keil and Delitzsch's view, which they themselves admitted, is that it cannot explain why 2 Chr 6:41–42 is not parallel with 1 Kgs 8:50–53 but with Ps 132:8–10.[82] When arguing for Solomonic authorship of the psalm in 2 Chr 6:41–42, these two commentators do not explain why there are two different endings of Solomon's prayer.

2 Chronicles 6:41–42 as Solomon's Words Taken from Psalm 132:8–10

Another view postulating 2 Chr 6:41–42 as Solomon's words holds that he adapted words from Ps 132:8–10. Payne argues that Solomon took vv. 8–10 of Ps 132, which he believes was composed by David at the time when the ark was transferred to Jerusalem (1 Chr 16), i.e., forty years before the reign of Solomon. Solomon quoted these three psalmic verses at the end of his prayer at the dedication of the temple. Payne argues that the prose ending of Solomon's prayer pertaining to the exile (// 1 Kgs 8:50b–53) is omitted by the Chronicler because these verses do not fit the postexilic context of his time.[83]

Payne's argument is problematic because it is based on the debatable supposition that David is the author of Ps 132. This psalm has been variously dated from the preexilic[84] to the postexilic[85] periods. The hypothesis of Davidic authorship of Ps 132 is based on the Early Biblical Hebrew (hereafter EBH) features (for example, מוֹשָׁב is an archaic form in Ps 132:13).[86] However, recent research on Late Biblical Hebrew has concluded that Ps 132 is a mixture of EBH and many linguistic forms of LBH (e.g., vv. 6, 11, 12, 13, 14, 17).[87] Also, the earliest preexilic date proposed for Ps 132 is in the time of Solomon rather than of David. This proposed date is based on the content of Ps 132 (for example, Ps 132:11–12 implies Solomon's

---

80. Keil and Delitzsch, *1 and 2 Kings*, 327–28.
81. Keil and Delitzsch, *1 and 2 Kings*, 14–15, 328.
82. Keil and Delitzsch, *1 and 2 Kings*, 328.
83. Payne, "1 and 2 Chronicles," 463.
84. Booij, "Psalm 132," 80–82.
85. Hossfeld and Zenger, *Psalms 101–150*, 459; Barbiero, "Psalm 132," 258.
86. Cross, *Canaanite Myth*, 97.
87. Carvalho, "Psalm 132," 647–48.

disobedience and the tragedy after Solomon's death).[88] Yet the same scholar who argues for this Solomonic date also admits that the psalm could alternatively be postexilic.[89] In light of all this, Payne's assumption of Davidic authorship of Ps 132 is highly uncertain. Consequently, one also doubts the hypothesis that Solomon himself adapted from Ps 132.

2 Chronicles 6:41–42 as the Chronicler's Work
Extracted from Psalm 132:8–10

Instead of postulating Solomon as either the original author of the words recorded in 2 Chr 6:41–42 or the adapter of lines from Ps 132:8–10, most scholars today espouse the view that the Chronicler incorporated Ps 132:8–10 as the last part of Solomon's prayer in 2 Chr 6:41–42. The first observation in support of this position includes the parallels between MT 2 Chr 6:41–42 and MT Ps 132:8–10 and the tradition of attributing untitled psalms to David and Solomon.[90] This argument is based on the assessment that the Chronicler is consistent in his literary adaptation. Like the composite psalm in 1 Chr 16:8–36, which is adapted from the three Pss 105, 96, and 106, here the Chronicler also adapts the extant Ps 132:8–10 to create the ending of Solomon's prayer in 2 Chr 6 that is different from the prose conclusion in 1 Kgs 8:23–53.[91] There are, however, not only similarities but also differences between the text of the psalm in 2 Chr 6 and Ps 132:8–10 as indicated in the table below.

---

88. Laato, "Psalm 132 and the Development," 66.

89. Laato concludes, "My aim was not to show that there is no logical 'possible world' in which Psalm 132 can be dated to the postexilic period, but to show that there are also logical possible worlds in which the Solomonic date for the contents of Psalm 132 is optional." Laato, "Psalm 132: A Case Study in Methodology," 33.

90. Berlin, "Psalms," 26; Curtis and Madsen, *Books of Chronicles*, 345; Noth, *Chronicler's History*, 105.

91. Beentjes, "Psalms and Prayers," 40; Japhet, *I and II Chronicles*, 601.

The Chronicler's General Methodology with Biblical Sources

Table 1. Textual Differences Between Psalm 132:8–10 and 2 Chronicles 6:41–42

Ps 132:8–10 (MT)	2 Chr 6:41–42 (MT)	Textual Differences	
		Ps 132:8–10	2 Chr 6:41–42
8 קוּמָה יְהוָה לִמְנוּחָתֶךָ אַתָּה וַאֲרוֹן עֻזֶּךָ	41 וְעַתָּה קוּמָה יְהוָה אֱלֹהִים לְנוּחֶךָ אַתָּה וַאֲרוֹן עֻזֶּךָ	מְנוּחָתֶךָ None	וְעַתָּה אֱלֹהִים נוּחֶךָ None
9 כֹּהֲנֶיךָ יִלְבְּשׁוּ־צֶדֶק וַחֲסִידֶיךָ יְרַנֵּנוּ	כֹּהֲנֶיךָ יְהוָה אֱלֹהִים יִלְבְּשׁוּ תְשׁוּעָה וַחֲסִידֶיךָ יִשְׂמְחוּ בַטּוֹב 42 יְהוָה אֱלֹהִים	צֶדֶק יְרַנֵּנוּ	יְהוָה אֱלֹהִים תְשׁוּעָה יִשְׂמְחוּ בַטּוֹב יְהוָה אֱלֹהִים
10 בַּעֲבוּר דָּוִד עַבְדֶּךָ אַל־תָּשֵׁב פְּנֵי מְשִׁיחֶךָ	בַּעֲבוּר דָּוִד עַבְדֶּךָ אַל־תָּשֵׁב פְּנֵי מְשִׁיחֶיךָ זָכְרָה לְחַסְדֵי דָּוִיד עַבְדֶּךָ	מְשִׁיחֶךָ	מְשִׁיחֶיךָ זָכְרָה לְחַסְדֵי דָּוִיד עַבְדֶּךָ

These textual differences are best attributed to the Chronicler's intentional editing. For example, the Chronicler adds the words וְעַתָּה ("and now," 2 Chr 6:41) to signify his transition, moving from the source text of 1 Kgs 8 to Ps 132:8–10.[92] The Chronicler adds the divine name יְהוָה אֱלֹהִים ("YHWH God") three times (2 Chr 6:41 [twice], 42) to emphasize the urgency of the petition by repeatedly calling on the divine name.[93] Through the three יְהוָה אֱלֹהִים (2 Chr 6:41, 42), the Chronicler also declares the praise of God: "YHWH is God, YHWH is God, YHWH is God."[94] The Chronicler replaces the word צֶדֶק ("righteousness," Ps 132:9) with תְשׁוּעָה ("salvation," 2 Chr 6:41) to imply that salvation was needed in the Chronicler's time even though the priests were being righteous.[95] The Chronicler turns the singular מְשִׁיחֶךָ ("your anointed one," Ps 132:10) into the plural מְשִׁיחֶיךָ ("your anointed ones," 2 Chr 6:42) to refer to both King David and King Solomon.[96] The Chronicler transfers the first phrase of Ps 132:10 to the last line of the prayer (2 Chr 6:42) to emphasize the petition that God remember David.[97]

The third observation supporting this view is that the Chronicler intentionally harmonizes the content of the psalm in 2 Chr 6:41–42 with

---

92. Klein and Hanson, *2 Chronicles*, 98.

93. Japhet, *I and II Chronicles*, 602; Klein, "Psalms in Chronicles," 271; Klein and Hanson, *2 Chronicles*, 98–99.

94. Japhet, *I and II Chronicles*, 602.

95. Klein and Hanson, *2 Chronicles*, 98–99.

96. Dillard, *2 Chronicles*, 51; Japhet, *I and II Chronicles*, 603–4.

97. Thompson, *1, 2 Chronicles*, 231.

its surrounding narrative in Chronicles. For example, the content of Ps 132:8–10 fits the narrative of 2 Chr 5–7, which mentions the event of the temple's dedication.[98] The Chronicler also changes וַחֲסִידֶיךָ יְרַנֵּנוּ ("let your pious men shout," Ps 132:9) to וַחֲסִידֶיךָ יִשְׂמְחוּ בַטּוֹב ("let your pious men rejoice in the goodness," 2 Chr 6:41) to echo Chronicles' theme of joy or rejoicing.[99] Moreover, when the Chronicler leaves out part of the source text of Solomon's prayer in 1 Kgs 8 and inserts Ps 132:8–10, he returns to the theme of the ark (1 Chr 13–16, 2 Chr 5–6), whereas the omitted passage of the source text (1 Kgs 8:50–53) does not mention this.[100] By doing this, the Chronicler completes his account of the two stages of transferring the ark to Jerusalem, which was started by David and completed by Solomon.[101]

The Chronicler's intentional editorial activity best explains the two different endings of Solomon's prayer in 1 Kgs 8 and 2 Chr 6. It also accounts for the textual differences between the psalm in 2 Chr 6:41–42 and Ps 132:8–10. Moreover, this hypothesis explains the harmonization between the psalm in 2 Chr 6:41–42 and its narrative context in Chronicles. Regarding Ps 132 itself, Schreiner has recently reinvestigated the linguistic features and structure of the psalm. He concludes that Ps 132:1–12 is a preexilic composition, while vv. 13–18 are a postexilic expansion.[102] The evidence for this is that, although both EBH and LBH appear in the psalm, most of the archaic linguistic features occur in vv. 1–12.[103] Moreover, vv. 1–12 focus on King David with an a–b–a structure (a = vv. 1– 5, announce the plea or the call for the Lord to remember David's deed // a = vv. 11–12, announce the Lord's answer to the plea in v. 1).[104] Verse 13 begins with the asseverative כִּי (indeed) to signify a new beginning, which is the postexilic expansion focused on the Lord's choice of Zion (vv. 13–18).[105] Schreiner's most recent study quite plausibly explains the mixture of EBH and LBH in Ps 132 and comports with the view that the Chronicler used Ps 132:8–10, which had been composed in preexilic times.

---

98. Dillard, *2 Chronicles*, 51.
99. Beentjes, "Psalms and Prayers," 41.
100. Klein and Hanson, *2 Chronicles*, 88.
101. Japhet, *I and II Chronicles*, 601.
102. Schreiner, "Double Entendre," 20.
103. Schreiner, "Double Entendre," 23–24.
104. Schreiner, "Double Entendre," 28–29.
105. Schreiner, "Double Entendre," 30–33.

Conclusion

The origins of the psalms in Chronicles have been examined by many scholars, resulting in diverse conclusions. Having critically examined each view on the origins of both the psalm in 1 Chr 16 and the psalm in 2 Chr 6, we conclude that the most persuasive position is that the Chronicler composes both psalms by adapting from Pss 105, 96, 106, and 132. This position is persuasive because it best explains the presence of both similarities and differences between the psalms in Chronicles and the four Psalms. In addition, this conclusion is supported by the semantic and thematic harmonization between Pss 105:1–15; 96:1–13; 106:1, 47–48 (which comprise the composite psalm of 1 Chr 16:8–36); Ps 132:8–10 (which formed the conclusion of Solomon's prayer in 2 Chr 6:41–42); and other parts of Chronicles. Furthermore, this conclusion is also sustained by the *silluq* evidence transmitted at Qumran.

The Chronicler's General Methodology

We have demonstrated in the previous sections that MT Samuel–Kings and MT Pss 105:1–15; 96:1–13; 106:1, 47–48; and 132:8–10 are sources of the Chronicler. We now consider how the Chronicler handles these texts. The above sections have not only argued that the similar MT Pss 96, 105, 106, and 132 are the *Vorlagen* of Chronicles, but also have demonstrated, albeit in a general fashion, how the Chronicler uses those psalms to serve his postexilic audience. This section will examine more closely the Chronicler's overall method in appropriating his biblical sources.

Although scholars use various terms to describe the nature of the Chronicler's literary work, this present study explores to what extent the Chronicler's reading is faithful to his biblical sources and also contextual in terms of what the texts mean to the Chronicler's contemporary readers in the postexilic period.

In the nineteenth century, the Chronicler was considered to be writing midrash. Based on the word מִדְרָשׁ (midrash) in 2 Chr 13:22 and 24:27, Wellhausen and later scholars argue that Chronicles is a midrash of the historical books as preserved for us in the canon.[106] Although there are different understandings of the term "midrash," it is agreed that "all midrash

---

106. Wellhausen, *Prolegomena*, xiv, 227; Welch, *Work of the Chronicler*, 54.

tries to interpret the Scriptures."[107] More specifically, Peter Ackroyd argues that the Chronicler performed exegesis of earlier materials[108] to produce a homiletic work in order to preach the doctrine of divine retribution, "failure and judgment, grace and restoration."[109] Ackroyd further observes that the Chronicler applies exegetical methods to earlier materials to provide a unified theological understanding of the past history for his own contemporaries. This explains the relationship between unbelief and national disaster to promote faith and restoration.[110] For instance, 1 Chr 10:1–12 is almost identical to 1 Sam 31:1–13, though the Chronicler adds a few minor details (e.g., the Chronicler adds the name of the place where Saul's head was hung [1 Chr 10:10]). In other words, the Chronicler faithfully reads the account of Saul's death in 1 Sam 31 because his reading closely follows 1 Sam 31:1–13 (// 1 Chr 10:1–12). While reading 1 Sam 31:1–13, the Chronicler adds an explanation for Saul's death, which is Saul's unfaithfulness (מעל) to YHWH, his disobedience to YHWH's command, and his consultation of a medium (1 Chr 10:13). Ackroyd indicates that the concept of unfaithfulness (מעל) to YHWH is common in Chronicles and links to the themes of conquest and exile in Deuteronomy. Indeed, Deut 32:51–52 tells of the Israelites' unfaithfulness to YHWH and consequently their failure to conquer the promised land. In the postexilic period, the Israelites' unfaithfulness to YHWH was often mentioned (e.g., Neh 1:8 and Ezra 9–10). Here, the Chronicler reads the narrative of Saul's death and failure to conquer his enemies with relevance to the people's unfaithfulness in the Chronicler's own time.[111]

Similarly, W. M. Schniedewind states, "There can be no doubt that Chr. was an interpreter of Scripture."[112] Chronicles, which includes various forms such as speeches, narratives, and theology, is like a sermon because its overall function is homiletical, to exhort the Chronicler's audience to seek the Lord.[113] For Schniedewind's example, 1 Chr 23:1–32 demonstrates a faithful reading of Num 4 and a relevant application of the Mosaic law to the Chronicler's period. Numbers 4:1–3 declare that Levites from thirty

---

107. See details in Tate, *Handbook for Biblical Interpretation*, 258–61.
108. Ackroyd, "Chronicler as Exegete," 24.
109. Ackroyd, *I and II Chronicles*, 27.
110. Ackroyd, "Chronicler as Exegete," 24; Ackroyd, *I and II Chronicles*, 27–28.
111. Ackroyd, "Chronicler as Exegete," 7.
112. Schniedewind, "Chronicler as an Interpreter," 179.
113. Schniedewind, *Word of God in Transition*, 250–52.

The Chronicler's General Methodology with Biblical Sources

years old to fifty years old are responsible for all the work in the tabernacle. First Chronicles 23 recounts how all the Levites who were thirty years old and above were gathered (1 Chr 23:3) to do the work in the house of the Lord. The following verses (1 Chr 23:4–23) list the names of all these Levites. This is a faithful reading of Num 4. Beyond that, 1 Chr 23:24–32 illustrates how the Chronicler applies the Mosaic law with relevance to the changed historical context of his postexilic period. Numbers 4 describes how the Levites should serve in the tabernacle, which was moveable, whereas 1 Chr 23 indicates how the Levites should serve in the house of the Lord, which was in a fixed location. To apply the law appropriately for the new historical context, in 1 Chr 23:24–32 the list also includes Levites from twenty years old and above. The reason is that the Levites were no longer to carry the tabernacle and other things for the movable worship services. The Levites had changed to working in the temple. The Chronicler points out that this change had been initiated by King David (1 Chr 23:22–27) and continued to apply in the postexilic period. In the time of Zerubbabel and Jeshua the son of Jozadak, all the Levites who returned from the captivity and were twenty years old and above had to serve in the temple (Ezra 3:8).[114]

Following numerous recent publications of studies on the Dead Sea Scrolls, some scholars have observed that Chronicles is similar to much of the Jewish literature from the Second Temple period in which the authors rewrote biblical passages in their own words. Such Second Temple literature has been designated as Rewritten Bible. George J. Brooke states that Chronicles is an example of Rewritten Bible though "the authoritative place of Chronicles as written forms of the earlier history books is unclear."[115] Philip Alexander states that Chronicles is "arguably the prototype of all the rewritten Bible texts."[116] Despite being named Rewritten Bible, this kind of literature does not merely rewrite the Scriptures. Interpretation of the received authoritative texts is also an indispensable aspect of these works. The general features of this type of literature are that authors rewrite selected biblical passages such as legal texts, narratives, Former and Latter

---

114. Schniedewind, "Chronicler as an Interpreter," 169–70.

115. Brooke, "Rewritten Bible," 778. Klein shows some differences between the Rewritten Bible literature and Chronicles. Although Klein objects to Chronicles being considered as Rewritten Bible, he agrees with the general consensus that the Chronicler did employ exegetical methods on the authoritative texts he received (see Klein and Hanson, *2 Chronicles*, 4–5).

116. Alexander, "Retelling the Old Testament," 100.

Prophets,[117] and implicitly give exegesis on the biblical texts[118] in order to both "draw out the sense of Scripture" and validate the tradition of the community of the author or readers of Rewritten Bible.[119] Thus, even if the term "Rewritten Bible" is applied to Chronicles, the Chronicler's general method is again to interpret biblical texts to display the meaning of the text and make it relevant to the tradition of the author's community. An example of rewritten texts is given by Pancratius C. Beentjes, who argues that the Chronicler rewrote genealogies from the book of Genesis. The genealogies (1 Chr 1:1—2:2) were rewritten in such a way as to make Israel the center of the nations from a geographical perspective,[120] and to make the three tribes of Judah, Benjamin (loyal to the house of David), and Levi (responsible for the temple services) dominant among the tribes. First Chronicles 2:3—9:44 lists more names from those three tribes than from any other tribes. The reason is that most of the Jewish people who constituted the Chronicler's postexilic community belonged to those three tribes.[121] Again, the Chronicler accurately reads or rewrites names and lines of descent from earlier materials and also makes them relevant to the historical context of his postexilic community.

Another popular way to characterize Chronicles is as a redactional work. What is the Chronicler's method if Chronicles is a redactional work? The activity of a redactor may be described as follows: "Selection of material, the editorial links, summaries and comments, expansions, additions, and clarifications which it is believed the biblical writer has introduced in the composition of his text"; these "reveal insights into the theology of the biblical author and the community of which he was a member."[122] This means that if the Chronicler is a redactor, he shapes biblical texts to communicate certain theological views to serve his postexilic community. Using redaction criticism to examine 2 Chr 8:11 // 1 Kgs 9:24,[123] Louis C.

---

117. Brooke, "Rewritten Bible," 778–79; Alexander, "Retelling the Old Testament," 99.

118. Brooke, "Rewritten Bible," 780.

119. Alexander, "Retelling the Old Testament," 118.

120. Beentjes, *Tradition and Transformation*, 22.

121. Beentjes, *Tradition and Transformation*, 17.

122. Law, *Historical Critical Method*, 181.

123. 1 Kgs 9:24: "Pharaoh's daughter went up from the city of David to her own house that Solomon had built for her; then he built the Millo." 2 Chr 8:11: "Solomon brought Pharaoh's daughter from the city of David to the house that he had built for her, for he said, 'My wife shall not live in the house of King David of

The Chronicler's General Methodology with Biblical Sources

Jonker argues that the Chronicler adds the clause "for he said my wife shall not live in the house of David King of Israel because the places where the ark of YHWH has come are holy," which is not found in the parallel source (1 Kgs 9:24), into 2 Chr 8:11. The purpose is to explain why Solomon's wife, who was Pharaoh's daughter, dwelt in places outside the city of David as stated in 1 Kgs 9:24.[124] Anti-exogamy traditions circulated in the postexilic era, as evidenced in Ezra 9–10 and Neh 13. Those traditions derived from the regulations found in Num 25. Jonker presents a detailed examination of Ezra 9–10 and Neh 13 and then concludes that the Chronicler's application, as demonstrated by the additional clause in 2 Chr 8:11, is closer to Neh 13 (no expelling gentile wives from the Israelite community) than to Ezra 9–10 (expelling gentile wives).[125] On the one hand, the Chronicler reads 1 Kgs 9:24 faithfully since he does not subvert the meaning of 1 Kgs 9:24, which states that Solomon built a house for Pharaoh's daughter separated from Jerusalem. On the other hand, through the added phrase, the Chronicler explains the texts in a way that is relevant to the traditions of his postexilic community concerning the attitude of anti-exogamy. In other words, even if the Chronicler is a redactor, the Chronicler reads 1 Kgs 9:24 faithfully to the source and contextually appropriates it to communicate what the text means to his postexilic community.

More recently, the designation "historiography" has been applied to Chronicles. If Chronicles is historiography, then what is the Chronicler's method? Isaac Kalimi, a leading scholar advocating this view, states that the Chronicler selects earlier biblical texts, connects various texts, interprets the meaning of the texts, and explains ambiguities and contradictions in the texts in order to derive lessons for the present and the future of the Chronicler's Israel.[126] Along these lines, the Chronicler's general method is to interpret his source texts and express their significance to his contemporary community. For instance, 2 Chr 36:9–10 // 2 Kgs 24:8–17 presents the reign of Jehoiachin, king of Judah. However, the account of Jehoiachin in Chronicles is shorter than the one in Kings because it omits the description of Jerusalem's destruction by the king of Babylon as well as the description of the people taken to Babylon.

Israel, for the places to which the ark of the Lord has come are holy.'"
    124. Jonker, "'My Wife,'" 42–45.
    125. Jonker, "'My Wife,'" 42–44, 46.
    126. Kalimi, *Ancient Israelite Historian*, 31–32.

Another significant difference is seen in Chronicles' information about the precious vessels of the house of YHWH brought to Babylon by king Nebuchadnezzar (2 Chr 36:10). In contrast to Chronicles, 2 Kgs 24:12–13 states that the king of Babylon carried off all the treasures of the house of YHWH and the treasures of the king's house, and cut in pieces all the vessels of gold in the temple of YHWH. Why does the account in Chronicles mention only the vessels and present the details differently from 2 Kgs 24:12–13? Isaac Kalimi and James D. Purvis point out that what happened to the vessels in the attack by the king of Babylon has also been narrated in other passages: Jer 27:16–22; 28:3, 6; 2 Kgs 25:13–17 // Jer 52:17–23. Jer 27:16–22; 28:3, 6 do not state that the vessels were cut into pieces, whereas 2 Kgs 24:12–13 says the vessels of gold in the temple were cut into pieces. The two scholars argue that the Chronicler had two sources. He followed both the Jeremiah tradition and 2 Kgs 24:12–13. Jeremiah 27:16–22 and 28:3, 6 tell of vessels (in general) being taken to Babylon. 2 Kings 24:12–13 specifies that vessels of *gold* were cut into pieces. Consequently, the Chronicler writes that *precious* vessels (instead of *gold*, though *precious* may hint at gold) were brought to Babylon (2 Chr 36:10).[127]

The remaining question is why the Chronicler omits other details of Jerusalem's destruction except for the vessels. Jeremiah 27:19–22 records Jeremiah's prophecy that one day YHWH would bring back the vessels from Babylon to the house of YHWH. In the postexilic period, Ezra 1:7–11; 5:13–15; and 6:5 narrate the story of the vessels being returned from Babylon to Jerusalem. However, the Second Temple in postexilic times was unimpressive and less splendid than the first temple built by Solomon (Hag 2:3; Ezra 3:12–13). It also lacked the ark of the covenant (2 Macc 2:5). Kalimi and Purvis argue that the Chronicler highlights the continuous use of these same vessels to promote the Second Temple during the Chronicler's period.[128] This example shows that even if Chronicles is characterized as a historiographical work, the Chronicler's general method is the same as if it were considered as a midrash, a sermon, a Rewritten Bible, or a redactional work: he reads his sources faithfully to what the text meant and he also shapes the text in a relevant fashion for his postexilic audience.

---

127. Kalimi and Purvis, "King Jehoiachin," 452–53.
128. Kalimi and Purvis, "King Jehoiachin," 454–55.

Chapter Conclusion

In view of all the above, we conclude that the Chronicler appropriated texts now reflected in MT Samuel–Kings and the four MT Pss 105:1–15; 96:1–13; 106:1, 47–48; and 132:8–10. Moreover, we also argue that although scholars have proposed a variety of ways to describe the nature of Chronicles, behind all of them, the Chronicler's general method in using existing biblical materials is the same: the Chronicler not only interprets his biblical sources, but also applies their messages with relevance to his postexilic community. Unlike most Western biblical interpretation, which focuses on what the text meant, the Chronicler's general method is akin to Asian biblical reading, i.e., holistically encompassing both what the text meant and what it means. This leads to the question of exactly *how* the Chronicler reads biblical passages in order to be faithful to what those passages meant while also making them relevant to his postexilic audience. This question will be addressed in chapters 4 and 5. In addition, those chapters will compare the Chronicler's reading of biblical materials with each of the two Asian models of biblical interpretation. To prepare for that, we must first examine those two models more closely. That will be our task in the next chapter.

3

Asian Contextual Reading and Postcolonial Reading of the Bible

THIS CHAPTER WILL PRESENT basic features of the two common models of Asian biblical interpretation. The term Asian biblical interpretation could refer either to how Asians interpret the Bible or how the Bible has been read in the light of an Asian context. The term "Asian" is very broad, encompassing many countries and peoples in Asia with diverse cultures, heterogeneous identities, distinct political issues, various social issues, and different histories of Christianity. With these backgrounds, Asian biblical interpretation has flourished in recent decades. Although the gospel came to each Asian country at different times, most Asians could not engage in biblical interpretation until the last two centuries when the Bible was translated into the local languages of Asia.[1] Bible translations and widespread printing of the Bible has only been done in the modern period by evangelical missionaries (e.g., in the nineteenth century for India[2] and in the twentieth century for Vietnam[3]). Philip Chia characterizes the Bible as an immigrant book to Asia because Christianity is not a traditional religion

---

1. Chia asks, "How can the Bible be discovered in a nonbiblical world when the peoples do not even have access to the Bible in their own language?" Chia, "Differences and Difficulties," 54.

2. Premnath, "Biblical Interpretation in India," 4.

3. Reimer, *Vietnam's Christians*, 28.

of most Asian countries. Consequently, the discipline of biblical studies in Asia has only emerged in the modern period through Western penetration and influence.[4]

Since "Asian" is a broad term, scholars have tried to categorize the various approaches to biblical interpretation among Asian peoples based on common features. Two models of Asian biblical interpretation have commonly been studied and discussed among Asian Christians: the Asian contextual model and the postcolonial model. These two reading models are widely employed by Asians and are demonstrated in many publications. Together they paint a general picture of Asian biblical reading. Thus, we select these two reading models to compare with the Chronicler's reading of biblical sources. We will present these comparisons in chapters 4 and 5. In this chapter, we will present the basic features of each of the two Asian models of biblical interpretation.

Dalit Biblical Reading: An Asian Contextual Approach

As mentioned in the literature review, although practitioners of the Asian contextual reading model have varied concerns and interests, they share the same reading principle. They use their contextual concerns and interests (e.g., the liberation and resistance to discrimination of marginal peoples, discrimination against tribal people, gender discrimination, social injustice, and so on) as keys to read the Bible and to make the Bible relevant to their readers' contexts.[5] Among practitioners of the Asian contextual model are Dalit biblical interpreters. Other reading approaches of the Asian contextual model, as presented in the literature review, have not been as widely used to interpret the whole Bible. Thus, Dalit biblical reading has been selected to compare with the Chronicler's reading in this present study. To prepare for the comparison, it is necessary to first examine Dalit biblical interpretation in greater detail than the above survey.

Dalit refers to the oppressed people in the lowest caste of Indian society who have not been categorized in the caste system.[6] There are about 250 million Dalit people.[7] The majority of Christians in India belong

---

4. Chia, "Biblical Studies," 90–91.

5. Kuan, "Asian Biblical Interpretation," 72–73; Lee, "Asian Biblical Interpretation," 68–69; Sugirtharajah, *Bible and Asia*, 210.

6. Clarke, "Dalit Theology," 64.

7. Massey, *One Volume*, xvii.

to the Dalit community; Melanchthon indicates that about 90 percent of Christians in India are Dalit people.[8] This section will discuss the general contextual issues faced by Dalits, why the Bible holds an important role among the Dalits, and how the Dalits interpret the Bible.

General Contextual Issues of Dalits

Although the caste system has undergone many changes throughout history, the basic features of the Indian caste system remain.[9] Owing to the dominant influence of Hinduism since ancient times, the society of India has been divided into four major castes as written in Hindu scriptures (*Vedas*): *Brahmin*, *Kshatriya*, *Vaishya*, and *Shudra*. *Brahmins* are called priests and teachers of the universal laws of the world. They are people of the highest caste in Indian society. *Kshatriya* are called warriors who defend and protect the community. *Vaishya* are called traders and farmers who run the business of the community. *Shudra* are called laborers and servants of the community.[10] Besides the four major castes, the fifth group of Indian people is the lowest rung of Indian society, which is outside the caste system. According to Hinduism, all Indian people who belong to outcaste collectives are called Dalits.[11] The word "Dalit" comes from the Sanskrit word *dal*, which means crushed, downtrodden, scattered, destroyed; the word has a theological background from Hinduism claiming that Dalits are "the people who were born from the dirt that God walked on" and are appointed to do jobs considered unclean from a religious perspective, such as dealing with dead bodies, cleaning rubbish and sewage, or processing animal skins for use.[12] Caste discrimination is based on the predetermined perception of unequal social structure according to the teachings of Hinduism.[13] Dalits are required to stay separate from upper castes in daily activities. For example, they are banned from coming to public places such as temples,

---

8. Melanchthon, "Dalits, Bible, and Method."
9. Milner, *Status and Sacredness*, 46.
10. Milner, *Status and Sacredness*, 46.
11. Clarke, "Dalit Theology," 64.
12. Bubash, "Dalit Theology," 37–38. Since Dalit protest movements have emerged in recent decades to reject the negative implications of the term Dalit, this term has been used with positive meaning to express "hope for recovery of their past identity." See Massey, *Down Trodden*, 3; Oommen, "Emerging Dalit Theology."
13. Kumari, "Untouchable 'Dalits,'" 10.

parks, village wells (where people draw water), and even the main streets of communities. Dalits are usually forced to perform the hardest and lowest-paid jobs.[14] Intercaste marriages are persecuted.[15] This phenomenon of segregation, called "untouchability," is the social norm, although the Indian government prohibits those practices.[16]

Although there are many theories of caste discrimination,[17] there is a common consensus that Dalits have suffered discrimination in Indian society because the Indian caste system or Hinduism hold that Dalits have the traditional (or theological) background of impurity, pollution, and filth.[18] Dalits suffer discrimination not only in Hindu society, but also among Christians (both Roman Catholics and Protestants) in India. For example, Dalit Christians rarely have opportunities to take part in church decision-making. The percentage of Dalit priests is less than 4 percent. Upper-caste priests are reluctant to visit the homes of Dalit Christians.[19] Religious doctrines emphasized by Christian leaders who belong to the upper castes do not address the concerns of Dalits.[20] Despite Indian legislation prohibiting caste discrimination and practices of untouchability in recent decades, anti-Dalit discrimination still exists in daily life. A recent BBC article reports that a lecturer at Delhi University came to a Rajasthan tea shop for a drink. When he had finished his drink and was ready to leave, the shop owner asked the customer which caste he belonged to. The lecturer said that he was a Dalit. Immediately, the shop owner refused to wash the cup which was used by the Dalit customer and instead asked the lecturer to wash the cup. Another Dalit man was refused a haircut by a local barber who belonged to an upper caste. A group of Dalit pupils were required to eat their lunch separately from their classmates who belonged to upper castes.[21]

In recent decades, Dalit issues have attracted international attention due to the rise of the internet and the explosion of mass communications. Caste discrimination has become a human rights concern.[22] Many Dalits

---

14. Kumari, "Untouchable 'Dalits,'" 10.
15. Bubash, "Dalit Theology," 38.
16. Kumari, "Untouchable 'Dalits,'" 9.
17. See details in Rajkumar, *Dalit Theology*, 5–18.
18. Rajkumar, *Dalit Theology*, 19.
19. Rajkumar, *Dalit Theology*, 20–21.
20. Bubash, "Dalit Theology," 39.
21. "India's Dalits Still Fighting."
22. Rawat and Satyanarayana, *Dalit Studies*, 7.

find that education can deliver them from poverty.[23] Consequently, the literacy rate of Dalits has risen from 37.41 percent in 1991[24] to 66 percent in 2011.[25] In terms of Christianity in India, inspired by Latin American liberation theology in 1970s, both the Roman Catholic and Protestant churches have worked on theologies for Dalit liberation and resistance since 1978.[26] Scholars have observed that the Bible has become the main foundation of Dalit theology[27] because the Bible is understood as affirming Dalit Christian identity.[28]

The Role of the Bible to Dalits

Many Dalit Christians have discovered their identity in the Bible. James Massey comments that although the two ancient languages, Hebrew and Sanskrit, are different from each other in terms of grammar and syntax, the root of the term Dalit (*dal*) shares similar meanings of negation with the same root in Hebrew. The Sanskrit root *dal* means "to crack, split, be broken or torn asunder, trodden down, scattered, crushed and destroyed."[29] He also indicates that "the Hebrew root דַּל (dal) which means hang down, to be languid, be weakened, be low and feeble," occurs fifty times in different grammatical forms in the Hebrew Bible to denote identity of people who have been rejected by dominant groups (e.g., Exod 23:3, 30:15; Lev 14:21; Job 34:28; Ps 83:3; Prov 22:16; Jer 40:7, 52:16; and others).[30] K. P. Aleaz shows that Dalits consider Jesus in the New Testament to be a Dalit when he came into the world. The "dalitness" of Jesus is demonstrated through his genealogy (his four outcaste female ancestors) and his suffering of rejection and ridicule (e.g., Mark 2:15–16, 8:31, 9:12, 10:45, and so on). The climax of Jesus' dalitness is demonstrated on the cross where Jesus was cursed,

---

23. "India's Dalits Still Fighting."
24. Clarke, "Viewing the Bible," 253.
25. Jaffrelot, "Dalits Still Left Out."
26. Hebden, *Dalit Theology*, 115–17; Rajkumar, *Dalit Theology*, 38–40.
27. Melanchthon, "Unleashing the Power," 55–56; Hebden, *Dalit Theology*, 117–18.
28. Melanchthon, "Unleashing the Power," 58.
29. Massey, "Dalits in India," 20.
30. Massey, *Towards Dalit Hermeneutics*, 3–7.

crushed, broken, and forsaken.³¹ On the cross, Jesus took the outcasteness (dalitness) of human beings upon himself.³²

Regarding the issue of impurity and pollution, Peniel Rajkumar notes that the Mosaic legislations concerning purity and impurity (e.g., Lev 13–15; Num 5:1–3; 19) never imputes uncleanness or disqualification to people (or even animals) on the basis of hierarchy.³³ This biblical teaching promotes Dalit identity because it contrasts with the Hindu teaching that considers Dalits as permanently impure and polluted based on the inequality inherent in the caste system. As for untouchability, healing stories in the New Testament frequently portray Jesus' healing by touching without regard for any risk of contamination by the impurity of patients and sinners. Jesus' touch made polluted outcastes whole and restored them to the community.³⁴ Thus, the healing narratives of the New Testament have challenged caste discrimination regarding touching uncleanness.³⁵

Moreover, the Bible plays a critical liberating role to Dalits not only due to its content but also for its physical tangibility as a sacred book. Since Dalits and tribal Indians are banned from reading and even touching the Hindu scriptures (as sacred texts), Clarke reports that even illiterate Dalit Christians and Indian tribal Christians would buy copies of the Bible to display in their houses.³⁶ Even holding the Bible (a sacred text) is a way to empower the identity of Dalits.³⁷ For understanding the Bible, most Dalits and Indian tribal people rely on biblical interpreters.³⁸ What does Dalit biblical interpretation look like? The next paragraphs will present the answer.

Method of Dalit Biblical Interpretation

Beyond possessing the Christian sacred text, the Dalits read the Bible to find equality in society, to be liberated from discrimination, and to resist the oppression of the caste system.³⁹ Dalit biblical interpretation combines

31. Aleaz, "Some Features," 148.
32. Aleaz, "Some Features," 162.
33. Rajkumar, *Dalit Theology*, 80–83.
34. Rajkumar, *Dalit Theology*, 99.
35. Rajkumar, *Dalit Theology*, 97–98.
36. Clarke, "Viewing the Bible," 253.
37. Rajkumar, "'How' Does the Bible," 412.
38. Clarke, "Viewing the Bible," 265.
39. Raja, "Dialogue," 40–50; Melanchthon, "Unleashing the Power," 61.

a range of approaches, such as historical-critical approaches, literary approaches, and reader-response methods.[40] Historical-critical and literary approaches help Dalit readers discern how God worked among marginalized and oppressed people (similar to Dalits) in the periods depicted in the Bible. The reader-response approach presents meaning through dialogue or interaction between a reader and a text.[41] Thus, the reader-response approach assists Dalits to discern how biblical messages are helpful to the defenseless and oppressed people in Indian society. The above summary of James Massey's understanding of the term "dalit" with the similar root in Hebrew and Sanskrit in detail[42] illustrates that

1. historical-critical (author-centered) approaches are employed to find the original meaning of this term in Hebrew,
2. a literary approach is used to discern how this root is used in the literary contexts in which the root occurs, and
3. a reader-response approach is used to show the interrelation between the use of the Hebrew term in the Bible and the Sanskrit term in the Indian context.

A succinct statement on the multifaceted methodology of Dalit biblical hermeneutics is provided by Maria Arul Raja: "A genuine Dalit interpretation of the Bible has to have the blend of the reader-centered, text-centered and also the author-centered approaches. They need not be exclusive of each other."[43]

Although Sugirtharajah opines that the Asian contextual model indeed helps Asian readers to interpret and apply the Bible in their contexts, he also points out that the issues of biblical interpretation pertain not only to the interpretative method but also to the sociopolitical nature of biblical texts.[44] He argues that many biblical books were written under the colonial system to encourage oppressed people to submit to dominant powers (e.g., Rom 13; 1 Pet 2:13–14; Titus 3:1).[45] Thus, Sugirtharajah proposes the postcolonial model, which we now consider.

---

40. Melanchthon, "Unleashing the Power," 58–59.
41. Tate, *Handbook for Biblical Interpretation*, 369.
42. Massey, *Towards Dalit Hermeneutics*, 3–34.
43. Raja, "Reading the Bible," 87.
44. Sugirtharajah, *Bible and Asia*, 222.
45. Sugirtharajah, *Asian Biblical Hermeneutics*, 19–20.

The Postcolonial Biblical Reading

The second common model of biblical interpretation practiced by Asians is the postcolonial model. Although the terms post-colonialism and postcolonialism are often used interchangeably, the former usually refers to the period after colonized countries have gained independence, whereas the latter usually denotes an academic discipline.[46] Postcolonialism studies the influence and legacy of imperialism on colonized nations and then seeks to resist the influence of imperialism, supremacy, inequality, or disparity across all aspects of society (e.g., politics, economics, history, literature, gender, culture, and so on).[47] Combining postcolonial studies and biblical studies, postcolonial biblical criticism examines colonial dominance in biblical studies and then seeks to resist those imperialist influences.[48] Postcolonial biblical criticism has been practiced all over the world, such as in Africa, Asia, and countries in South, Central, and North America (by Asian American scholars), to serve different aims (e.g., feminist criticism, Marxist criticism, liberation, or identity of diaspora [hybridity]).[49] For instance, Kwok Pui-lan, a Chinese woman born in Hong Kong, applies this model to interpret the Bible from her Asian feminist perspective.[50] She uses this reading approach[51] to present a feminist interpretation of the Bible because postcolonial reading helps women to resist oppression resulting not only from gender discrimination but also from multiple forms of social, economic, and ethnic discrimination.[52] Regarding postcolonial biblical criticism in Asia, Ralph Broadbent calls R. S. Sugirtharajah,[53] a Sri Lankan, "the Sage of Postcolonialism" and "the founding father of postcolonialism" among the biblical and theological community in Asia as well as all over

---

46. Crowell, "Postcolonial Studies," 218.

47. Ching, "Postcolonialism," 169–70.

48. Moore and Segovia, "Postcolonial Biblical Criticism," 10–11.

49. Moore and Segovia, "Postcolonial Biblical Criticism," 2–3. For detail on different aims and perspectives, see Moore and Segovia, "Postcolonial Biblical Criticism," 12–19.

50. Kwok, *Introducing Asian Feminist Theology*, 59.

51. For the postcolonial reading model, this study uses the term "model" and "approach" interchangeably because this reading model does not have various approaches with different names like the Asian contextual model.

52. Kwok, *Introducing Asian Feminist Theology*, 62; Kwok, "Making the Connections," 48.

53. R. S. Sugirtharajah was born and grew up in Sri Lanka. He studied theology in India and the UK and he has taught theology at Birmingham University.

the world.[54] How do we discern whether an interpreter practices postcolonial biblical reading? Let us now examine the basic differences between the discipline of Asian contextual reading and postcolonial biblical reading.

Basic Difference: Postcolonial versus Asian Contextual Reading

The postcolonial reading approach suggests that Asian readers not only employ the Bible to liberate readers themselves but also to deliver readers from the Bible itself "to find meaning and solace beyond its brutal and offending tendencies."[55] Although the postcolonial model shares with the contextual model the feature of bringing Asian contextual issues to interpret the Bible (e.g., liberating Asian readers from the domination and discrimination of social class, gender, and race),[56] Sugirtharajah points out differences between the two models as follows. The Asian contextual model generally upholds the authority of the Bible. Practitioners of this model may hold to the hegemonic authority of the Bible while reinterpreting the Bible to elevate Asian contextual issues within the scope of Christianity. The postcolonial model holds that the problems of biblical reading also include the Bible itself because it was written in colonial periods with imperial ideologies. Thus, unlike the contextual model, the postcolonial model insistently considers the authority of the Bible to be equal to that of other religious texts.

Furthermore, the contextual model reads the Bible through the lens of the oppressed people of God (e.g., oppressed Hebrews, suffering Jews) and neglects the suppression of other peoples (e.g., Canaanites, Egyptians) in these same biblical accounts. In contrast, the postcolonial model concerns emancipation for all peoples. The postcolonial interpreters do not stop at the deliverance of the Israelites; they are also concerned with the oppression against the Canaanite peoples as well as the Israelite practice of slavery (Exod 21:1–11). Thus, they see the Bible's endorsement of both liberation and enslavement as problems. Moreover, unlike the Asian contextual model, which demonstrates a Christian-centric hermeneutic, the postcolonial model espouses a pluralism-centric hermeneutic. For example, from the point of view of the poor, the contextual model interprets Mark 12:41–44 as saying that Jesus complimented the poor widow on her wholehearted offering, and thus making her an example of ideal devotion. However, the

54. Broadbent, "One Step Beyond," 297.
55. Sugirtharajah, *Bible and Asia*, 223.
56. Sugirtharajah, "Postcolonial Biblical Interpretation," 77.

postcolonial model reads this passage as meaning that Jesus did not commend the window's offering but rather condemned the exploitation exercised by the temple treasury authorities.[57] The following subsections will consider why scholars employ postcolonial biblical interpretation and what its general method of this model entails.

Reasons for the Postcolonial Biblical Interpretation

Sugirtharajah indicates that, although official colonies have almost ceased to exist in the last two decades, colonialism still survives and tends to revive itself because weak countries and strong countries are interdependent and need one another. Moreover, after the terrorist attacks of September 11 in America, imperialism has clearly reemerged in actions taken in the name of protecting the US and its allies from countries deemed to pose threats to their security. The revival of colonialism is also called neocolonialism. Yee expounds, "Neocolonialism refers to replication of colonial rule and exploitation by an indigenous elite brought to power in a newly independent nation that has thrown off its Western colonizer."[58] Sugirtharajah adds that because of this revival of imperialism, postcolonialism becomes an increasingly important tool for resistance.[59]

For biblical studies, Sugirtharajah argues that the legacy of imperialism has been propagated through Bible commentaries, Bible translations, sermons, articles, journals, and so on. He has conducted many studies of such literature to demonstrate how biblical interpretation has supported colonial ideologies. For example, Sugirtharajah observes that although the words *'am* (עַם) and *goy* (גּוֹי) in Hebrew denotes various meanings such as people, nation, tribe, land, and inhabitants, the King James Version (KJV) translated all those words as "nation." Similarly, the KJV translated the words *ethnos* (ἔθνος) and *genos* (γένος) as "nation," even though those two words in Greek carry many meanings such as nation, people, race, and offspring. Consequently, the term "nation" occurs 454 times in the KJV, while this term in Latin (*natio*) occurs 100 times in the Vulgate. He states the reason is that British translators of the King James Version were influenced by a common colonial ideology that Great Britain was God's chosen nation

---

57. Sugirtharajah, "Postcolonial Biblical Interpretation," 78–79.
58. Yee, "Postcolonial Biblical Criticism," 194.
59. Sugirtharajah, *Postcolonial Reconfigurations*, 96–100.

to spread the gospel all over the world.⁶⁰ Sugirtharajah cites another example of biblical recolonization after the 2004 tsunami tragedy in Asia. He argues that scriptural recolonization occurred when several Bible societies in the West quickly sent Bibles to the Asian countries impacted by the tsunami. He asserts that the flood story in the first eleven chapters of the Bible (Gen 1–11) could be used to strengthen imperialism with two theological responses: the tsunami may be God's punishment and a consequence of human sin.⁶¹

Another reason for postcolonial biblical criticism is that not only do many biblical interpretations support colonial ideologies, but so does the Bible itself. Sugirtharajah argues that the colonial perspective is embedded in the Bible itself because the Bible was written or composed in colonial periods (e.g., during the Assyrian and Persian empires for the Old Testament and the Roman empire for the New Testament) to respond to those imperialist powers.⁶² For example, the book of Esther narrates the story of the Jews under the subjugation of the Persian Empire. This colonial story instructs colonized people how to survive through working in cooperation with the imperialist ruler. In the New Testament, the apostles (e.g., Paul and Peter) lived under the hegemony of the Roman Empire, so their epistles tend to support colonial rule. They called Christians to live submissively and peacefully with colonizers (Rom 13; 1 Pet 2:13–14; Titus 3:1).⁶³ Many such instances of colonial perspectives embedded in biblical texts and numerous examples of the influence of colonial ideologies on biblical interpretation are presented in Sugirtharajah's works.⁶⁴ Thus, postcolonial biblical interpretation aims to expose colonial perspectives embedded in the biblical texts and to resist biblical interpretations supporting colonialism. Moreover, scholars acknowledge the contributions of postcolonial biblical interpretation in terms of providing new insights when reading the Bible through the lens of colonized people who are marginalized or suffering many kinds of discrimination (e.g., gender, race, culture, social class).⁶⁵

---

60. Sugirtharajah, "Master Copy," 512.

61. Sugirtharajah, "Tsunami, Text, and Trauma," 122–28.

62. Sugirtharajah, *Bible and Asia*, 212.

63. Sugirtharajah, *Asian Biblical Hermeneutics*, 19–20.

64. For more illustrations, see Sugirtharajah, *Bible and the Third World*; Sugirtharajah, *Bible and Empire*; Sugirtharajah, *Troublesome Texts*.

65. Lau, "Back Under Authority," 134–35; Sugirtharajah, *Bible and the Third World*, 7; Wright, *Mission of God*, 39.

Method of Postcolonial Biblical Interpretation

To achieve those purposes, postcolonial biblical readers employ an interpretive method involving the following steps. First, they use historical-critical approaches to identify the colonial perspectives embedded by biblical authors or final redactors in biblical texts when they composed or redacted the Bible.[66] Sugirtharajah discerns four kind of "codes" in biblical narratives:

1. The hegemonic code refers to biblical texts about the ruling classes such as kings, officials, rich and powerful people, and their activities (e.g., 2 Sam 9–20; 1 Kgs 1–2).
2. The professional code indicates texts describing laws, traditions, and practices of those rulers to promote the interests of the ruling class.
3. The negotiated code denotes texts about the theological interpretation of certain events to respond to new situations or new contexts (e.g., Mark 12:28–34; Matt 22:34–40; Luke 10:25–37).
4. The oppositional (protest) code refers to texts about marginalized people (e.g., Num 27:1–11; Exod 1:15–19).[67]

Sugirtharajah stipulates that historical-critical approaches need to be employed to discover the colonial ideologies embedded in those biblical texts. For example, when reading biblical passages about household codes (Eph 5:1—6:9; Col 3:18—4:1; 1 Pet 2:18—3:7), he instructs readers to refer to commentaries to discover the historical background of the household codes.[68]

Another example is Philip Chia's postcolonial reading of Dan 1. To describe the colonial power of Babylon, he uses historical-critical reading to reconstruct the historical background of Dan 1 in order to show King Nebuchadnezzar's colonial policies through segregation, language, education, and change of names.[69] He also engages in a philological investigation to elucidate the narrator's resistance to the colonizer (Babylon) by performing word study of בָּא (come, take, and place, Nebuchadnezzar's actions in Dan 1:1-2). He contrasts the Babylonian king's actions with YHWH's will and command for the people to come to the Jerusalem temple for worship (Deut 12:5, 31:11; 2 Sam 7:18; 1 Kgs.8:41; Isa 30:29; Jer 7:2; Pss 5:7 [v. 8 in

---

66. Crowell, "Postcolonial Studies," 233.
67. Sugirtharajah, *Postcolonial Criticism*, 79–86.
68. Sugirtharajah, *Postcolonial Criticism*, 82. For this reading, Sugirtharajah suggests the work of Aune, *Greco-Roman Literature*.
69. Chia, "On Naming the Subject" 172–77.

Hebrew], 42:2 [v. 3 in Hebrew]) to demonstrate that the narrator's ironic resistant voice asserts that it was actually YHWH, the Lord of the colonized, who gave victory to the colonizer (Nebuchadnezzar) (Dan 1:2). Thus, the "voices of the colonized shall be heard, and the identity of the colonized as a superior subject, rather than a subjugated subject will be articulated."[70] Crowell comments, "Chia's reading of this chapter is an insightful example of how postcolonial theory can inform historical-critical and literary readings of the text."[71]

After detecting colonial perspectives contained in biblical texts, reception history is necessary to examine how prior biblical interpretations supported colonialism.[72] This step will help postcolonial readers realize how marginalized or colonized voices have been ignored by colonial interpretations.

Postcolonial readers then reinterpret the Bible through the lens of colonized people to address postcolonial interests such as liberation, discrimination (gender, ethnicity, social class, or religion), identity (multinational and multicultural perspectives), and so on.[73] Sugirtharajah concludes that postcolonial biblical hermeneutics is a combination of different methods (from historical-critical approaches to contemporary literary approaches). It is "interdisciplinary in nature and pluralistic in its outlook."[74]

In Asia, practitioners of postcolonial biblical reading often call their approach by different names. For example, Lily Fetalsana-Apura reads Josh 1–9 in the Filipino context. Although she describes her work as "resistant reading," her method is actually a postcolonial reading because she clearly states that she is examining the colonial perspectives embedded in the biblical text itself, reviewing scholarly interpretations of the passage that were influenced by imperialist ideologies, and then reinterpreting the biblical text in the Filipino context.[75] Sugirtharajah affirms that there are "some well-established practitioners of postcolonial criticism and a few scholars

---

70. Chia, "On Naming the Subject," 172–74.

71. Crowell, "Postcolonial Studies," 235.

72. Yee, "Postcolonial Biblical Criticism," 206–7; Sugirtharajah, *Bible and the Third World*, 255–57.

73. Sugirtharajah, *Bible and the Third World*, 252–53.

74. Sugirtharajah, *Bible and the Third World*, 258.

75. Fetalsana-Apura, *Filipino Resistance Reading*, 15–22.

Asian Contextual Reading and Postcolonial Reading of the Bible

who may not call themselves postcolonial, but whose work resonates with the preoccupations of postcolonialism."[76]

In summary, the Asian contextual model and the postcolonial model lean on historical-critical approaches, literary approaches, and biblical theology as the first steps of their reading method. They then take on the feature of Asian biblical interpretation, which involves reading the Bible in an Asian context.

Chapter Conclusion

This chapter has presented the two models of Asian biblical reading that have been widely used in Asian communities. They are the Dalit biblical reading approach (representing the Asian contextual model) and the biblical reading approach of the postcolonial model. In terms of interpretive steps in practice, the methods of the two reading models are different. In terms of purposes of interpretation, however, both models of Asian reading belong to the "contextual umbrella" because they all deal with Asian contextual issues and concerns. Together, these two common models of biblical reading paint a general picture of Asian biblical hermeneutics.

Philip Chia claims that biblical studies in China and India are largely representative of the whole of Asian practice, which includes interfaith dialogues between Christianity and the traditional religions of Asian countries, as well as dialogues between the Bible and contextual issues in terms of Asian social, cultural, political, and economic issues (e.g., racial and ethnic conflicts, poor and oppressed people).[77] Chia's perspective is supported by the fact that pioneers of postcolonial biblical reading are from China and India (e.g., Archie Lee, Kwok Pui-lan, and R. S. Sugirtharajah, in his works focusing on the Indian context). The two reading models presented in this chapter actually covered more than the geographical scope named by Philip Chia. Asian Christians living in the US also employ the two models to read the Bible. Recently published, the *T&T Clark Handbook of Asian American Biblical Hermeneutics* covers the two Asian reading models discussed in this chapter.[78] It also shows that although the two Asian reading models attempt to read the Bible in Asian contexts, they all employ some Western

---

76. Sugirtharajah, *Postcolonial Biblical Reader*, 2.

77. Chia, "Biblical Studies," 91–92.

78. Kim and Yang, *T&T Clark Handbook*; see also Liew, *Asian American Biblical Hermeneutics*, 12–16, 76, 92, 115–16.

approaches (e.g., historical-critical approaches, grammatical-historical approaches, literary study, or rhetorical discourse) in the initial steps of interpretation. These are then followed by dialogues between the Bible and the Asian readers' contexts. In other words, the two models of Asian biblical reading build on and extend Western biblical reading; they do not stop with studying what the text meant. The Asian biblical reading proceeds further and always looks for what the text means to contemporary Asian readers.

Having surveyed the landscape of Asian biblical interpretation by looking at the two common interpretive models, we now turn to examine each one more thoroughly and compare each model with the way the Chronicler handled his sources. This will be our task for the next chapters.

4

Comparing the Chronicler's Reading and Postcolonial Biblical Reading

ALTHOUGH FORMAL COLONIAL GOVERNMENTS ceased to exist roughly two decades ago, and we are now living in the postcolonial era, the legacy of colonialism still remains in many areas of modern society, including biblical studies. Postcolonial biblical reading emerged in the 1990s as a tool to resist the influence of colonialism in biblical interpretation.[1] As indicated in chapter 3, although practitioners of postcolonial biblical hermeneutics all over the world have different interests, they share a common interpretive procedure when using this approach to read the Bible. Postcolonial biblical readers employ a method involving the following steps. First, reception history is employed to examine how prior interpretations supported colonialism. Second, historical-critical approaches are used to identify any colonial perspectives embedded in biblical texts. The aforementioned two steps need not be done in that order; they may be reversed. Finally, postcolonial interpreters reread the Bible through the lens of colonized people to address postcolonial readers' interests such as liberation, discrimination (gender, ethnicity, social class, or religion), and cultural and ethnic identity.

To present a full picture of the postcolonial reading approach, this chapter will first illustrate in detail how a postcolonial reader implements

---

1. Yee, "Postcolonial Biblical Criticism," 204–5.

those three steps. Uriah Kim's study, which uses postcolonial hermeneutics to read 2 Kgs 21:19—23:30 concerning the King Josiah account, is selected as an illustration.[2] However, our evaluation of the postcolonial approach will also engage other studies practicing postcolonial biblical hermeneutics, including postcolonial biblical commentaries, to give a fuller assessment of this approach. Uriah Kim's work is selected to illustrate the postcolonial approach because 2 Kgs 21:19—23:30 is also read by the Chronicler (2 Chr 33:21—35:27). Thus, this selection provides a common basis for our hermeneutical comparison between the postcolonial biblical reading and the Chronicler's reading. Moreover, unlike most studies of postcolonial biblical reading, which are short essays, Uriah Kim's treatment of 2 Kgs 22–23 is a monograph that thoroughly demonstrates all three steps of postcolonial interpretation.[3] After discussing Kim's work, we will consider whether the Chronicler reads his sources through the lens of his postexilic colonized context in ways similar to the postcolonial biblical reading approach.

Description of a Postcolonial Biblical Reading (2 Kings 21:19—23:30)

As mentioned above, the first step of a postcolonial reading of the Bible is usually a reception history to examine how prior interpretations supported colonialism. Similarly, Kim's postcolonial reading of 2 Kgs 21:19—23:30 begins with a reception history to investigate how previous studies of the Josiah account supported colonialism.

Reception History of the Josiah Account

By examining the reception history of the Josiah account in 2 Kgs 22–23, Kim demonstrates how past studies of the Josiah account have supported colonialism. Kim concurs with the common consensus of scholarship that the account of Josiah (2 Kgs 22–23) belongs to the Deuteronomistic History (DH). He discerns two major views on the DH composition. First,

---

2. Kim, *Decolonizing Josiah*.

3. Kim has written another monograph employing postcolonial biblical interpretation (Kim, *Identity and Loyalty*). However, many of the biblical passages Kim uses to read in this study were not used in the Chronicler's reading (e.g., 1 Sam 1–30; 2 Sam 2; 3:6–39; 4; 13–21:14; 1 Kgs 1:1—2:9, 13–46). Thus, this present study focuses on Kim's postcolonial reading of 2 Kgs 21:19—23:30.

Comparing the Chronicler's Reading and Postcolonial Biblical Reading

Kim states that F. M. Cross and his followers suggest that the DH was composed during the reign of Josiah, before the exilic time. Alternatively, Rudolf Smend and his followers adopt Martin Noth's view that the DH was composed in the exilic period.[4] A few scholars attempt to combine the two views.[5] Kim observes that although scholars have proposed various views on these issues, and also different views on the boundaries of Josiah's kingdom and the extent to which the king expanded his reforms to the north, these debates over details do not matter from the postcolonial perspective.[6] The reason is that scholars have employed Western ideologies in terms of dominant perspectives from which to interpret the Josiah account.[7] Kim states, "DH is viewed as the first and archetypical Western history that describes the creation of an all-Israel state in Palestine as a nation."[8] Kim cites many scholars to illustrate the point that scholars "saw ancient Israel as the model of the nation the West imitated and fulfilled."[9]

Kim observes that Martin Noth's study of the DH has proposed "an all-Israel state in Palestine as a nation" and that other scholars have followed Noth in studying ancient Israel with the concepts of nationalism and orientalism.[10] The concepts of orientalism and nationalism derived from Western imperialism in the early nineteenth century. Kim explains that the nationalism in the Western mindset defines a nation in terms of a legitimate union of people with a central government in a land.[11] In Western imperialism, orientalism supports the dominance of the West and justifies a perception that non-Western people are inferior or weaker in relation to Westerners.[12] For example, Kim indicates that Gary N. Knoppers, a leading scholar on the DH, lets nationalism influence his reading of the Josiah account and uses the term "crusade" to describe Josiah's reforms, which aimed to reunite the two kingdoms and to restore the empire of David and

---

4. Kim, *Decolonizing Josiah*, 2. Kim cites both Cross, *Canaanite Myth*, 274–89; and Smend, "Law and the Nations," 95–110.
5. Kim, *Decolonizing Josiah*, 3; Kim quotes Campbell, "Martin Noth," 31–62.
6. Kim, *Decolonizing Josiah*, 4, 159.
7. Kim, *Decolonizing Josiah*, 5, 58–59.
8. Kim, *Decolonizing Josiah*, 111.
9. Kim, *Decolonizing Josiah*, 58, 110.
10. Kim, *Decolonizing Josiah*, 111.
11. Kim, *Decolonizing Josiah*, 6–10.
12. Kim, *Decolonizing Josiah*, 19–20.

Solomon.¹³ Kim points out that past studies of the Josiah account have used those Western concepts to read the narrative.

Although scholars disagree on the extent of Josiah's kingdom, they all assume that the state of Israel in the time of David and Solomon was a nation that dominated the land of Palestine and that Josiah's reforms aimed to restore the empire of David and Solomon by reuniting the two nations.¹⁴ In Kim's opinion, the reason why those views reflect both the concepts of nationalism and orientalism is that they consider the state of ancient Israel to be similar to the hegemony of the West in Palestine and Syria, and they consider the non-Israelites who lived in the land of the former northern kingdom of Israel to be inferior to the Israelites.¹⁵ For instance, Kim quotes the words of Van Seters, stating that the Deuteronomistic historian was "the first Israelite historian, and the first known historian in Western civilization."¹⁶ In addition, Kim points out that the claim that Josiah attempted a reunion of the two nations is based on scholars' general assumption. The assumption is that during Josiah's period, there was no strongly dominant power controlling the territory that was formerly the land of the northern kingdom of Israel. Kim adds that this assumption reflects the situation in which the territories of powerless peoples were colonized by the West in past centuries on the pretext that they were "empty."¹⁷ For Kim, such views are not persuasive because they are based not only on biblical narratives but also on the imagination of scholars, which is shaped by Western cultural and political contexts rather than empirical evidence. Kim believes that there are no empirical data (e.g., archeological evidence and nonbiblical ancient texts) to support those assertions.¹⁸ Therefore, Kim rejects the claim that Josiah was a powerful king who sought to reunite the nation and restore the Davidic empire.¹⁹

---

13. Kim, *Decolonizing Josiah*, 136–38; Kim quotes Knoppers, *Two Nations Under God*, 2:71.

14. Kim, *Decolonizing Josiah*, 116–17.

15. Kim, *Decolonizing Josiah*, 126–28.

16. Kim, *Decolonizing Josiah*, 56; Kim cites Van Seters, *In Search of History*, 362.

17. Kim states, "The West equated the lack of perceived central power with the land being 'empty.'" Kim, *Decolonizing Josiah*, 118.

18. Kim, *Decolonizing Josiah*, 126–29.

19. Kim, *Decolonizing Josiah*, 179–81.

Proposing a Postcolonial Reading of the Josiah Account

After pointing out the long-debated studies reconstructing ancient Israel based on biblical texts, nonbiblical texts, and archeological evidence, Kim declares that he would not reject past studies portraying Josiah's kingdom through the lens of Western ideologies. However, since the long-debated studies provide no firm conclusions concerning the condition of the ancient state of Israel, Kim proposes an alternative reading that is different from the earlier readings influenced by Western imperialism.[20] Kim employs postcolonial biblical hermeneutics to read the Josiah account through the lens of Asian Americans.[21] He suggests that Josiah's reign was under Assyrian-Egyptian hegemony and that Josiah's people lived in an interracial and multicultural context.

From this understanding, Kim proposes that, from political and ideological perspectives, the condition of Josiah's people was inferior to that of the non-Israelite people living under Assyrian imperialism.[22] Although Kim admits that he also cannot provide empirical data to support his view, his proposal is based on the following evidence: Josiah could not expand his kingdom deeply into the province of Samerina (the former territory of the northern kingdom of Israel). Moreover, Egypt was strong enough to control the trade routes connecting Egypt, Palestine, Syria, and Mesopotamia but was not powerful enough to occupy Judah and the province of Samerina. Those areas were still under the control of the Assyrian empire, though Assyrian political and military power had been weakening since Josiah's time.[23] Thus, Kim infers that Josiah's reform expanded to the former northern kingdom but that was not to fill a power vacuum as supposed by the past studies influenced by Western dominion ideology.

Identifying Colonial Perspectives in the Josiah Account

Kim identifies a colonial perspective which he believes was embedded in the biblical text when the DH, including the Josiah account, was composed. After reviewing past studies of the Josiah account, Kim concludes that Josiah's kingdom was only a small state. Consequently, Josiah's people

20. Kim, *Decolonizing Josiah*, 118.
21. Kim, *Decolonizing Josiah*, 17, 182.
22. Kim, *Decolonizing Josiah*, 168, 180–82.
23. Kim, *Decolonizing Josiah*, 177.

experienced exploitation under Neo-Assyrian imperialism. From the political, ethnic, and ideological perspectives, they were considered inferior people and adversaries vis-à-vis the imperial forces of the Neo-Assyrian Empire, the rising Egyptians, and the Babylonians-Medes.[24]

Kim suggests that after the discovery of the book of the law and probably other writings as well, Josiah's courtiers used those materials to write the DH to present their history as being independent of those imperial forces. Kim agrees with previous studies indicating that the aims of the DH are to "legitimate the ruling house of David" and to advocate for religious activities being performed mainly in the temple (Deut 12:1–14).[25] Kim adds that another purpose of the DH is to affirm the identity of Josiah's people through their faithfulness to YHWH (religious perspective) and their differentiation from other ethnic peoples. He cites the example of circumcision to demonstrate the people's identity. Kim admits that, although circumcision was common among the ancient Near East (hereafter ANE) people, this practice plays a special role in Hebrew biblical narratives. After entering Canaan, the Israelites were required to perform circumcision as a mark of religious identity (Josh 5:1–8). The Hebrew Bible often calls non-Israelites the uncircumcised people (e.g., Judg 14:3; 15:8; 1 Sam 14:6; 17:26, 36; 31:4; 2 Sam 1:20), clearly indicating that circumcision was also a mark of ethnic identity for the Israelites.[26] The fact that the DH needed to assert that independence implies that the situation in which the DH was composed was colonial, thereby requiring the anticolonial perspectives embedded in the DH. Detecting those colonial perspectives embedded in the biblical text is the basis for Kim to reread the Josiah account through the lens of a postcolonial reader.

A Postcolonial Reading of King Josiah's Death

The account of King Josiah's death (2 Kgs 21:19–26 and 23:28–30) is a main focus of Kim's postcolonial reading. Kim points out that the Josiah account begins with Amon's death (2 Kgs 21:19–26) and ends with Josiah's death (2 Kgs 23:28–30). In his reading, Kim uses the term "*Realpolitik* of liminality," by which he means "the danger and promise of being situated in a location

---

24. Kim, *Decolonizing Josiah*, 206, 210–12.

25. Kim, *Decolonizing Josiah*, 222–28; Kim quotes Coote and Coote, *Power*, 3, 61; Kim mentions a study by Cho, "Josianic Reform."

26. Kim, *Decolonizing Josiah*, 229–31.

not of one's own making."²⁷ The death of King Amon of Israel and the death of Josiah both demonstrate the *Realpolitik* of liminality which Judah suffered.

Second Kings 21:20–21 states that the King Amon followed all the ways of his father (Manasseh). Kim interprets this to mean that Amon followed Manasseh by being loyal to the Assyrians. Kim's argument is based on ancient records of Assyria and Babylon stating that the Assyrian kings, Esarhaddon and his son Ashurbanipal (668–27 BCE), summoned twenty-two kings of the Hatti and the seacoast, which supposedly included King Manasseh of Judah, to engage in building projects for the Assyrians and to fight against the Egyptians. From this, Kim concludes that Manasseh was loyal to the Assyrians during his reign.²⁸

Concerning 2 Chr 33:10–13, which states that Manasseh was captured and brought to Babylon and then was released and reigned again in Judah, Kim argues that this was a policy of the Assyrians. He indicates that when Necho, the king of Egypt, and the Egyptians rebelled against the Assyrians, Ashurbanipal defeated the Egyptian rebels and killed all of them except Necho. Ashurbanipal then reinstated Necho to reign in Egypt. This is an Assyrian tactic to make the vassal loyal to the Assyrians for the rest of the Egyptian king's life. In view of this, Kim infers from 2 Chr 33:10–13 that Manasseh was similarly exiled to Babylon for his rebellion against the Assyrians and then released and reinstated as king in Judah.²⁹ Since Manasseh's son, Amon, followed the political strategy of his father, which included loyalty to the Assyrians, Kim reads 2 Kgs 21:23 as meaning that Amon's servants who killed Amon belonged to an anti-Assyrian faction. Thus, the people who killed those who murdered Amon (2 Kgs 21:24) were the pro-Assyrian faction. Kim suggests that two infighting factions, namely, the anti-Assyrian and the pro-Assyrian groups, existed in Judah. To maintain the vassal's loyal policy to the Assyrian empire, the infighting factions "might be a result of Assyria's tactic," and as described above, Judah is "a good illustration of the *Realpolitik* of liminality."³⁰

Turning to the circumstances surrounding Josiah's death, Kim observes that the Assyrian Empire had been weakening for a while when Josiah came to meet the Egyptian Pharaoh Necho II at Megiddo (2 Kgs 23:29). After Ashurbanipal passed away, the Egyptians and Assyrians formed an

27. Kim, *Decolonizing Josiah*, 17.
28. Kim, *Decolonizing Josiah*, 215–17.
29. Kim, *Decolonizing Josiah*, 209–10, 216.
30. Kim, *Decolonizing Josiah*, 218–19.

alliance to confront the rising Neo-Babylonians and Medes. Second Kings 22–23 does not indicate any reason why Necho II killed Josiah. Kim is aware of the common view that Josiah died while fighting "against" Necho II. However, Kim points out the ambiguous preposition עַל (2 Kgs 23:29), which means either "against" or "for," and then states that this verse is ambiguous as to whether Pharaoh Necho II came to "help" the Assyrians or to "fight against" the Assyrians. Moreover, the following phrase וַיֵּלֶךְ הַמֶּלֶךְ יֹאשִׁיָּהוּ לִקְרָאתוֹ ("and King Josiah went to encounter him [Necho II]," 2 Kgs 23:29) does not clearly indicate whether Josiah came to meet Necho II for war or a friendly purpose. Regarding this incident, 2 Chr 35:20–22 states that Josiah came to fight against Necho II and was killed because Josiah did not listen to God's words through Necho. Kim observes that other Jewish texts, such as 1 Esdras, Josephus, *Ant.* 10:73–77, and LXX 2 Kgs 23:29, follow the Chronicler's reading and provides further elaboration. But as Kim points out, 2 Chr 35:20–22 still does not explicitly state whether Necho II came to support or to fight against the Assyrians.[31]

Based on these observations, Kim argues that Josiah's death as narrated in the DH (2 Kgs 23:29–30a) was not due to a war. Kim suggests that Josiah's reforms (which called all the Israelites to Jerusalem for the Passover in order to encourage the people to live a life devoted to YHWH) demonstrated an anti-Assyrian attitude during the time when the Assyrian empire had been weakening. Consequently, Josiah was suspected of treachery.[32] Thus, Kim contends that Josiah's death was the result of "a court-martial based on sovereign-vassal relations" rather than the consequence of a war. Josiah was caught up in the conflict between two powerful forces, namely, Assyria-Egypt and Babylonia-Medes. In other words, Josiah's death in 2 Kgs 22–23 indicates that Josiah and his people were in a situation of *Realpolitik* liminality under imperialism. Kim's point is that the people who lived in that context were in a dangerous and life-threatening situation whether they followed a pro-Assyrian policy or an anti-Assyrian policy.[33]

What does Kim's postcolonial reading of 2 Kgs 21:19–26 and 23:28–30 mean to his readers today? Kim finds similarity between the context of Josiah's people and that of Asian Americans. Like Josiah's people who lived in the space and experience of *Realpolitik* liminality, Asian Americans are

---

31. Kim, *Decolonizing Josiah*, 211, 219–21.

32. Kim, *Decolonizing Josiah*, 238; Kim cites Nakanose, *Josiah's Passover*, 51, 64, 73, 106, 110.

33. Kim, *Decolonizing Josiah*, 218–21.

Comparing the Chronicler's Reading and Postcolonial Biblical Reading

located in a similar space of liminality and have endured similar experiences.[34] Kim observes that although Asian Americans have been present in the US for more than 150 years, they are still considered immigrants. Kim elaborates that, historically, most American citizens today have ancestors who immigrated from other lands to the US. However Asian Americans are still viewed as foreigners or immigrants who are inferior to white Americans. Consequently, they continue to suffer discrimination. Kim presents numerous illustrations of discrimination against Asian Americans in the US. For example, the US Congress issued the Chinese Exclusion Act of 1882, which was renewed in 1902, to ban Chinese from coming to reside in the US.[35] This Act also prohibited Chinese Americans, even those who have lived in the US for ten years, from attaining US citizenship. In contrast, Western Europeans have immigrated much more easily into the US.[36]

For another instance, Asian Americans, particularly Korean Americans, suffered disproportionately during the Los Angeles riots in 1992. Kim observes that although the riots aimed to protest against the acquittal of four white Los Angeles policemen who had brutally beaten an African American, rioters attacked numerous buildings, shops, and properties owned not only by white Americans but also by Asian Americans in the city. The Los Angeles police focused on protecting the white community but let the rioters burn, rob, and destroy shops and properties of Asian Americans. Korean Americans sustained half of the total material damages.[37]

Illustrating discrimination in daily conversations, Kim observes that when an Asian American is asked "where are you from?" by other Americans, the inquirers usually do not stop after receiving an answer concerning the current hometown in the US. The American inquirers are often only satisfied when they receive an answer concerning the Asian American's original hometown in Asia. He states that this kind of questioning may be wittingly or unwittingly "based on the premise that Asians or people of Asian descent are aliens in this nation."[38] Moreover, Asian Americans in the US are stuck between the white and black communities since they are yellow in terms of racial politics. Kim observes that although Asian Americans may have more opportunities than black people, "Asian Americans

---

34. Kim, *Decolonizing Josiah*, 17, 182–84.
35. This Act was repealed in 1943, but Kim does not mention this in his book.
36. Kim, *Decolonizing Josiah*, 35–36, 124–26.
37. Kim, *Decolonizing Josiah*, 188–89.
38. Kim, *Decolonizing Josiah*, 183.

were often used by whites to punish blacks and other minorities," and thus, Asian Americans are in a state of liminality.[39]

In summary, Kim uses postcolonial hermeneutics to read Josiah's account intercontextually in dialogue with the context of Asian Americans. This kind of reading makes the text concerning Josiah's story meaningful to Kim's Asian American readers. Like Josiah's people who lived in state of liminality in terms of interracialism and mixed culture, Asian Americans have coped with similar experiences. Like Josiah's people who were caught between the dominant people of the Assyrian empire and other peoples in the ANE, Asian Americans have been caught between the black and white communities in America and thus have also experienced dangerous situations.[40]

Evaluation of Postcolonial Biblical Reading

Having described a certain postcolonial reading of the Bible, this section will now evaluate the postcolonial biblical reading as follows.

Reading Both What the Text Meant and What the Text Means

The description above has demonstrated that postcolonial biblical reading considers both what the text meant and what the text means. It is a combination of author-centered and reader-response approaches. Kim begins his postcolonial interpretation with the examination of previous studies of the Josiah story relating to colonial perspectives. He demonstrates that past studies of the Josiah account employed the dominant ideologies of the West to interpret this biblical narrative. He also argues that such interpretations lack empirical supporting evidence. This review of past scholarship is the first step.

Kim's second step in postcolonial reading begins by identifying the colonial perspectives embedded in the DH when the Josianic editor(s) composed the DH, including the Josiah narrative. It explores the historical-cultural contexts of the biblical passage concerning the formation and intentions of the text relating to the colonial perspective. In particular, the DH was composed to present the history and identity of Josiah's people as being independent from the dominant empires. Kevin Vanhoozer states

---

39. Kim, *Decolonizing Josiah*, 182–84.
40. Kim, *Decolonizing Josiah*, 184–87.

Comparing the Chronicler's Reading and Postcolonial Biblical Reading

that studying the original meaning of the text is "to confine the text to its own time."[41] This second step of postcolonial reading is an attempt to study what the text meant or the original meaning of the text by highlighting the colonial perspectives embedded in the text.

The second step has established a historical context for Kim's third step, which is the rereading of the Josiah narrative through the lens of oppressed and discriminated people to serve the concern of his postcolonial readers. Kim has established that Josiah's people suffered in the conflict between the imperial forces of Assyria-Egypt and Babylonia-Medes. They were in the context of the *Realpolitik* of liminality. This historical-cultural context, Kim asserts, is similar to the context of Kim's Asian American readers. From this, he attempts to investigate what the text means to his postcolonial readers. In other words, the first and second steps of postcolonial biblical hermeneutics focus on authorial intention. The third step is the reader-response perspective, which reads the biblical text through the lens of Kim's readers. This feature has also been displayed in postcolonial biblical commentaries. For example, a postcolonial commentator reads the narratives of Jael (Judg 4) and Jephthah's daughter (Judg 10–12) in the book of Judges. The commentator interprets the stories as depicting "survival in the context of oppressive powers."[42] This is what the text meant. Gossai and García-Alfonso then explain how those stories are meaningful to their Cuban readers.[43] This is what the text means to defenseless Cubans who "find the power and agency to face their daily lives" for their survival.[44]

In summary, postcolonial biblical reading examines not only what the text meant but also considers what the text means to postcolonial readers.

Seeking Parallel Situations

Postcolonial biblical hermeneutics seeks to make relevant contextualization by finding parallel situations between the original context of the biblical text and the postcolonial readers' contexts. This feature is clearly demonstrated in Kim's postcolonial reading of the Josiah account. Kim

---

41. Vanhoozer, *Is There a Meaning*, 421.

42. Gossai, "Introduction," 4.

43. As mentioned above, although practitioners of postcolonial biblical reading around the world have different purposes when they employ this approach, the principles of this reading are the same.

44. García-Alfonso, "Judges," 119–20; Gossai, "Introduction," 4.

argues that Josiah's people were considered inferior to non-Israelite people by the imperial forces. Like Josiah's people, who were in an unsafe situation due to living in the tension between powerful forces (e.g., Assyria-Egypt and Babylonia-Medes), Asian Americans have been in an unsafe environment because they have been deliberately or inadvertently looked down upon by white Americans and are also stuck between the white and black communities in terms of racial politics. Just as Josiah's courtiers composed the DH, including the Josiah account, to form a history and identity for Josiah's people independent from the imperial power, Kim suggests that Asian Americans need to find ways to construct their own subjectivity and identity separate from the dominant national identity.[45]

Seeking parallel situations is a regular feature presented in postcolonial biblical commentaries. In the foreword to the Old Testament volume of the postcolonial commentary, Samuel E. Balentine encourages postcolonial readers to find similarities between readers' contexts and voices and biblical contexts and voices. He challenges the readers: "Do we identify with the colonizers or the colonized? Do we find our voice with those who speak or with those whose voice the text or tradition has muted?"[46] Balentine does not mean a fusion of the two horizons between the text and its reader as defined by Gadamer,[47] but rather that postcolonial readers need conceptualization in their interpretation.

This feature has also been displayed in postcolonial commentaries on the New Testament. For instance, Efraín Agosto uses historical-literary reading to establish that residents of the city of Philippi (a Roman colony) became citizens of the Roman Empire in Paul's time. This could bring both advantages and disadvantages to the Philippians. For example, they could have the benefits of taxation and military protection. However, they had to be loyal to the Roman Empire unconditionally. Consequently, they lost their national identity. Paul reminded the Philippian Christians that they had heavenly citizenship in the heavenly kingdom and that they must be loyal to Jesus Christ their most high king (Phil 3:20).[48] Agosto finds this to be parallel to the context of Puerto Rican people. The people of Puerto Rico

---

45. Kim, *Decolonizing Josiah*, 242–43.

46. Balentine states, "Postcolonial biblical perspectives provide a lens for conceptualizing and critiquing the intersection of power and politics in ancient texts and, consequentially, the moral and ethical commitments they undergird or undermine in their readers." Balentine, "Foreword," 9.

47. Gadamer, *Truth and Method*, 370.

48. Agosto, "Letter to the Philippians," 288–89.

have US citizenship. This brings them benefits such as getting jobs and good living conditions in the US. They have, however, experienced a deficiency in lacking a defined nationhood and their territory has been struggling in terms of economic development and political administration. Therefore, Paul's exhortation to the Philippian Christians concerning heavenly citizenship (Phil 3:20) is also relevant to Puerto Rican Christians.[49] Agosto states that the people of Puerto Rico found a citizenship "that superseded the technicality of US citizenship and the lack of a defined nationhood."[50]

In summary, postcolonial biblical interpretation investigates the original contexts of biblical texts to find parallel circumstances to those of postcolonial readers today. These parallel situations typically pertain to experiences of struggle under powers of domination.

Selective Reading

Since postcolonial biblical interpreters look for parallel situations between the original context of the Bible and postcolonial readers' contexts, they focus on selecting biblical texts that contain colonial issues relating to postcolonial contexts for their interpretation. Selection is necessary because not all biblical texts relate to colonial perspectives. Sugirtharajah affirms, "The focus of some biblical texts falls outside the concerns of postcolonialism."[51]

This feature of selective reading is demonstrated in postcolonial biblical commentaries. The two volumes of postcolonial commentaries on the Old Testament (Gossai) and New Testament (Moore and Segovia) do not touch on every chapter of the Bible. The main task of the postcolonial commentators in these two volumes is to detect colonial perspectives embedded in certain passages of each biblical book. The commentators then focus on interpreting those biblical passages that contain colonial issues relating to modern concerns of their postcolonial contexts.

For example, the book of Judges has been interpreted by two commentators, namely, Cristina García-Alfonso and Diandra Chretain Erickson. García-Alfonso detects the issue of struggle for survival in the colonial context in Judg 4:1–23 and 10:6—12:7. She then focuses on interpreting those biblical passages. This reading relates to the issue of survival in daily

---

49. Agosto, "Letter to the Philippians," 290–91.
50. Agosto, "Letter to the Philippians," 291.
51. Sugirtharajah, *Exploring Postcolonial Biblical Criticism*, 53.

life in the Cuban context.[52] Erickson discerns the identities of the colonized Israelites in Judg 4, 13–16, 19–21 in terms of mimicry,[53] ambivalence,[54] and hybridity.[55] Erickson focuses on reading those passages to explain the above three perspectives of colonized identity. Finally, she argues that her interpretation is helpful to readers who are minoritized and colonized.[56]

In contrast, the book of Leviticus has been interpreted in order, chapter by chapter, because the colonial issue of hereditary priesthood being co-opted by colonizers is embedded in almost every chapter.[57] To explain this method of selective reading, Gossai, the editor of the postcolonial commentary volume on the Old Testament, states that postcolonial commentators do not always interpret biblical books chapter by chapter because "postcolonial perspectives and insights are neither dependent on biblical order, nor are they essentially dependent on all of the books."[58]

The same applies to the postcolonial commentary volume on the New Testament. For example, the postcolonial commentary on Matthew discusses the biblical text chapter by chapter in order because the colonial perspective of resistance to the dominion of the Roman Empire is embedded in most chapters through themes such as the gospel's proclamation, power and role, God's kingdom and reign, the victorious death and resurrection of Jesus, and so on.[59] However, the postcolonial commentary on the book of Revelation focuses on reading only those chapters in which colonial

---

52. García-Alfonso, "Judges," 106–20.

53. Erickson states, "The colonizer compels the colonized to 'mimic' the colonizer's culture, values, and characteristics." Erickson, "Judges," 124. For Erickson, colonizers use mimicry as a tool to manipulate and control their colonized people.

54. Erickson explains that colonial mimicry leads the colonized people to ambivalence which "disrupts the clear-cut authority of colonial domination because it disturbs the simple relationship between colonizer and colonized" and "creates a slippage that compromises the binary between the colonizer and the colonized." Erickson, "Judges," 124.

55. Erickson indicates that hybrid identity is the outcome of colonial mimicry and ambivalence. She writes, "Mimicry and ambivalence create hybrid identities that disrupt the boundaries between insiders/outsiders, us/them, and center/periphery. . . . When the colonizer and the colonized interact through mimicry, the ambivalence within these interactions creates liminal spaces where both the dominant and peripheral groups experience transformations of their subjectivities." Erickson, "Judges," 124.

56. Erickson, "Judges," 123–40.

57. Laffey, "Leviticus," 27–56.

58. Gossai, "Introduction," 7.

59. Carter, "Gospel of Matthew," 69–104.

perspectives are embedded, such as Rev 2–3 (colonial issue of hybridity), Rev 4–5 (Jesus, the divine emperor in the guise of the lamb), Rev 13 and 17 (mimicry), and Rev 21–22 (hyperidealized, the new metropolis).[60]

In summary, postcolonial interpreters focus on interpreting only those biblical passages in which they find colonial perspectives in the text. They interpret several books (e.g., Leviticus, Matthew) chapter by chapter because they find colonial issues embedded in every chapter. For other biblical books, they interpret only those passages in which they find colonial perspectives. Thus, postcolonial biblical interpretation is a *selective* reading.

Reader's Context Defining Biblical Meaning

Although postcolonial readers seek parallel situations between the original contexts of biblical texts and the readers' contexts for interpretation, they sometimes let postcolonial readers' contexts take control and even subvert what biblical texts meant to serve the postcolonial readers' concerns. The reason is that postcolonial readers do not hold a high view of the Christian Bible. Sugirtharajah states that the authority of the Christian Bible is equal to that of the sacred texts of other religions such as Hinduism, Buddhism, or Confucianism.[61] He adds that the Christian Bible does not contain exclusive truth.[62] He also advises practitioners of postcolonial reading to apply this principle in biblical interpretation.[63] This is a typical feature of postcolonial biblical hermeneutics.

For example, Kim states that 2 Chr 35:20–25 gives an inaccurate version of events and that 2 Kgs 23:29–30 is more historically reliable.[64] For Kim, the Chronicler's reading (2 Chr 35:20–25) is just a mistaken interpretation of 2 Kgs 23:29–30, and so are all other Second Temple texts (LXX 2 Kgs 23:29–30;[65] LXX 2 Chr 35:19–25; 1 Esd 1:25–31; *Ant.* 10:74–83) that identify the reason for Josiah's death similarly to the Chronicler's perspective. Kim advocates the view that the Chronicler's reading (2 Chr 35:20–25)

---

60. Moore, "Revelation to John," 436–54.
61. Sugirtharajah, "From Orientalist to Post-Colonial," 25–26.
62. Sugirtharajah, "Bible and Its Asian Readers," 65; Sugirtharajah, *Exploring Postcolonial Biblical Criticism*, 123, 127.
63. Sugirtharajah states, "This I think should be the aim of all those who are involved in the task of biblical interpretation." Sugirtharajah, "Bible and Its Asian Readers," 66.
64. Kim, *Decolonizing Josiah*, 221. Kim uses the word "fictitious."
65. This version also seems to suggest a hostile encounter between Josiah and Necho.

is fictional. Kim rightly points out that 2 Kgs 23:28–30a does not state a clear reason for Josiah's death, since we cannot know whether the preposition עַל (2 Kgs 23:29) means either "against" or "for."[66] However, if 2 Kgs 23:28–30a does not clearly tell the reason for Josiah's death, how could Kim be sure that the Chronicler's interpretation is wrong? Moreover, the fact that all other Second Temple literature conforms to the Chronicler's reading does not support the contention that the Chronicler's reading is wrong. Conversely, since all readers in the same postexilic context agree on the same reason for Josiah's death, this reason provided by the Chronicler should be accepted as correct through the lens of the postexilic context. Kim's negative evaluation of 2 Chr 35:20–25 with the adjective "fictitious" makes readers assume some parts of the Bible are fictional and not reliable as to what the texts say. Consequently, Kim's postcolonial reading subverts what the biblical text meant. The section below evaluating the Chronicler's reading will show why the Chronicler's reading is relevant and reliable for Jewish readers in the postexilic context.

Before turning to that, let us consider another example. Laura E. Donaldson finds colonial perspectives in the book of Ruth. She indicates that Ruth and Orpah belonged to the indigenous people before the Israelites had come to possess the land. Ruth was later assimilated into Israel through intermarriage with Boaz. Ruth's assimilation is demonstrated through her son, Obed, who was legally transferred to Naomi and Boaz, two Israelites. Donaldson finds this parallel to her Cherokee women's context. The Cherokee people were native Americans but were assimilated into the European settlers when they came to possess the American land.[67] Thus, Donaldson uses the postcolonial reading approach to interpret the book of Ruth.

Donaldson disagrees with most commentators who read Orpah negatively and read Ruth positively, and she states those readers just "mimic the biblical text."[68] For Donaldson, Orpah is "the story's central character," and her decision to leave Naomi and go back to her mother's house is prudent and resistant to assimilation. She indicates that because Orpah does not relinquish her traditions and ancestors, "Orpah connotes hope rather than perversity" for the Cherokee women.[69] Yet according to the literary context of the Ruth narrative, Orpah is mentioned only twice in the whole narrative

---

66. Kim, *Decolonizing Josiah*, 219–21.
67. Donaldson, "Sign of Orpah," 138–40.
68. Donaldson, "Sign of Orpah," 141.
69. Donaldson, "Sign of Orpah," 142–43.

(Ruth 1:4 and 14), whereas Ruth and Naomi are mentioned many times in all chapters of the book. Scholars observe that Orpah is just a minor character and functions as a foil for Ruth. The major characters in the narrative are Ruth, Naomi, and Boaz.[70] Although Donaldson herself admits that the name Orpah occurs only twice in the book,[71] she nonetheless reads Orpah as the main character in the book to make the Ruth narrative significant to the context of Cherokee women.[72] Peter Lau points out that Donaldson lets the reader's context become the final arbiter to determine the meaning of the biblical text,[73] and thus distorts what the biblical text meant.[74]

Writers of postcolonial biblical commentaries also demonstrate this feature. For instance, Gordon Zerbe and Muriel Orevillo-Montenegro observe that Western interpreters commonly read Col 1:13, 22 and 2:13 concerning spiritual salvation with a spiritual connotation. The two postcolonial commentators also affirm the spiritual meanings in accordance with the literary context of Col 1–2.[75] When using postcolonial biblical hermeneutics, however, these postcolonial readers interpret the verses as an encouragement to resist the unjust regimes and dominating powers of their context. The two readers state that employing postcolonial reading of the epistle to the Colossians "would make the reader realize that God in Christ Jesus and those who lived Christ-like lives have 'disarmed the rulers and authorities,' giving courage to the colonized to resist dominating and stifling powers."[76] In short, postcolonial readers let their present context control the derivation of meaning from biblical texts to serve their interests.

Conclusion

Since not every biblical chapter contains colonial perspectives, postcolonial biblical interpretation operates with selectivity. Postcolonial biblical reading demonstrates the typical feature of Asian biblical reading, which is the study of both what the text meant and what the text means. Practitioners of the postcolonial reading all over the world, including Asian postcolonial

---

70. Berlin, *Poetics and Interpretation*, 83–86; Lau, "Back Under Authority," 136.
71. Donaldson, "Sign of Orpah," 141.
72. Donaldson, "Sign of Orpah," 143–44.
73. Lau, "Back Under Authority," 137.
74. Lau, "Back Under Authority," 135.
75. Zerbe and Orevillo-Montenegro, "Letter to the Colossians," 299–300.
76. Zerbe and Orevillo-Montenegro, "Letter to the Colossians," 301.

readers, have similar principles of interpretation. The reason is that postcolonial biblical interpretation studies the world behind the text to detect colonial perspectives embedded in the text when it was composed. This helps the postcolonial readers to understand what the text meant. Moreover, the postcolonial readers also study the world in front of the text to find out how the biblical text relates to the reader's postcolonial concerns. This helps the readers understand what the text means.

Nonetheless, there is a conflict within postcolonial biblical hermeneutics. Practitioners of this reading model let the reader's context control or even subvert what biblical texts meant to serve the postcolonial reader's interests, particularly freedom from oppression. Postcolonial biblical readers do not hesitate to derive meanings from biblical texts which could be inappropriate in the literary context of those texts. When practitioners of the postcolonial approach make serving the reader's postcolonial issues the top priority, this causes a conflict within the postcolonial reading itself. Peter Lau rightly argues that in "superimposing a postcolonial ideology over and against the biblical text..., the [postcolonial reading] strategy becomes its own oppression."[77] Ironically, while practitioners of this reading model attempt to deliver biblical readers from all kinds of oppression, they can sometimes let their reading strategy become an oppressive force on biblical texts.

Evaluation of the Chronicler's Reading Through Colonial Perspectives

As mentioned in chapter 2, the Chronicler's postexilic context was "colonial" because the Chronicler's community lived under the rule of foreign empires. This section will examine whether and how the Chronicler reads his sources through his colonial perspectives from his postexilic context, akin to the postcolonial reading approach. To achieve this aim, this chapter begins with a discussion on the colonial perspectives stemming from the Chronicler's postexilic context.

Colonial Perspectives in the Postexilic Context

Broadly speaking, due to disagreements among scholars about the historical reliability of particular sources, reconstructing the historical contexts of

---

77. Lau, "Back Under Authority," 144.

the ancient Israelites and the postexilic Jewish community is a long-debated issue. The debate can be viewed from two polar positions: maximalists and minimalists. Maximalists hold to the historicity of biblical narratives and use the Bible to reconstruct the historical context from which the biblical texts originated. Conversely, minimalists reject the biblical stories as reliable historical sources.[78] This challenge also pertains to the reconstruction of the Chronicler's historical context.[79]

Philip Davies claims that a biblical narrative cannot be demonstrated to be historical if we do not have other extrabiblical supporting evidence, but it can reflect the ideologies of its writer and its first readers in terms of why it was written.[80] For instance, Davies observes that the books of Ezra and Nehemiah tell stories of the postexilic community in the fifth century. Since these books were composed in the postexilic period, studying them will help us detect the thinking of rulers of the Yehud province, the thinking of Israel in the past, as well as the contemporary context of the authors.[81]

Other scholars hold a middle position. For example, Lester L. Grabbe explains that he uses all potential sources, but since biblical texts are usually problematic, he gives "priority to primary sources such as archeology and epigraphic sources."[82] Grabbe uses archeological evidence to examine all Persian decrees and letters mentioned in the book of Ezra (Ezra 1:2–4; 4:8–16, 17–22; 5:7–17; 6:2–5, 6–12; 7:12–26). He concludes that those biblical passages were composed from original Persian documents with the compiler's ideology embedded in them to reflect the Jewish community's attitude toward Persian rule.[83] For example, Grabbe argues that the general policy of the Persian Empire was that the emperor allowed exiled people to return and reconstruct their temples and statues if those people would continue to submit to Persian rule. This is evidenced by the Babylonian Chronicles, the Cyrus Cylinder, and some other inscriptions. Although those sources of evidence do not state either the name of the Jews or Cyrus's specific support of the returning Jews, we can infer that the Jews were indeed among the peoples whom the emperor allowed to return to their home countries and rebuild their temples. Thus, Cyrus's decree, narrated in

---

78. Knauth, "Israel," 514; Hill, "History of Israel 3," 445.

79. Duke, "Chronicles," 163.

80. Davies, *History of Ancient Israel*, 141.

81. Davies, *History of Ancient Israel*, 79.

82. Grabbe, *History of the Jews*, 1:16.

83. Grabbe, "'Persian Documents,'" 563.

Ezra 1:2–4 and stating support for the exiled Jews to return and rebuild the temple, would be based on authentic Persian documents while simultaneously also reflecting the ideology of the compiler of Ezra (Ezra 1:1, stating that this decree fulfills Jeremiah's prophecy).[84]

Without becoming embroiled in the debate over which of the three positions described is the best one to take when examining the biblical texts, this study will focus on those biblical narratives that have support from archeological or epigraphic evidence to affirm their historicity. In other words, this selection of biblical texts should satisfy both the minimalist and maximalist positions, as well as the mediating position. With that in mind, let us now turn to a surveys of the Chronicler's historical context with a focus on its colonial perspectives.

Attitudes of the Postexilic Community Toward Imperial Rule

This section will demonstrate three attitudes of the postexilic community toward foreign dominion: a pro-empire attitude, an anti-empire attitude, and an attitude of passive and quiet resistance.

A pro-empire attitude existed in the postexilic community. Christine Mitchell compares the Testament of Darius (DNa and DNb, dated early fifth century BCE) and the narratives of foreign kings in Chronicles. She finds that the decree of Cyrus in 2 Chr 36:22–23 (// Ezra 1:1–3) is reflected in this ancient Persian text.[85] Scholars agree that Ezra-Nehemiah and Chronicles reveal a Jewish pro-Persian attitude because these biblical books describe positively the foreign emperor who granted the exiled Jews permission to return to their home country, rebuild the temple, and worship YHWH.[86] This empire "is treated positively because it fulfills the purposes of Yahweh."[87] Those Jews holding this perspective accepted the Persian Empire as God's agent to fulfill God's promise of restoring the temple and nation.[88]

---

84. Grabbe, "'Persian Documents,'" 540–43.

85. Mitchell, "Testament of Darius," 363–64, 377–78.

86. Ben Zvi, "When The Foreign Monarch Speaks," 227–28; Davies, *History of Ancient Israel*, 88; Wilson, "Yahweh's Anointed," 346.

87. Boda, "Identity and Empire," 270.

88. VanderKam, *Introduction to Early Judaism*, 186; Boda, "Identity and Empire," 252, 270.

Comparing the Chronicler's Reading and Postcolonial Biblical Reading

On the other hand, scholars also detect in these biblical books evidence reflecting an anti-empire attitude. Ben Zvi finds that although four out of five descriptions of foreign kings in Chronicles are positive, one of them is very negative (2 Chr 32:10–15, on Sennacherib).[89] Boda points out that the Jewish attitude was anti-empire when empires were described as evil and against YHWH (2 Chr 32:13–19).[90] People with this attitude expected YHWH to intervene mightily to destroy such imperial powers and restore the Davidic house along with a Jewish community more glorious than the one before (Hag 1–2; Zech 1–8).[91] Duke also argues that Ezra 6:21 reflects the two groups, pro-empire and anti-empire, among the people who did not go into exile and remained in the land. This verse tells that one group was accepted by Nehemiah and separated from the other group which was rejected by Nehemiah.[92] Philip Davies also indicates that the Jewish pro-empire group (including Nehemiah and the Jewish returners who were sent back by the Persian emperor) had enemies who already dwelled in the homeland. These enemies were also YHWH worshipers, but they opposed Nehemiah's leadership and thus harbored an anti-imperial attitude. Later on, the Hasmoneans joined this group and fought against the imperial rule of their time.[93]

Besides the two attitudes mentioned above, there were also people who appeared to follow the pro-empire faction but implicitly rebelled against it. Those people demonstrated an attitude of passive and quiet resistance, a combination of both pro- and anti-empire attitudes oriented toward quiet rebellion. The voice of such intertwined pro-empire and anti-empire sentiment is implicitly reflected in the words of Nehemiah's subordinate officers spoken in the form of a penitential prayer during a public meeting (Neh 9:36). Leo G. Perdue and Warren Carter point out that although Nehemiah and his subordinate officers demonstrated their submission to their Persian

---

89. Ben Zvi indicates that in the book of Chronicles, Huram of Tyre (2 Chr 2:10–15), the Queen of Sheba (2 Chr 9:5–8), Necho of Egypt (2 Chr 35:21), and Cyrus of Persia (2 Chr 36:23) submitted to the authority of the God of Israel. However, Sennacherib of Assyria did not. The Chronicler describes Sennacherib as being evil and blasphemous against YHWH (2 Chr 32:10–15). Ben Zvi, "When The Foreign Monarch Speaks," 210–15.

90. Boda, "Identity and Empire," 266.

91. Janzen, *Chronicles*, 193–94; VanderKam, *Introduction to Early Judaism*, 186.

92. Duke, "Chronicles," 165.

93. Davies, *In Search of "Ancient Israel,"* 103–4.

overlords, their words (Neh 9:36) imply that these Persians were oppressive rulers over the Jews, who were their slaves.[94]

Scholars who have conducted archeological surveys agree that Yehud was a small and impoverished province in the Persian Empire and that the emperor-appointed governors of this province had to collect taxes to pay annual tribute to the imperial rulers. This duty persisted throughout the Second Temple period under all imperial rulers.[95] There is no evidence that the temple in Yehud was supported by the Persians; in fact, the "Persian policy was to reduce the income of temples."[96] Marbury studies nonbiblical sources of the Persian period concerning Persian policies on the temples in Babylon and Egypt and discovers that those temples were overburdened and struggled because of the Persian practice of levying heavy taxes on the temples. He finds no evidence that the Persians exempted the Jewish temple from taxes. Thus, the temple in the small and poor Yehud province had to cope with significant economic pressures.[97]

From this, it is logical that Nehemiah's subordinate officers in Yehud would lament that they were slaves to the Persians (Neh 9:36). The reason for this attitude of quiet resistance is that the scribes who wrote these books were supported by the governing institution and the temple.[98] Davies points out that public libraries containing literature from Judah have been found in Athens (fourth century BCE), in Alexandria and Antioch (third century BCE), and in Pergamon (mid-second century BCE). Moreover, 2 Macc 2:13 records that Nehemiah founded a library and collected books for himself.[99] The imperial rulers allowed colonized scribes to write and explain the colonized history and religious practices under imperial review.[100] Although the scribal works were to serve the interests of the monarchs and the temple, they also attempted to evaluate and even criticize the regime,[101] though the latter critical voice is much more muted. That is why both pro-empire and anti-empire voices appeared implicitly in those books. This

---

94. Perdue and Carter, *Israel and Empire*, 120–21.

95. Grabbe, *History of the Jews*, 1:154, 355; Perdue and Carter, *Israel and Empire*, 108, 116.

96. Grabbe, *History of the Jews*, 1:216; Grabbe, "'Persian Documents,'" 540.

97. Marbury, "Reading Persian Dominion," 167.

98. Snyman, "Chronicler's Narrative," 183.

99. Davies, *In Search of "Ancient Israel*," 146.

100. Snyman, "Chronicler's Narrative," 178, 182.

101. Davies, *In Search of "Ancient Israel*," 93–94.

Identity of the Chronicler's Community

To compare Kim's postcolonial reading concerning his readers' identity with the Chronicler's reading, it is necessary to explore the identity of the Chronicler's community. In the Chronicler's time, the Jews were scattered in many places. When the Persian Empire allowed the exiled Jews to return to their homeland, not all of the Jews did. Both biblical books (e.g., Esther, Daniel, Ezra, and Nehemiah) and nonbiblical data indicate that the Jews were living in numerous locations such as the former northern kingdom, Babylon, Egypt, and Mesopotamia.

For example, Aramaic papyri (dated to the fifth century BCE) in Elephantine mention that there was a temple of the Jews in Egypt dedicated to the Yahwistic cult.[102] Archeological data also show that there was a Samaritan temple for worshiping YHWH (dated to the end of the fifth century BCE) on Mount Gerizim.[103] This present study argues that the identity of the Chronicler's community in the postexilic time is that they were Jews living under Persian dominion in Yehud or other Persian provinces (e.g., in Samaria, Babylon, Egypt, and Mesopotamia),[104] whether they followed the practices of Yahwistic religion or not.[105] Evidence from the Elephantine papyri shows that when the Jewish temple in Egypt was attacked (around 410 BCE), the Jews from Elephantine sent letters to the Judean and Samaritan authorities, including the high priest in Jerusalem, to seek support for rebuilding the temple in Egypt. The temple in Egypt was then rebuilt with support from the two Jewish communities in Judea and Samaria.[106]

From the biblical data, we see that while Ezra and Nehemiah advocated for the Yehud community to separate from other neighboring peoples living in the land of the former northern kingdom, those who opposed

---

102. Murphy, "Second Temple Judaism," 63.

103. Stern, "Religious Revolution," 202.

104. Berquist, "Constructions of Identity," 54–56; Kessler, "Persia's Loyal Yahwists," 94–95.

105. Berquist, "Constructions of Identity," 57.

106. VanderKam, *Introduction to Early Judaism*, 8–9; Davies, *Rethinking Biblical Scholarship*, 115; Weingart, "What Makes an Israelite," 173.

to Nehemiah's program continued to build relationships with Nehemiah's enemies (e.g., Tobiah and Sanballat) when Nehemiah was away from Yehud (Neh 13:4–6).[107] Tobiah and Sanballat were somehow related to the Israelite and Judahite people and their Yahwistic religion. For example, Tobiah's name means "my good is YHWH," and Tobiah's son married into a notable family in Judah (Neh 3:4, 30).[108] The same is true of Sanballat, who, being the governor of Samaria and possibly an Ephraimite according to the Horonite epithet, also worshiped YHWH.[109]

Knoppers supports a view that is similar to the Chronicler's view concerning the identity of the postexilic Israelite community. The Chronicler portrays the pro-empire Israelites, including all the tribes, as comprising the community of Yehud.[110] For example, while Neh 11:4 states that the inhabitants of Jerusalem included only descendants of the two tribes of Judah and Benjamin, 1 Chr 9:3 states that the inhabitants of Jerusalem included various tribes of Israelites such as Judah, Benjamin, Ephraim, and Manasseh.[111] Grabbe contends that Ezra-Nehemiah and Chronicles (with the genealogical list including all Israel tribes in 1 Chr 1–9) reveal the "all Israel" perspective of the identity of the Jews in the Persian period and throughout the Second Temple period.[112] While Weingart argues that the main component of Israelite identity in the Persian period is the *ethnic* element (ethnos),[113] evidence from both nonbiblical data and biblical data (Ezra, Nehemiah, Chronicles) as mentioned above indicate another important component to form the identity of the Chronicler's community, namely, the *religious* concerns that could unite all Jews living in different provinces of the Persian empire.

---

107. Knoppers, "Nehemiah and Sanballat," 330–31.
108. Knoppers, "Nehemiah and Sanballat," 317, 323.
109. Knoppers, "Nehemiah and Sanballat," 325–26.
110. Knoppers, "Nehemiah and Sanballat," 330.
111. Knoppers, "Nehemiah and Sanballat," 321–22.
112. Grabbe, *History of the Jews*, 1:170–71.
113. Weingart emphasizes the ethnic component because he uses only two biblical passages in Chronicles: 2 Chr 13 (Abijah's speech) and 1 Chr 1–9 (the genealogical lists). Weingart, "What Makes an Israelite," 169, 175.

Conclusion

Based on the above discussion, we conclude that the identity of the Chronicler's community in the postexilic era is that they were all the ethnic Israelites or Jews living under Persian imperial dominion. The Chronicler demonstrated an idealized presentation of "all Israel" in his work (e.g., 1 Chr 1–9; 2 Chr 13). In reality, both biblical and nonbiblical data indicate that ethnic and religious concerns were able to unite all Jews in the Persian empires. There were varied attitudes within the Chronicler's community toward imperial dominion: pro- and anti-empire attitudes, as well as an attitude of passive and quiet resistance.

The Chronicler's Reading Through a Colonial Lens

After demonstrating the colonial perspectives stemming from the Chronicler's postexilic context, this section will investigate whether and how the Chronicler reads his sources through his colonial perspectives, akin to the postcolonial reading approach.

Reading Through the Lens of a Victim of the *Realpolitik* of Liminality

Kim has shown that the historical context of Josiah's people was the conflict between Assyria-Egypt and Babylonia-Medes. Kim calls this context the *Realpolitik* of liminality under imperialism. The people who lived in this liminal context were in a risky situation regardless of which imperial forces they followed. Josiah died because he was a victim of the *Realpolitik* of liminality.[114] This present study has demonstrated that the Chronicler's community also lived in a similar context of *Realpolitik* of liminality. They experienced the conflict between the imperial forces (the forces from Egypt and others, either Persian or Greek). The Chronicler's reading of Josiah's death (2 Kgs 23:28–30a // 2 Chr 35:20–25) is through the lens of such a context.

During the Persian Empire (538–332 BCE), the Egyptians often rebelled against Persian dominion. The Egyptians even drove out the Persians for sixty years before the end of the Persian era (404–343 BCE).[115] Since Yehud was a Persian province, the Egyptians often attacked Yehud.[116] In the

---

114. Kim, *Decolonizing Josiah*, 218–19, 221.
115. Perdue and Carter, *Israel and Empire*, 122–23.
116. Perdue and Carter, *Israel and Empire*, 115.

Hellenistic period, the Jews were stuck between different Greek factions, which included Egypt during this time. Scholars indicate that although the Greek Empire dominated the world in this period (332–63 BCE), it was divided by the successors of Alexander the Great (e.g., Plotemy, Seleucus, and Antigonus Gonatas) after he died in 323 BCE. The Ptolemaic dynasty was based in Egypt and controlled its surrounding areas. This dynasty claimed that the land of the Jews was a colony of Egypt and took over the Palestine area.[117] The Seleucid dynasty was based in Syria and Mesopotamia and controlled the surrounding areas. The Seleucid dynasty also wished to control the whole of Palestine, including the territory of Judea. Consequently, these two imperial forces frequently fought against each other.[118] The Palestine area and the Yehud province became a buffer zone between the two competing imperial forces.[119] As a result, the Chronicler's postexilic Jewish community lived in the context of *Realpolitik* liminality throughout most of the Second Temple period. No matter when during the Second Temple period one dates the Chronicler's audience, this community was stuck between powerful forces, either between the Egyptians and the Persians in the Persian era, or between the Ptolemaic dynasty (forces from Egypt) and the Seleucid dynasty (in Syria and Mesopotamia) in the Hellenistic period.

Concerning the Chronicler's reading of the account of Josiah's death (2 Kgs 23:29–30a // 2 Chr 35:20–25), scholars debate whether the Chronicler's presentation is true history. For example, Williamson holds that the Chronicler's reading is true history because this reading provides the location of Carchemish (the Chronicler's source, 2 Kgs 23:29–30a, does not mention this location), which is evidenced in the Babylonian Chronicles. Thus, Williamson argues that the Chronicler's account of Josiah's death is more historically accurate than the Kings version (2 Kgs 23:29–30a), and the Chronicler's account is also an expanded version of the Kings account.[120] Conversely, other scholars claim that the Chronicler's portrait is fictional. For example, Talshir argues that the Chronicler's reading might refer to Jer 46:2 concerning the location of Carchemish rather than referring to other sources such as the Babylonian Chronicles. Consequently, according to

---

117. Mendels, "Palestine Among the Empires," 147; VanderKam, *Introduction to Early Judaism*, 12.

118. Mendels, "Palestine Among the Empires," 147; Perdue and Carter, *Israel and Empire*, 137–38; VanderKam, *Introduction to Early Judaism*, 11–12, 16.

119. Mendels, "Palestine Among the Empires," 147.

120. Williamson, *1 and 2 Chronicles*, 408–10.

Talshir's reading, the Chronicler misunderstood the event of Josiah's death and created the fictitious war to explain it.[121] Talshir suggests that Necho killed Josiah because Josiah's religious reforms expanded into the territory of the former northern kingdom (2 Kgs 23:15–20) and thus made Necho suspect that Josiah was rebelling against the imperial dominion.[122] Other scholars hold a middle position. For example, Japhet examines historical facts of the account of Josiah's death. She states, "no conclusive statement may be made."[123] The account only shows that the Chronicler's reading adds a theological comment to explain why Josiah was killed. The king died because of his sin of disobedience to God's will.[124]

This present study does not discuss the historicity of Josiah's death. Instead, it aims to examine whether the Chronicler's reading is faithful to his source (2 Kgs 23:29–30a) and how he presents his reading through the lens of his postexilic colonial perspective. In other words, this section suggests an alternative explanation of the Chronicler's reading of Josiah's death through the lens of a colonial perspective in terms of *Realpolitik* liminality. Let us take a look at the parallel texts.

Table 2. The Chronicler's Reading of 2 Kings 23:29–30a

2 Kings 23:29–30a	2 Chronicles 35:20–25
בְּיָמָיו עָלָה פַרְעֹה נְכֹה מֶלֶךְ־מִצְרַיִם עַל־מֶלֶךְ אַשּׁוּר עַל־נְהַר־פְּרָת וַיֵּלֶךְ הַמֶּלֶךְ יֹאשִׁיָּהוּ לִקְרָאתוֹ	אַחֲרֵי כָל־זֹאת אֲשֶׁר הֵכִין יֹאשִׁיָּהוּ אֶת־הַבַּיִת עָלָה נְכוֹ מֶלֶךְ־מִצְרַיִם לְהִלָּחֵם בְּכַרְכְּמִישׁ עַל־פְּרָת וַיֵּצֵא לִקְרָאתוֹ יֹאשִׁיָּהוּ׃
	21 וַיִּשְׁלַח אֵלָיו מַלְאָכִים לֵאמֹר מַה־לִּי וָלָךְ מֶלֶךְ יְהוּדָה לֹא־עָלֶיךָ אַתָּה הַיּוֹם כִּי אֶל־בֵּית מִלְחַמְתִּי וֵאלֹהִים אָמַר לְבַהֲלֵנִי חֲדַל־לְךָ מֵאֱלֹהִים אֲשֶׁר־עִמִּי וְאַל־יַשְׁחִיתֶךָ׃ 22 וְלֹא־הֵסֵב יֹאשִׁיָּהוּ פָנָיו מִמֶּנּוּ כִּי לְהִלָּחֵם־בּוֹ הִתְחַפֵּשׂ וְלֹא שָׁמַע אֶל־דִּבְרֵי נְכוֹ מִפִּי אֱלֹהִים
וַיְמִיתֵהוּ בִמְגִדּוֹ כִּרְאֹתוֹ אֹתוֹ׃	וַיָּבֹא לְהִלָּחֵם בְּבִקְעַת מְגִדּוֹ׃ 23 וַיֹּרוּ הַיֹּרִים לַמֶּלֶךְ יֹאשִׁיָּהוּ וַיֹּאמֶר הַמֶּלֶךְ לַעֲבָדָיו הַעֲבִירוּנִי כִּי הָחֳלֵיתִי מְאֹד׃

---

121. Talshir, "Three Deaths of Josiah," 214–15, 219.
122. Talshir, "Three Deaths of Josiah," 218.
123. Japhet, *I and II Chronicles*, 1044.
124. Japhet, *I and II Chronicles*, 1041–42.

Reading the Bible as a Postexilic Biblical Author Read

2 Kings 23:29–30a	2 Chronicles 35:20–25
30 וַיַּרְכִּבֻהוּ עֲבָדָיו מֵת מִמְּגִדּוֹ וַיְבִאֻהוּ יְרוּשָׁלַם וַיִּקְבְּרֻהוּ בִּקְבֻרָתוֹ	24 וַיַּעֲבִירֻהוּ עֲבָדָיו מִן־הַמֶּרְכָּבָה וַיַּרְכִּיבֻהוּ עַל רֶכֶב הַמִּשְׁנֶה אֲשֶׁר־לוֹ וַיּוֹלִיכֻהוּ יְרוּשָׁלַם וַיָּמָת וַיִּקָּבֵר בְּקִבְרוֹת אֲבֹתָיו
	וְכָל־יְהוּדָה וִירוּשָׁלַם מִתְאַבְּלִים עַל־יֹאשִׁיָּהוּ׃
	25 וַיְקוֹנֵן יִרְמְיָהוּ עַל־יֹאשִׁיָּהוּ וַיֹּאמְרוּ כָל־הַשָּׁרִים ׀ וְהַשָּׁרוֹת בְּקִינוֹתֵיהֶם עַל־יֹאשִׁיָּהוּ עַד־הַיּוֹם וַיִּתְּנוּם לְחֹק עַל־יִשְׂרָאֵל וְהִנָּם כְּתוּבִים עַל־הַקִּינוֹת
(In his days Pharaoh Neco king of Egypt went up to the king of Assyria to the river Euphrates. King Josiah went to meet him;	(After all this, when Josiah had set the temple in order, King Neco of Egypt went up to fight at Carchemish on the Euphrates, and Josiah went out against him.
	21 But he[125] sent messengers to him, saying, "What have I to do with you, king of Judah? I am not coming against you today, but against the house with which I am at war; and *elohim*[126] (God/gods) has commanded me to hurry. Stop opposing *elohim*,[127] who is with me, so that he will not destroy you."
	22 But Josiah did not turn away from him, when he disguised himself in order to fight with him. He did not listen to the words of Neco from the mouth of *elohim*,[128]
but when Pharaoh Neco met him at Megiddo, he killed him.	but joined battle in the plain of Megiddo. 23 The archers shot King Josiah; and the king said to his servants, "Take me away, for I am badly wounded."
30 His servants carried him dead in a chariot from Megiddo, brought him to Jerusalem, and buried him in his own tomb.)	24 So his servants took him out of the chariot and carried him in his second chariot and brought him to Jerusalem. There he died, and was buried in the tombs of his ancestors.
	All Judah and Jerusalem mourned for Josiah.
	25 Jeremiah also uttered a lament for Josiah, and all the singing men and singing women have spoken of Josiah in their laments to this day. They made these a custom in Israel; they are recorded in the Laments.)

125. Translation follows MT 2 Chr 35:21, which reads וַיִּשְׁלַח (he sent).
126. Translation follows MT 2 Chr 35:21, which reads וֵאלֹהִים (and elohim).
127. Translation follows MT 2 Chr 35:21, which reads מֵאֱלֹהִים.
128. Translation follows MT 2 Chr 35:22, which reads אֱלֹהִים.

Comparing the Chronicler's Reading and Postcolonial Biblical Reading

Second Kings 23:29–30a narrates that Josiah went out to meet Necho at Meggido when the Egyptian king marched through Judah on his way to meet the king of Assyria somewhere along the river Euphrates. When Necho met Josiah at Meggido, Necho killed Josiah (v. 29). Josiah's servants carried the king from Meggido to Jerusalem and buried Josiah in his tomb at Jerusalem (v. 30). The Chronicler's source (2 Kgs 23:29–30a) does not tell why Necho killed Josiah. While reading 2 Kgs 23:29–30a, the Chronicler explains that Carchemish is the location on the river Euphrates where Necho was heading to fight, and Josiah went to meet Necho on the way (2 Chr 35:20).

Regardless of which sources the Chronicler referred to (e.g., the Babylonian Chronicles, Jer 46:2) to provide the destination of Necho on the Euphrates (Carchemish), most scholars agree that the Chronicler reading is correct because this encounter is corroborated by nonbiblical data.[129] Following his source, the Chronicler faithfully narrates that Josiah was eventually killed from his encounter with Necho at Meggido. While the Chronicler's source does not show why and how Josiah was killed, the Chronicler expounds the why and the how (2 Chr 35:21–24). Moreover, although modern scholars have not yet found archeological evidence to prove the historicity of the Chronicler's reading concerning the reason for Josiah's death, the postexilic community accepted the Chronicler's reading as reliable because the Jewish literature in the Second Temple period identified the reason for Josiah's death similarly to the Chronicler's reading (LXX 2 Kgs 23:29–30; LXX 2 Chr 35:19–25; 1 Esd 1:25–31; *Ant.* 10:74–83). In short, the Chronicler's reading does not subvert nor distort what 2 Kgs 23:29–30a meant concerning the story of Josiah's death in his encounter with Necho.

Additionally, the Chronicler has provided further explanation on the why and the how in his reading of Josiah's death through the lens of the *Realpolitik* of liminality context in the postexilic period. Since the Chronicler's community lived in the conflict zone between imperial forces (i.e., the Egyptians and others) during most of the Second Temple period, they would be unsafe regardless of which imperial forces they supported. Thus, they would do well to please all imperial forces, if that were even possible. If Necho came to Carchemish to support the Assyrians in fighting against the newly emerged forces, namely, the Babylonians and the Medes (Persians) according to the Babylonian Chronicles, the Chronicler's explanation that

---

129. Grayson, *Assyrian and Babylonian Chronicles*, 99.

Josiah went to fight against Necho (2 Chr 35:20) would make the Persians pleased. The Chronicler, however, further elaborates that *elohim* was with Necho in that war and Necho then killed Josiah, who wanted to stop Necho in the battle. This explanation of the Chronicler would please the Egyptians since it states that the Egyptian fight was supported by *elohim*. Nevertheless, the Chronicler's reference to אֱלֹהִים (3x, 2 Chr 35:21–22) is ambiguous because the term אֱלֹהִים can refer either to foreign gods or to the God of Israel. Janzen rightly asks: Who is this god? The God of Israel or the gods of Egypt?[130] This ambiguity has caused much debate among scholars.[131] The Chronicler describes Necho's words referring to אֱלֹהִים ambiguously and makes readers realize Josiah's difficulty. How could Josiah know whether Necho's words were true and whether YHWH would support the alliance of Assyrian-Egyptian forces or the other newly emerged coalition? The Chronicler's interpretation illustrates the difficulty of people living in the context of the *Realpolitik* of liminality. From this, the Chronicler provides his own conclusion that Josiah deserved great sympathy and lament from his people (2 Chr 35:24–25). We do not know what lamentations the people spoke concerning Josiah's death, yet Josiah "is the only king for whom all Israel mourns; no other king is mourned in death."[132]

Even though we are not sure whether Josiah disobeyed God by going up, people still mourned for Josiah because he was overall a very good king, even if his last act of going to war against Necho were not God's will. The mourning of people does not only respond to Josiah's tragic death but also to their lamentable situation of living in the context of the *Realpolitik* of liminality. Josiah was killed because he lived in a zone of conflict between imperial forces, yet his death fulfilled YHWH's prophecy through Huldah. YHWH had foretold Josiah's death in peace with his fathers (i.e., not being exiled) through Huldah (2 Kgs 22:19–20 // 2 Chr 34:27–28). Thus, regardless of whether Josiah supported or fought against Necho, the Chronicler's presentation of Josiah's death via the use of ambiguous words and the people's lamentation (2 Chr 35:21–22, 24–25) has demonstrated Josiah's

---

130. Janzen, *Chronicles*, 142.

131. Klein and Hanson argues that the Chronicler meant Israel's God (see Klein and Hanson, *2 Chronicles*, 526). Japhet argues that v. 21 refers to the Egyptian gods, while v. 22 refers to Israel's God, who allowed Necho's message, revealed by the Egyptian gods, to be sent to Josiah (see Japhet, *I and II Chronicles*, 1056–57). McConville does not reject a possibility that both vv. 21–22 indicate Egyptian gods (see McConville, *I and II Chronicles*, 264).

132. Ristau, "Reading and Rereading Josiah," 238.

Comparing the Chronicler's Reading and Postcolonial Biblical Reading

dilemma under the context of *Realpolitik* of liminality. In conclusion, the Chronicler is reading through the lens of his postexilic community living in the difficulty of the *Realpolitik* of liminality.

Reading Through the Lens of Explicitly Pro-Imperial Rule and Implicitly Pro-Davidic Hope

The Chronicler lived in a context of imperial dominion. On the one hand, the Chronicler's reading demonstrated submission and appreciation to the empire that allowed the exiled people to return to their homeland. On the other hand, the Chronicler's reading implicitly resisted the Persian Empire as it looked forward to the full restoration of the Davidic house as promised by God to David. For example, the Chronicler's interpretation of Jeremiah's prophecy demonstrates this twofold attitude (2 Chr 36:22–23 // Ezra 1:1–3). Second Chronicles 36:22–23 is an interpretation of Jeremiah's prophecy (Jer 29:10), which the Chronicler has stated earlier (2 Chr 36:21). Regardless of whether the Chronicler is using the words of Ezra 1:1–3 or another source, 2 Chr 36:22–23 demonstrates the Chronicler's point of view and advocates this interpretation of Jer 29:10 when he includes this passage in Chronicles. Jeremiah 29:10 states that YHWH will visit his people, fulfill his promise, and bring them back to Jerusalem. Second Chronicles 36:22–23 illustrates a faithful reading of Jer 29:10 and explains how this prophecy would be fulfilled through Cyrus, the king of Persia, as well as how and why YHWH would bring his people back to Jerusalem through Cyrus's edict. This passage clearly communicates the Chronicler's support for the Persian king because it claims that Cyrus was used by God to fulfill God's words through the prophet Jeremiah. Verses 22b and 23 imply that obeying Cyrus's written commandment is obeying God's will. However, as Wilson points out, God's requirement for a king reigning over God's people is that he should be an Israelite and must not be a foreigner (Deut 17:15–20). Yet the Chronicler repeatedly specifies Cyrus's ethnic identity as Persian (כּוֹרֶשׁ מֶלֶךְ פָּרַס [3x], 2 Chr 36:22–23).[133] Wilson states that this creates tension for anyone supporting Cyrus as YHWH's agent, akin to a Davidic king, since this contradicts

---

133. Isa 44:28, 45:1, and 45:13 also state that Cyrus would be used by YHWH and Cyrus was even called "the anointed." However, these verses in Isaiah do not specify Cyrus's Persian ethnicity. In contrast, the Chronicler does not designate him as "the anointed."

the Deuteronomic law.[134] The Chronicler's emphatic identification of Cyrus as Persian implies that God's promise to David concerning an eternal Davidic dynasty was yet to be completely fulfilled and thus the readers should still expect the full restoration of the Davidic house. In short, 2 Chr 36:22–23 presents a faithful interpretation of Jer 29:10 through a lens similar to the postcolonial perspective, namely, resistance to imperial dominion. Here, the Chronicler's reading is *explicitly* in favor of Cyrus's imperial rule but *implicitly* in resistance to permanent imperialism and in favor of the restoration of the Davidic house. This kind of reading is also found in the Chronicler's reading of the account of King Manasseh (2 Kgs 21:1–18 // 2 Chr 33:1–20), which will be presented in the following section.

Reading Through the Lens of Belief in the Deliverance
and Supremacy of YHWH over Imperial Forces

The Chronicler's postexilic community lived under the rule of colonial powers. This present study demonstrates that, while reading his sources concerning accounts of God's people being oppressed by colonial empires, the Chronicler implicitly presents an attitude of resistance to foreign empires (e.g., the Assyrians, Chaldeans, and Persians) when he describes YHWH's supremacy and control over the activities of imperial forces. The Chronicler often hints at the means by which YHWH will deliver his people from foreign dominion, thereby espousing YHWH's supremacy over all human empires.

The Chronicler demonstrates YHWH's supremacy over the Assyrians in the following ways. He explains that the God of Israel had used the Assyrians as God's tool to exile the Israelites (1 Chr 5:26). Here the Chronicler asserts that YHWH had ultimate sovereignty over the Assyrians' treatment of his people, even when God allowed them to oppress and exile the northern kingdom of Israel. In other respects, the Chronicler's reading of the Hezekiah account indicates a voice of resistance. When Hezekiah renewed observance of the Passover, he sent messengers to all Israel (under the reign of Hoshea at that time) and throughout his southern kingdom to call all the people to return to YHWH because only the God of Abraham, Isaac, and Israel could deliver them from the Assyrians (2 Chr 30:6). Here the Chronicler indicates the way for the Israelites to be delivered from Assyrian oppression. Unfortunately, most of the Israelites of the northern kingdom

---

134. Wilson, "Yahweh's Anointed," 334–35, 349–50.

Comparing the Chronicler's Reading and Postcolonial Biblical Reading

rejected this solution (2 Chr 30:10). After the Assyrians exiled the northern kingdom and then invaded the southern kingdom, the Chronicler again shows this kind of reading in terms of YHWH's sovereignty and supremacy through his interpretation of Sennacherib's invasion of Judah (2 Kgs 18:13—19:37 [or Isa 36:1—37:38] // 2 Chr 32:1-23). The following table demonstrates the textual evidence for this.

Table 3. The Chronicler's Reading of 2 Kings 18:13—19:37

2 Kings 18:13—19:37	Isaiah 36:1—37:38	2 Chronicles 32:1-23
Verse 13:	Verse 1:	Verse 1:
וּבְאַרְבַּע עֶשְׂרֵה שָׁנָה לַמֶּלֶךְ חִזְקִיָּה עָלָה סַנְחֵרִיב מֶלֶךְ־אַשּׁוּר עַל כָּל־עָרֵי יְהוּדָה הַבְּצֻרוֹת וַיִּתְפְּשֵׂם	וַיְהִי בְּאַרְבַּע עֶשְׂרֵה שָׁנָה לַמֶּלֶךְ חִזְקִיָּהוּ עָלָה סַנְחֵרִיב מֶלֶךְ־אַשּׁוּר עַל כָּל־עָרֵי יְהוּדָה הַבְּצֻרוֹת וַיִּתְפְּשֵׂם	אַחֲרֵי הַדְּבָרִים וְהָאֱמֶת הָאֵלֶּה בָּא סַנְחֵרִיב מֶלֶךְ־אַשּׁוּר וַיָּבֹא בִיהוּדָה וַיִּחַן עַל־הֶעָרִים הַבְּצֻרוֹת וַיֹּאמֶר לְבִקְעָם אֵלָיו
(In the fourteenth year of King Hezekiah, King Sennacherib of Assyria came up against all the fortified cities of Judah and captured them.)	(In the fourteenth year of King Hezekiah, King Sennacherib of Assyria came up against all the fortified cities of Judah and captured them.)	(After these things and these acts of faithfulness, King Sennacherib of Assyria came and invaded Judah and encamped against the fortified cities, thinking to win them for himself.)
Verse 22:	Verse 7:	Verse 11b–12:
וְכִי־תֹאמְרוּן אֵלַי אֶל־יְהוָה אֱלֹהֵינוּ בָּטָחְנוּ הֲלוֹא־הוּא אֲשֶׁר הֵסִיר חִזְקִיָּהוּ אֶת־בָּמֹתָיו וְאֶת־מִזְבְּחֹתָיו וַיֹּאמֶר לִיהוּדָה וְלִירוּשָׁלִַם לִפְנֵי הַמִּזְבֵּחַ הַזֶּה תִּשְׁתַּחֲווּ בִּירוּשָׁלִָם	וְכִי־תֹאמַר אֵלַי אֶל־יְהוָה אֱלֹהֵינוּ בָּטָחְנוּ הֲלוֹא־הוּא אֲשֶׁר הֵסִיר חִזְקִיָּהוּ אֶת־בָּמֹתָיו וְאֶת־מִזְבְּחֹתָיו וַיֹּאמֶר לִיהוּדָה וְלִירוּשָׁלִַם לִפְנֵי הַמִּזְבֵּחַ הַזֶּה תִּשְׁתַּחֲווּ	לֵאמֹר יְהוָה אֱלֹהֵינוּ יַצִּילֵנוּ מִכַּף מֶלֶךְ אַשּׁוּר: 12 הֲלֹא־הוּא יְחִזְקִיָּהוּ הֵסִיר אֶת־בָּמֹתָיו וְאֶת־מִזְבְּחֹתָיו וַיֹּאמֶר לִיהוּדָה וְלִירוּשָׁלִַם לֵאמֹר לִפְנֵי מִזְבֵּחַ אֶחָד תִּשְׁתַּחֲווּ וְעָלָיו תַּקְטִירוּ
(but if you say to me, "We rely on the Lord our God,"	(but if you say to me, "We rely on the Lord our God,"	(saying,[135] "the Lord our God will save us from the hand of the king of Assyria"?
is it not he whose high places and altars Hezekiah has removed,	is it not he whose high places and altars Hezekiah has removed,	12 Was it not this same Hezekiah who took away his high places and his altars and commanded Judah and Jerusalem, saying, "Before one altar you shall worship, and upon it you shall make your offerings"?)
saying to Judah and to Jerusalem, "You shall worship before this altar in Jerusalem"?)	saying to Judah and to Jerusalem, "You shall worship before this altar"?)	

---

135. Translation follows MT 2 Chr 32:11, which reads לֵאמֹר.

Reading the Bible as a Postexilic Biblical Author Read

2 Kings 18:13—19:37	Isaiah 36:1—37:38	2 Chronicles 32:1-23
2 Kings 19:35-37	Isaiah 37:36-38	2 Chronicles 32:21-23
וַיְהִי בַּלַּיְלָה הַהוּא וַיֵּצֵא ׀ מַלְאַךְ יְהוָה וַיַּךְ בְּמַחֲנֵה אַשּׁוּר מֵאָה שְׁמוֹנִים וַחֲמִשָּׁה אָלֶף וַיַּשְׁכִּימוּ בַבֹּקֶר וְהִנֵּה כֻלָּם פְּגָרִים מֵתִים:	וַיֵּצֵא ׀ מַלְאַךְ יְהוָה וַיַּכֶּה בְּמַחֲנֵה אַשּׁוּר מֵאָה וּשְׁמֹנִים וַחֲמִשָּׁה אָלֶף וַיַּשְׁכִּימוּ בַבֹּקֶר וְהִנֵּה כֻלָּם פְּגָרִים מֵתִים:	וַיִּשְׁלַח יְהוָה מַלְאָךְ וַיַּכְחֵד כָּל־גִּבּוֹר חַיִל וְנָגִיד וְשָׂר בְּמַחֲנֵה מֶלֶךְ אַשּׁוּר וַיָּשָׁב בְּבֹשֶׁת פָּנִים לְאַרְצוֹ
36 וַיִּסַּע וַיֵּלֶךְ	37 וַיִּסַּע וַיֵּלֶךְ	וַיָּבֹא בֵּית אֱלֹהָיו וּמִיצִיאָו מֵעָיו שָׁם הִפִּילֻהוּ בֶחָרֶב:
וַיָּשָׁב סַנְחֵרִיב מֶלֶךְ־אַשּׁוּר וַיֵּשֶׁב בְּנִינְוֵה:	וַיָּשָׁב סַנְחֵרִיב מֶלֶךְ־אַשּׁוּר וַיֵּשֶׁב בְּנִינְוֵה:	
37 וַיְהִי הוּא מִשְׁתַּחֲוֶה בֵּית ׀ נִסְרֹךְ אֱלֹהָיו וְאַדְרַמֶּלֶךְ וְשַׂרְאֶצֶר הִכֻּהוּ בַחֶרֶב וְהֵמָּה נִמְלְטוּ אֶרֶץ אֲרָרָט וַיִּמְלֹךְ אֵסַר־חַדֹּן בְּנוֹ תַּחְתָּיו	38 וַיְהִי הוּא מִשְׁתַּחֲוֶה בֵּית ׀ נִסְרֹךְ אֱלֹהָיו וְאַדְרַמֶּלֶךְ וְשַׂרְאֶצֶר בָּנָיו הִכֻּהוּ בַחֶרֶב וְהֵמָּה נִמְלְטוּ אֶרֶץ אֲרָרָט וַיִּמְלֹךְ אֵסַר־חַדֹּן בְּנוֹ תַּחְתָּיו	
(That very night the angel of the LORD set out and struck down one hundred eighty-five thousand in the camp of the Assyrians; when morning dawned, they were all dead bodies.	(Then the angel of the LORD set out and struck down one hundred eighty-five thousand in the camp of the Assyrians; when morning dawned, they were all dead bodies.	(And the LORD sent an angel who cut off all the mighty warriors and commanders and officers in the camp of the king of Assyria.
36 Then King Sennacherib of Assyria left, went home, and lived at Nineveh. 37 As he was worshiping in the house of his god Nisroch, his sons Adrammelech and Sharezer killed him with the sword, and they escaped into the land of Ararat. His son Esar-haddon succeeded him.)	37 Then King Sennacherib of Assyria left, went home, and lived at Nineveh. 38 As he was worshiping in the house of his god Nisroch, his sons Adrammelech and Sharezer killed him with the sword, and they escaped into the land of Ararat. His son Esar-haddon succeeded him.)	So he returned in disgrace to his own land. When he came into the house of his god, some of his own sons struck him down there with the sword.)
		22 ׀ וַיּוֹשַׁע יְהוָה אֶת־יְחִזְקִיָּהוּ וְאֵת יֹשְׁבֵי יְרוּשָׁלַ͏ִם מִיַּד סַנְחֵרִיב מֶלֶךְ־אַשּׁוּר וּמִיַּד־כֹּל וַיְנַהֲלֵם מִסָּבִיב
		23 וְרַבִּים מְבִיאִים מִנְחָה לַיהוָה לִירוּשָׁלַ͏ִם וּמִגְדָּנוֹת לִיחִזְקִיָּהוּ מֶלֶךְ יְהוּדָה וַיִּנַּשֵּׂא לְעֵינֵי כָל־הַגּוֹיִם מֵאַחֲרֵי־כֵן

Comparing the Chronicler's Reading and Postcolonial Biblical Reading

2 Kings 18:13—19:37	Isaiah 36:1—37:38	2 Chronicles 32:1-23
		(22 So the LORD saved Hezekiah and the inhabitants of Jerusalem from the hand of King Sennacherib of Assyria and from the hand of all his enemies; he gave them rest on every side.
		23 Many brought gifts to the LORD in Jerusalem and precious things to King Hezekiah of Judah, so that he was exalted in the sight of all nations from that time onward.)

The Chronicler indicates that YHWH is the supreme ruler and emphasizes God's salvation through Hezekiah's words that YHWH will deliver his people from the hand of the Assyrians (2 Chr 32:11b). Moreover, the Chronicler concludes his reading by highlighting that YHWH's deliverance of his people from Assyria has been fulfilled and that the king of Judah was even exalted among all nations from that time (2 Chr 32:23). For the whole account of Sennacherib's invasion into the kingdom of Judah, the Chronicler reads this narrative faithfully to his sources (2 Kgs 18:13—19:37 [// Isa 36:1—37:38]) and then provides a theological commentary, repeatedly emphasizing that the people of the kingdom of Judah were rescued from Assyria by YHWH (2 Chr 32:22).

This type of reading by the Chronicler is even more evident in his presentation of the account of Manasseh (2 Kgs 21:1-18 // 2 Chr 33:1-20).

Table 4. The Chronicler's Reading of 2 Kings 21:1-18

2 Kings 21:1-18	2 Chronicles 33:1-20
Verse 1:	Verse 1:
בֶּן־שְׁתֵּים עֶשְׂרֵה שָׁנָה מְנַשֶּׁה בְמָלְכוֹ וַחֲמִשִּׁים וְחָמֵשׁ שָׁנָה מָלַךְ בִּירוּשָׁלָםִ וְשֵׁם אִמּוֹ חֶפְצִי־בָהּ	בֶּן־שְׁתֵּים עֶשְׂרֵה שָׁנָה מְנַשֶּׁה בְמָלְכוֹ וַחֲמִשִּׁים וְחָמֵשׁ שָׁנָה מָלַךְ בִּירוּשָׁלָםִ
(Manasseh was twelve years old when he began to reign; he reigned fifty-five years in Jerusalem. His mother's name was Hephzibah.)	(Manasseh was twelve years old when he began to reign; he reigned fifty-five years in Jerusalem.)

Reading the Bible as a Postexilic Biblical Author Read

2 Kings 21:1–18	2 Chronicles 33:1–20
Verses 8–10:	Verses 8–16:
וְלֹא אֹסִיף לְהָנִיד רֶגֶל יִשְׂרָאֵל מִן־הָאֲדָמָה אֲשֶׁר נָתַתִּי לַאֲבוֹתָם רַק ׀ אִם־יִשְׁמְרוּ לַעֲשׂוֹת כְּכֹל אֲשֶׁר צִוִּיתִים וּלְכָל־הַתּוֹרָה אֲשֶׁר־צִוָּה אֹתָם עַבְדִּי מֹשֶׁה: 9 וְלֹא שָׁמֵעוּ וַיַּתְעֵם מְנַשֶּׁה לַעֲשׂוֹת אֶת־הָרָע מִן־הַגּוֹיִם אֲשֶׁר הִשְׁמִיד יְהוָה מִפְּנֵי בְּנֵי יִשְׂרָאֵל: 10 וַיְדַבֵּר יְהוָה בְּיַד־עֲבָדָיו הַנְּבִיאִים לֵאמֹר	וְלֹא אוֹסִיף לְהָסִיר אֶת־רֶגֶל יִשְׂרָאֵל מֵעַל הָאֲדָמָה אֲשֶׁר הֶעֱמַדְתִּי לַאֲבֹתֵיכֶם רַק ׀ אִם־יִשְׁמְרוּ לַעֲשׂוֹת אֵת כָּל־אֲשֶׁר צִוִּיתִים לְכָל־הַתּוֹרָה וְהַחֻקִּים וְהַמִּשְׁפָּטִים בְּיַד־מֹשֶׁה: 9 וַיֶּתַע מְנַשֶּׁה אֶת־יְהוּדָה וְיֹשְׁבֵי יְרוּשָׁלִָם לַעֲשׂוֹת רָע מִן־הַגּוֹיִם אֲשֶׁר הִשְׁמִיד יְהוָה מִפְּנֵי בְּנֵי יִשְׂרָאֵל: 10 וַיְדַבֵּר יְהוָה אֶל־מְנַשֶּׁה וְאֶל־עַמּוֹ וְלֹא הִקְשִׁיבוּ: 11 וַיָּבֵא יְהוָה עֲלֵיהֶם אֶת־שָׂרֵי הַצָּבָא אֲשֶׁר לְמֶלֶךְ אַשּׁוּר וַיִּלְכְּדוּ אֶת־מְנַשֶּׁה בַּחֹחִים וַיַּאַסְרֻהוּ בַּנְחֻשְׁתַּיִם וַיּוֹלִיכֻהוּ בָּבֶלָה: 12 וּכְהָצֵר לוֹ חִלָּה אֶת־פְּנֵי יְהוָה אֱלֹהָיו וַיִּכָּנַע מְאֹד מִלִּפְנֵי אֱלֹהֵי אֲבֹתָיו: 13 וַיִּתְפַּלֵּל אֵלָיו וַיֵּעָתֶר לוֹ וַיִּשְׁמַע תְּחִנָּתוֹ וַיְשִׁיבֵהוּ יְרוּשָׁלִַם לְמַלְכוּתוֹ וַיֵּדַע מְנַשֶּׁה כִּי יְהוָה הוּא הָאֱלֹהִים: 14 וְאַחֲרֵי־כֵן בָּנָה חוֹמָה חִיצוֹנָה ׀ לְעִיר־דָּוִיד מַעְרָבָה לְגִיחוֹן בַּנַּחַל וְלָבוֹא בְשַׁעַר הַדָּגִים וְסָבַב לָעֹפֶל וַיַּגְבִּיהֶהָ מְאֹד וַיָּשֶׂם שָׂרֵי־חַיִל בְּכָל־הֶעָרִים הַבְּצֻרוֹת בִּיהוּדָה: 15 וַיָּסַר אֶת־אֱלֹהֵי הַנֵּכָר וְאֶת־הַסֶּמֶל מִבֵּית יְהוָה וְכָל־הַמִּזְבְּחוֹת אֲשֶׁר בָּנָה בְּהַר בֵּית־יְהוָה וּבִירוּשָׁלִָם וַיַּשְׁלֵךְ חוּצָה לָעִיר: 16 וַיִּכֶן אֶת־מִזְבַּח יְהוָה וַיִּזְבַּח עָלָיו זִבְחֵי שְׁלָמִים וְתוֹדָה וַיֹּאמֶר לִיהוּדָה לַעֲבוֹד אֶת־יְהוָה אֱלֹהֵי יִשְׂרָאֵל

Comparing the Chronicler's Reading and Postcolonial Biblical Reading

2 Kings 21:1–18	2 Chronicles 33:1–20
("I will not cause the feet of Israel to wander any more out of the land that I gave to their ancestors, if only they will be careful to do according to all that I have commanded them, and according to all the law that my servant Moses commanded them."	("I will never again remove the feet of Israel from the land that I appointed for your ancestors, if only they will be careful to do all that I have commanded them, all the law, the statutes, and the ordinances given through Moses."
But they did not listen; Manasseh misled them to do more evil than the nations had done that the LORD destroyed before the people of Israel.	9 Manasseh misled Judah and the inhabitants of Jerusalem, so that they did more evil than the nations whom the LORD had destroyed before the people of Israel.
The LORD said by his servants the prophets. . . .)	10 The LORD spoke to Manasseh and to his people, but they gave no heed.
	11 Therefore the LORD brought against them the commanders of the army of the king of Assyria, who took Manasseh captive in manacles, bound him with fetters, and brought him to Babylon.
	12 While he was in distress he entreated the favor of the LORD his God and humbled himself greatly before the God of his ancestors.
	13 He prayed to him, and God received his entreaty, heard his plea, and restored him again to Jerusalem and to his kingdom. Then Manasseh knew that the LORD indeed was God.
	14 Afterward he built an outer wall for the city of David west of Gihon, in the valley, reaching the entrance at the Fish Gate; he carried it around Ophel, and raised it to a very great height. He also put commanders of the army in all the fortified cities in Judah.
	15 He took away the foreign gods and the idol from the house of the LORD, and all the altars that he had built on the mountain of the house of the LORD and in Jerusalem, and he threw them out of the city.
	16 He also restored the altar of the LORD and offered on it sacrifices of well-being and of thanksgiving; and he commanded Judah to serve the LORD the God of Israel.)

The Chronicler reads 2 Kgs 21:1–18 (// 2 Chr 33:1–20) concerning Manasseh leading his people and doing more evil than all the nations that

YHWH has destroyed because of their sins (2 Kgs 21:9 // 2 Chr 33:9). The Chronicler again interprets that YHWH ultimately controlled the oppressive activities of imperial force when the Lord employed the Assyrians to punish Manasseh and exile him (2 Chr 33:11). The Chronicler then provides the important information that Manasseh humbly repented and YHWH restored him to the throne in Jerusalem. Although the Assyrian Empire claimed hegemony over the world, the empire was still under YHWH's control. The Lord used this empire to punish his people and then YHWH sovereignly restored his people according to his will. More importantly, as Mark Boda points out, the Chronicler also hints at a future restoration of the Davidic dynasty through the Manasseh narrative. The Chronicler describes how Manasseh and Jehoiakim were exiled in humiliation to Babylon in an identical way (2 Chr 33:11 and 36:6), but Manasseh humbly and wholeheartedly repented and was restored, whereas Jehoiakim did not.[136] Through this difference, the Chronicler is teaching how true repentance led to deliverance, as stated in the letter of the godly king Hezekiah sent to all Israel and Judah (2 Chr 30:1–9).[137] The Chronicler also reads 2 Kgs 21:7–8 (// 2 Chr 33:7–8) faithfully to remind his postexilic readers about YHWH's eternal promise to David and Solomon and about repentance as the key to deliverance and restoration. In summary, the Chronicler's presentation of Manasseh's life (exile and then restoration) parallels the Chronicler's readers' context (exile and restoration) and also offers a model of how "a royal figure in exile is restored to [his] rule."[138]

Similarly, regarding the Chaldeans and then the Persians, the Chronicler implicitly demonstrates his reading of resistance to those imperial powers by proclaiming YHWH's supremacy over them and his plan to deliver his people from their dominion. For instance, the Chronicler's reading of the Zedekiah account (2 Kgs 24:18–20 // 2 Chr 36:11–21) includes a summarization of what his source meant (2 Kgs 24:18–20 // 2 Chr 36:11–13a) as well as a voice of resistance (2 Chr 36:13b–21).

---

136. Boda, "Identity and Empire," 268.
137. Boda, "Identity and Empire," 267.
138. Boda, "Identity and Empire," 267.

Comparing the Chronicler's Reading and Postcolonial Biblical Reading

Table 5. The Chronicler's Reading of 2 Kings 24:18–20

2 Kings 24:18–20	2 Chronicles 36:11–21
Verse 18: בֶּן־עֶשְׂרִים וְאַחַת שָׁנָה צִדְקִיָּהוּ בְמָלְכוֹ וְאַחַת עֶשְׂרֵה שָׁנָה מָלַךְ בִּירוּשָׁלָם	Verse 11: בֶּן־עֶשְׂרִים וְאַחַת שָׁנָה צִדְקִיָּהוּ בְמָלְכוֹ וְאַחַת עֶשְׂרֵה שָׁנָה מָלַךְ בִּירוּשָׁלָם
(Zedekiah was twenty-one years old when he began to reign; he reigned eleven years in Jerusalem.)	(Zedekiah was twenty-one years old when he began to reign; he reigned eleven years in Jerusalem.)
Verse 19: וַיַּעַשׂ הָרַע בְּעֵינֵי יְהוָה כְּכֹל אֲשֶׁר־עָשָׂה יְהוֹיָקִים:	Verse 12: וַיַּעַשׂ הָרַע בְּעֵינֵי יְהוָה אֱלֹהָיו לֹא נִכְנַע מִלִּפְנֵי יִרְמְיָהוּ הַנָּבִיא מִפִּי יְהוָה:
(he did what was evil in the sight of the LORD, just as Jehoiakim had done.)	(he did what was evil in the sight of the LORD his God. He did not humble himself before the prophet Jeremiah who spoke from the mouth of the LORD.)
Verses 20b: וַיִּמְרֹד צִדְקִיָּהוּ בְּמֶלֶךְ בָּבֶל	Verses 13–20: וְגַם בַּמֶּלֶךְ נְבוּכַדְנֶאצַּר מָרָד אֲשֶׁר הִשְׁבִּיעוֹ בֵּאלֹהִים וַיֶּקֶשׁ אֶת־עָרְפּוֹ וַיְאַמֵּץ אֶת־לְבָבוֹ מִשּׁוּב אֶל־יְהוָה אֱלֹהֵי יִשְׂרָאֵל: 14 גַּם כָּל־שָׂרֵי הַכֹּהֲנִים וְהָעָם הִרְבּוּ לִמְעָל־מַעַל כְּכֹל תֹּעֲבוֹת הַגּוֹיִם וַיְטַמְּאוּ אֶת־בֵּית יְהוָה אֲשֶׁר הִקְדִּישׁ בִּירוּשָׁלָם: 15 וַיִּשְׁלַח יְהוָה אֱלֹהֵי אֲבוֹתֵיהֶם עֲלֵיהֶם בְּיַד מַלְאָכָיו הַשְׁכֵּם וְשָׁלוֹחַ כִּי־חָמַל עַל־עַמּוֹ וְעַל־מְעוֹנוֹ: 16 וַיִּהְיוּ מַלְעִבִים בְּמַלְאֲכֵי הָאֱלֹהִים וּבוֹזִים דְּבָרָיו וּמִתַּעְתְּעִים בִּנְבִאָיו עַד עֲלוֹת חֲמַת־יְהוָה בְּעַמּוֹ עַד־לְאֵין מַרְפֵּא: 17 וַיַּעַל עֲלֵיהֶם אֶת־מֶלֶךְ כַּשְׂדִּיִּים וַיַּהֲרֹג בַּחוּרֵיהֶם בַּחֶרֶב בְּבֵית מִקְדָּשָׁם וְלֹא חָמַל עַל־בָּחוּר וּבְתוּלָה זָקֵן וִישֵׁשׁ הַכֹּל נָתַן בְּיָדוֹ: 18 וְכֹל כְּלֵי בֵּית הָאֱלֹהִים הַגְּדֹלִים וְהַקְּטַנִּים וְאֹצְרוֹת בֵּית יְהוָה וְאֹצְרוֹת הַמֶּלֶךְ וְשָׂרָיו הַכֹּל הֵבִיא בָבֶל: 19 וַיִּשְׂרְפוּ אֶת־בֵּית הָאֱלֹהִים וַיְנַתְּצוּ אֵת חוֹמַת יְרוּשָׁלָם וְכָל־אַרְמְנוֹתֶיהָ שָׂרְפוּ בָאֵשׁ וְכָל־כְּלֵי מַחֲמַדֶּיהָ לְהַשְׁחִית: 20 וַיֶּגֶל הַשְּׁאֵרִית מִן־הַחֶרֶב אֶל־בָּבֶל וַיִּהְיוּ־לוֹ וּלְבָנָיו לַעֲבָדִים עַד־מְלֹךְ מַלְכוּת פָּרָס:

Reading the Bible as a Postexilic Biblical Author Read

2 Kings 24:18–20	2 Chronicles 36:11–21
(Zedekiah rebelled against the king of Babylon.)	(He also rebelled against King Nebuchadnezzar, who had made him swear by God; he stiffened his neck and hardened his heart against turning to the Lord, the God of Israel.
	14 All the leading priests and the people also were exceedingly unfaithful, following all the abominations of the nations; and they polluted the house of the Lord that he had consecrated in Jerusalem.
	15 The Lord, the God of their ancestors, sent persistently to them by his messengers, because he had compassion on his people and on his dwelling place;
	16 but they kept mocking the messengers of God, despising his words, and scoffing at his prophets, until the wrath of the Lord against his people became so great that there was no remedy.
	17 Therefore he brought up against them the king of the Chaldeans, who killed their youths with the sword in the house of their sanctuary, and had no compassion on young man or young woman, the aged or the feeble; he gave them all into his hand.
	18 All the vessels of the house of God, large and small, and the treasures of the house of the Lord, and the treasures of the king and of his officials, all these he brought to Babylon.
	19 They burned the house of God, broke down the wall of Jerusalem, burned all its palaces with fire, and destroyed all its precious vessels.
	20 He took into exile in Babylon those who had escaped from the sword, and they became servants to him and to his sons until the establishment of the kingdom of Persia.)

For the event that the Chaldeans completely defeated the kingdom of Judah and destroyed the city and temple of Jerusalem, the Chronicler comments that YHWH allowed Judah's kingdom to be destroyed and exiled by the Chaldeans (2 Chr 36:17–19) and then brought under the dominion of the Persians (2 Chr 36:20). The reason for YHWH's punishment is because God's people had persistently rejected God's prophets, disobeyed, and been unfaithful to YHWH (2 Chr 36:12b–14). Here the Chronicler interprets that all the Chaldeans' oppressive activities and then the Persian dominion over his people were completely under YHWH's control and with his permission. According to the Chronicler, YHWH is the real supreme ruler who permitted both the Chaldeans and the Persians to subjugate God's people (2 Chr 36:13b–21). Moreover, the Chronicler also teaches that God's mercy provided a way for God's people to escape from the imperial domination, i.e., via repentance. Tragically, God's people repeatedly rejected the prophets' call to return to him (2 Chr 36:15–16). Here the Chronicler's reading presents God's people with the possibility of deliverance from the imperial subjugation based on God's sovereignty and compassion, if only they would follow God's way.

The Chronicler's Portrayal of Jewish Identity for His Postexilic Community

Scholars agree that the theme of "all Israel" is an important one in Chronicles. The book of Chronicles shows that all people dwelling in the promised land (both the northern and the southern kingdoms) are all Israel through the use of genealogical lists of all Israelite tribes from Adam to the postexilic era (1 Chr 1–9). "All Israel" is mentioned in both the united kingdom (e.g., 1 Chr 11:1, 4; 13:1–6; 28:1; 2 Chr 7:8; and so on) and the divided kingdom (e.g., 2 Chr 11:16; 15:9–10; 30:11, 18, 21, 25).[139]

Grabbe also contends that the Second Temple biblical literature (e.g., Ezra, Nehemiah, Chronicles) often identifies the Jewish postexilic community as "all Israel."[140] This present study holds that the Chronicler portrays the identity of the Jewish postexilic community as all Israel and as needing to faithfully follow YHWH. For the Chronicler's postexilic audience, regardless of where they lived in the Persian provinces, they would never want to be destroyed (e.g., by the threat of destruction narrated in the book of Esther if they lived outside Yehud) nor to go into exile again (if they lived in the Yehud province). Therefore, by repeatedly noting that God's people suffered greatly and went into exile because of their unfaithfulness

---

139. Thompson, *1, 2 Chronicles*, 35; Klein and Krüger, *1 Chronicles*, 46; Japhet, *I and II Chronicles*, 46; Williamson, *Israel*, 139–40.

140. Grabbe, *History of the Jews*, 1:170–71.

to YHWH (e.g., 2 Chr 29:4–11; 30:6–9), the Chronicler presents all Israel as having the responsibility to faithfully follow YHWH. The Chronicler exhibits this view on his community's identity when he narrates that since the last years of the northern kingdom (right before its destruction and exile), the godly kings of the southern kingdom (Hezekiah and then Josiah) aimed to draw all Israelites back to YHWH.

An example is the Chronicler's presentation of Hezekiah (2 Kgs 18–20 // 2 Chr 29–32). While the Chronicler's source only briefly states that Hezekiah implemented religious reforms with a focus on the destruction of idols (2 Kgs 18:4) and that he faithfully followed YHWH's commands in general (2 Kgs 18:6), the Chronicler provides the details of Hezekiah's religious reforms (2 Chr 29:3—31:21) and of how the king appealed to all Israelites to participate (2 Chr 29:20–25; 30:1—31:10). Shortly before the northern kingdom was destroyed and its population exiled, the Chronicler tells us that Hezekiah offered sin offerings for all Israelites of both the northern and the southern kingdoms (2 Chr 29:20–36) because Hezekiah had acknowledged that the people would be destroyed and go into exile due to their unfaithfulness to YHWH (2 Chr 29:4–11; 30:6–9). Hezekiah then sent messengers to all areas of the two kingdoms to call all Israelites to participate in the observance of Passover (2 Chr 30:1–27). Some Israelites from the north kingdom accepted Hezekiah's call (2 Chr 30:11).

Similarly, the Chronicler reads the narrative of King Josiah (2 Kgs 22:1—23:30 // 2 Chr 34:1—35:26) and conveys his view that the identity of "all Israel" is one of a community needing to faithfully follow YHWH. The table below shows evidence of this identity.

Table 6. The Chronicler's Reading of 2 Kings 22:1—23:30

2 Kings 22:1—23:30	2 Chronicles 34:1—35:26
Verse 1:	Verse 1:
בֶּן־שְׁמֹנֶה שָׁנָה יֹאשִׁיָּהוּ בְמָלְכוֹ וּשְׁלֹשִׁים וְאַחַת שָׁנָה מָלַךְ בִּירוּשָׁלָ͏ִם	בֶּן־שְׁמוֹנֶה שָׁנִים יֹאשִׁיָּהוּ בְמָלְכוֹ וּשְׁלֹשִׁים וְאַחַת שָׁנָה מָלַךְ בִּירוּשָׁלָ͏ִם
(Josiah was eight years old when he began to reign; he reigned thirty-one years in Jerusalem.)	(Josiah was eight years old when he began to reign; he reigned thirty-one years in Jerusalem.)

Comparing the Chronicler's Reading and Postcolonial Biblical Reading

2 Kings 22:1—23:30	2 Chronicles 34:1—35:26
	Verses 3–7:
	וּבִשְׁמוֹנֶה שָׁנִים לְמָלְכוֹ וְהוּא עוֹדֶנּוּ נַעַר הֵחֵל לִדְרוֹשׁ לֵאלֹהֵי דָּוִיד אָבִיו וּבִשְׁתֵּים עֶשְׂרֵה שָׁנָה הֵחֵל לְטַהֵר אֶת־יְהוּדָה וִירוּשָׁלִַם מִן־הַבָּמוֹת וְהָאֲשֵׁרִים וְהַפְּסִלִים וְהַמַּסֵּכוֹת:
	4 וַיְנַתְּצוּ לְפָנָיו אֵת מִזְבְּחוֹת הַבְּעָלִים וְהַחַמָּנִים אֲשֶׁר־לְמַעְלָה מֵעֲלֵיהֶם גִּדֵּעַ וְהָאֲשֵׁרִים וְהַפְּסִלִים וְהַמַּסֵּכוֹת שִׁבַּר וְהֵדַק וַיִּזְרֹק עַל־פְּנֵי הַקְּבָרִים הַזֹּבְחִים לָהֶם:
	5 וְעַצְמוֹת כֹּהֲנִים שָׂרַף עַל־מִזְבְּחוֹתִים וַיְטַהֵר אֶת־יְהוּדָה וְאֶת־יְרוּשָׁלִָם:
	6 וּבְעָרֵי מְנַשֶּׁה וְאֶפְרַיִם וְשִׁמְעוֹן וְעַד־נַפְתָּלִי בְּהַר בָּתֵּיהֶם סָבִיב:
	7 וַיְנַתֵּץ אֶת־הַמִּזְבְּחוֹת וְאֶת־הָאֲשֵׁרִים וְהַפְּסִלִים כִּתַּת לְהֵדַק וְכָל־הַחַמָּנִים גִּדַּע בְּכָל־אֶרֶץ יִשְׂרָאֵל וַיָּשָׁב לִירוּשָׁלִָם
	(3 For in the eighth year of his reign, while he was still a boy, he began to seek the God of his ancestor David, and in the twelfth year he began to purge Judah and Jerusalem of the high places, the sacred poles, and the carved and the cast images.
	4 In his presence they pulled down the altars of the Baals; he demolished the incense altars that stood above them. He broke down the sacred poles and the carved and the cast images; he made dust of them and scattered it over the graves of those who had sacrificed to them.
	5 He also burned the bones of the priests on their altars, and purged Judah and Jerusalem.
	6 In the towns of Manasseh, Ephraim, and Simeon, and as far as Naphtali, in their ruins all around,
	7 he broke down the altars, beat the sacred poles and the images into powder, and demolished all the incense altars throughout all the land of Israel. Then he returned to Jerusalem.)

2 Kings 22:1—23:30	2 Chronicles 34:1—35:26
Verse 3:	Verse 8:
וַיְהִי בִּשְׁמֹנֶה עֶשְׂרֵה שָׁנָה לַמֶּלֶךְ יֹאשִׁיָּהוּ שָׁלַח הַמֶּלֶךְ אֶת־שָׁפָן בֶּן־אֲצַלְיָהוּ בֶן־מְשֻׁלָּם הַסֹּפֵר בֵּית יְהוָה לֵאמֹר . . . לְחַזֵּק בֶּדֶק הַבָּיִת	וּבִשְׁנַת שְׁמוֹנֶה עֶשְׂרֵה לְמָלְכוֹ לְטַהֵר הָאָרֶץ וְהַבָּיִת שָׁלַח אֶת־שָׁפָן בֶּן־אֲצַלְיָהוּ וְאֶת־מַעֲשֵׂיָהוּ שַׂר־הָעִיר וְאֵת יוֹאָח בֶּן־יוֹאָחָז הַמַּזְכִּיר לְחַזֵּק אֶת־בֵּית יְהוָה אֱלֹהָיו
(In the eighteenth year of King Josiah, the king sent Shaphan son of Azaliah, son of Meshullam, the secretary, to the house of the LORD... to repair the damages of the house.)	(In the eighteenth year of his reign, when he had purged the land and the house, he sent Shaphan son of Azaliah, Maaseiah the governor of the city, and Joah son of Joahaz, the recorder, to repair the house of the LORD his God.)

While the Chronicler's source (2 Kgs 22:3—23:27) only depicts King Josiah's activities of religious reform in the eighteenth year of his reign (when the king was twenty-six years old, 2 Kgs 22:3—23:27 // 2 Chr 34:8—35:19), the Chronicler provides the additional information that after being enthroned at eight years old (2 Kgs 22:1 // 2 Chr 34:1), the king began to seek the God of David when he was sixteen years old (in the eighth year of his reign, 2 Chr 34:3). Then, the Chronicler states that at the age of twenty (in the twelfth year of his reign), Josiah started his religious reforms by destroying idols in both the southern and northern kingdoms (2 Chr 34:3b-7). Here the Chronicler expounds that Josiah's religious reform derived from his godliness rather than from the threat of punishment for the sins narrated in the rediscovered book of the Torah.[141]

Moreover, Josiah could initiate the religious reform only when he was mature (twenty years old) and no longer under a regent.[142] The Chronicler provides additional important information about the extent of Josiah's religious purification, which took place not only in Jerusalem and Judah, but also in the towns of four tribes (Manasseh, Ephraim, Simeon, and Naphtali) and even covered all the land of Israel (2 Chr 34:6-7, בְּכָל־אֶרֶץ יִשְׂרָאֵל).[143] Scholars indicate that the territories of those four tribes covered the border of the northern kingdom in the western area of the Jordan river. The land of the two and a half tribes on the eastern side of the Jordan river was lost and out of Josiah's reach until the Chronicler's time (1 Chr 5:26).[144]

---

141. Japhet, *I and II Chronicles*, 1020.
142. Dillard, *2 Chronicles*, 277.
143. Also Japhet, *I and II Chronicles*, 1023.
144. Japhet, *I and II Chronicles*, 1024; Klein and Hanson, *2 Chronicles*, 498.

From his perspective of having been colonized, the Chronicler implies that after the exile happened, godly kings always desire for all God's people (all Israel) to return to YHWH and to follow him faithfully. That is why the Chronicler describes how, even before the discovery of the Torah, Josiah's religious reform, which expanded to the former northern kingdom of Israel, derived from his piety (2 Chr 34:3–7). The finding of the Torah book only encouraged Josiah to keep on destroying idolatry in all the territories of the two kingdoms and to continue reinforcing the message that all the people should serve YHWH (2 Chr 34:32–33). In short, the identity that the Chronicler's postexilic readers should pursue and take on was that of the "all Israel" that should return to YHWH and follow him. This was also the desire of all the godly kings of Judah as portrayed by the Chronicler.

Conclusion

The Chronicler and his community lived amid the conflict between the imperial forces (the forces from Egypt and others, whether Persian or Greek). Thus, the Chronicler read his biblical sources through the lens of such a context. His reading of Josiah's death (2 Kgs 23:28–30a // 2 Chr 35:20–25) is one instance demonstrating that they were victims of the *Realpolitik* of liminality. The Chronicler's use of ambiguous wording and his description of the postexilic community's lamentation for Josiah manifest the tragedy of the victims in this difficult context.

Living in a colonized context, the Chronicler could not display an explicit mode of resistance to the imperial forces. Nonetheless, the Chronicler and his postexilic community have persistently looked forward to the full restoration of the Davidic house as promised by YHWH to David. Consequently, the Chronicler demonstrates an implicit mode of resistance to the imperial dominion through his reading of biblical sources. On one hand, the Chronicler's reading may seem, on the surface, to be a capitulation to Persian imperial power, a compromise with non-Yahwistic dominion. On the other hand, the Chronicler's Davidic royal ideology or expectation is implicit. The Chronicler portrays the identity which his postexilic readers should pursue and embrace as the "all Israel" turning back to YHWH and following the Lord faithfully. That is the Chronicler's remedy for God's people to be delivered from imperial dominion.

Comparison and Suggestions

This chapter demonstrates that the Chronicler interprets certain passages in his sources through the lens of colonial perspectives, which serve his postexilic interests. Although the Chronicler did not live in the modern post-colonial era, his readings still reflect some principles of postcolonial biblical reading. The Chronicler does not engage in the first two steps of the postcolonial approach, namely, literature review and the detection of colonial perspectives in the source texts. But the Chronicler's interpretation of certain passages does resemble the third step of the postcolonial approach: reading through the lens of the colonized people within the Chronicler's postexilic context.

Comparison Between the Two Biblical Readings

Just as a postcolonial reading communicates resistance to imperial hegemony, the Chronicler's reading also presents a voice of resistance against imperial powers, frequently pointing out that the God of Israel controls all the oppressive activities of imperial forces and that there is a path to deliverance and restoration for God's people. Similar to how Uriah Kim's postcolonial reading serves his readers' context of *Realpolitik* liminality, the Chronicler interprets some passages through the lens of a victim of *Realpolitik* liminality in the postexilic context. Yet while postcolonial biblical interpreters present an *explicitly* resistant voice against the legacy of imperialism, the Chronicler's reading exhibits an *implicitly* resistant voice because the Chronicler's postexilic readers were still under imperial dominion. The Chronicler's context of *Realpolitik* liminality was far more dangerous than the contexts of most present-day postcolonial biblical interpreters. One of the biggest determinative factors in the different contexts of the Chronicler and the Asian postcolonial interpreters is that the former writes as one still colonized, while the latter mostly work in post-colonial societies where they can speak freely and explicitly. Thus, while the Chronicler's reading *explicitly* and understandably presents a favorable attitude toward imperial rule, it also *implicitly* hopes for the restoration of the Davidic dynasty. Moreover, just as postcolonial interpretation is a selective reading, the Chronicler also reads select passages through the lens of colonial perspectives to serve his postexilic concerns. As demonstrated by his attitude and approach, the Chronicler promotes the Jewish identity of his postexilic community in their colonial

Comparing the Chronicler's Reading and Postcolonial Biblical Reading

context as *all Israel who should return to following YHWH faithfully*. Though not explicitly stated, the Chronicler implies that maintaining this identity would eventually lead to the restoration of the Davidic house.

Suggestions for Postcolonial Reading

The Chronicler's reading and the postcolonial model of biblical interpretation both aim to understand what the text meant and present what it means. Yet while the Chronicler's reading reflects closely what his sources meant, practitioners of postcolonial reading often overlook the world of the text (e.g., the structures of the biblical books, the literary context of biblical passages, etc.) to serve their postcolonial concerns. This is a typical feature of postcolonial biblical interpretation, exemplified by Sugirtharajah, a leading exponent and founder of this approach, who encourages postcolonial interpreters to liberate themselves even from the biblical texts themselves.[145] Therefore, Peter Lau rightly states that postcolonial biblical hermeneutics is only profitable if it also examined the world of the text.[146] One main purpose of postcolonial reading is to resist oppression. If practitioners of postcolonial biblical interpretation do not adjust their reading strategy and continue to ignore the world of the text, Lau argues that these interpreters end up superimposing their postcolonial ideology on the text, and "the strategy becomes its own oppression; the voice of the text is suppressed by the grip of postcolonial ideology. The essential impulse of postcolonialism is thus undermined."[147] In other words, although postcolonial reading aims to provide freedom from every kind of oppression,[148] its reading strategy can actually oppress the biblical text. Unless practitioners of postcolonial biblical hermeneutics cease making their ideology an imperializing force, this kind of reading will be self-defeating as it becomes a textual form of colonization.

---

145. Sugirtharajah, *Bible and Asia*, 223.
146. Lau, "Back Under Authority," 138–40.
147. Lau, "Back Under Authority," 144.
148. Yee, "Postcolonial Biblical Criticism," 196.

5

Comparing the Chronicler's Reading and the Asian Contextual Reading

BROADLY SPEAKING, ORDINARY CHRISTIANS read the Bible daily to receive relevant messages for life application. Grant Osborne states that "the goal of evangelical hermeneutics is quite simple—to discover the intention of the Author/author."[1] Yet discovering what the text meant is just a starting point, for the task of hermeneutics is completed when the reader understands what the text means to them today.[2] Contextualization is another term to describe the task of discovering what the text means to readers today.[3] The issue of what the text means to readers today is the reader-response perspective, which is subjective and depends on the aims, interests, questions, and pre-understanding of readers.[4] How can we obtain a relevant interpretation that is faithful to what the Bible meant and also relevant to readers today? Rene Padilla observes that the intuitive approach to the Bible focuses on the immediate personal application of readers today and ignores the original biblical context. Conversely, historical-critical and literary approaches focus on understanding a biblical text in its original

---

1. Osborne, *Hermeneutical Spiral*, 24.
2. Klein et al., *Introduction*, 61–62; Osborne, *Hermeneutical Spiral*, 23.
3. Osborne, *Hermeneutical Spiral*, 21–22.
4. Thiselton, *New Horizons*, 515, 588; Osborne, *Hermeneutical Spiral*, 22.

historical and literary contexts while neglecting the contemporary contexts of interpreters. The contextual model of biblical interpretation is a combination of the two above approaches. It seeks to study a biblical text in its original context to discern its message and then appropriately transfer or apply that message according to the context of present-day readers.[5] Dalit biblical reading approach belongs to the contextual model.

As presented in chapter 3, the Dalit Bible Commentary series (hereafter DBC) illustrates the Asian contextual model. James Massey,[6] the chief editor of the DBC, indicates that the Chronicler's method of using biblical material (e.g., Samuel–Kings) with relevance to the Chronicler's contemporary audience is a good model for Dalit biblical reading because the historical context of the Chronicler in the fourth century BCE was similar to the Dalits' context in the present day. The Chronicler's postexilic community had just been released from exile, yet the people were still suffering oppression and discrimination. Similarly, although the Dalit people had officially gained citizenship after Indian independence in 1947, they continued to be oppressed and discriminated against because of the caste system.[7]

Therefore, the main question this chapter seeks to answer is: To what extent did the Chronicler address postexilic contextual issues in his reading of biblical materials in ways similar to the Dalit biblical reading, and vice versa? In this chapter, we will evaluate Dalit biblical reading and then compare the Dalits' reading with the Chronicler's reading. This chapter will demonstrate how both the Chronicler's reading and the Asian contextual reading achieve the twofold goal of biblical interpretation. The chapter will also offer suggestions on ways to improve the Asian contextual approach.

---

5. Padilla, "Interpreted Word," 297–98.

6. Massey is an advocate of Dalit biblical hermeneutics (see Massey, *Towards Dalit Hermeneutics*). He has recruited other Dalit scholars to contribute to the DBC. He has also written commentaries on several books for the DBC, such as Exodus, Judges, 1 and 2 Samuel, 1 and 2 Chronicles, and so on. Massey is a Dalit Indian and received academic training in the West. He earned a PhD from Johann Wolfgang Goethe University in Frankfurt, Germany, and a postdoctoral academic degree from the same university. He is a pastor and theologian with many published books in this field. See Massey, *One Volume*, xv.

7. Massey, "History," 65–66.

Evaluation of Dalit Biblical Reading

Having presented the methodology of Asian contextual reading in chapter 3, we now turn to an evaluation of this approach. Asian contextual interpreters seek to achieve relevant contextualization in the following ways.

Seeking Parallel Situations

One way Bible interpreters attain relevant contextualization that is also faithful to what the Bible meant is by identifying particular contexts of modern readers that parallel the original contexts of biblical passages.[8] In this respect, Mark J. Hatcher asserts that whatever questions or issues the readers "bring to a biblical text must have some correspondence with the subject matter of the text."[9] Jackson Wu clarifies that reading the Bible with Eastern eyes is not about reading into the Bible. This contextual reading aims to understand biblical passages in their original contexts. However, since readers today cannot have direct access to the biblical writers' world, "we compare similar cultural contexts that we can more easily understand. This positions us to approximate concerns or themes that were important to the Bible's original readers."[10] Dalit biblical interpreters employ this comparative strategy. They search for parallels between the biblical world and the Asian world to achieve relevant contextualization.

In the DBC, the introductions to both the Old Testament and the New Testament clearly state that the DBC's general interpretative method focuses on both the biblical context and the Dalit context. Since these two contexts differ, interpreters seek meeting points between the world of the Bible and the world of Dalits.[11] These meeting points are common issues or parallel situations between the two worlds. Editors of the DBC call this practice the "Dialogical-Contextual-Approach" to find biblical messages relevant to the Dalit community.[12] For instance, while reading the book of Genesis, A. Maria Arul Raja states, "This dialogue seeks to envisage the promotion

---

8. Klein et al., *Introduction*, 64; Osborne, *Hermeneutical Spiral*, 423, 432–33.

9. Hatcher, "Biblical Interpretation," 79. Hatcher quotes Hordern, "Systematic Theology," 75.

10. Wu, *Reading Romans*, 13.

11. Massey, "Jeremiah," xviii; John and Massey, *One Volume*, xvi.

12. Massey, "Jeremiah," xviii; John and Massey, *One Volume*, xvi.

of the culture of freedom from the clutches of the culture of casteism."[13] Raja identifies many parallel situations between stories in Genesis and Dalit contextual concerns.[14] Reading the first chapters of Genesis, Raja points out that after the fall of man, sinful human beings created systems of discrimination in the human world. Powerful people pounce on weak people to satisfy the indulgences of the powerful group. Raja understands Gen 6:1–6 as teaching that God's purpose in creation did not intend for women's bodies to be lusted after by the sons of God (the powerful people). From this, Raja draws a parallel with the Dalit context. The Dalit woman's body should not be worthless and must not become "the gratis site of giving vent to masculine lust" in the caste discrimination of India.[15]

In his reading of the book of Samuel, Massey cites another example of parallels between the world of Samuel and the world of the Dalits. Hannah's life (1 Sam 1–2) is similar to the life of Dalit women. Hannah suffered humiliation because of her barrenness. From the story of Hannah's liberation from her suffering, Dalit readers search for relevant messages concerning liberation from oppression and discrimination.[16] These instances demonstrate the type of relevant contextualization espoused by Dalit biblical interpretation.

Using the Concept of the Abstraction Ladder

If biblical interpreters cannot find a similarity between the biblical situation and the reader's situation to facilitate application of the biblical message to the reader's context, they may use the ladder of abstraction. The abstraction ladder is a way to distill a general principle from the biblical text to apply to the reader's situation.[17] For example, interpreters seek general principles about God's nature, God's character, and the relationship between humankind and God. Then they apply those teachings from the biblical passages to the reader's situation.[18]

Dalit biblical interpretation employs the ladder of abstraction. For example, 1 Sam 17:1–58 tells the story of how David defeated Goliath. The

13. Raja, "Creating Caste-Free Humanity," 3.
14. Raja, "Creating Caste-Free Humanity," 3–14.
15. Raja, "Genesis," 153–54.
16. Massey, "Relevance," 51.
17. Kaiser, *Toward Rediscovering*, 164–66.
18. Robinson, "Heresy of Application."

Dalit interpreter discerns that David was able to defeat Goliath because of his unwavering faith in the Lord and his commitment to his people. These two factors are crucial for the Dalits in their pursuit of liberation for their community.[19] In this case, the interpreter cannot apply the biblical situation of fighting in a violent war directly to Dalit readers. Therefore, the interpreter seeks biblical teachings related to the God-human relationship behind David's victory and applies these principles to its readers.

Similarly, commenting on 2 Sam 5:17–25, the passage concerning David's defeat of the Philistines, the Dalit interpreter presents the lesson that the reason David was able to defeat the Philistines was his faith in the Lord. From this, Dalits should also have faith in the Lord as they relentlessly pursue liberation for their community, for the Lord will surely support the Dalit people who trust firmly in him.[20] In numerous similar instances, Dalit interpreters use the abstraction ladder to achieve relevant contextualization in biblical interpretation.

Using Biblical Theology

Although scholars define biblical theology differently, broadly speaking, any study of concepts, ideas, or thoughts based on the Bible may be termed "biblical theology."[21] For this present study, as defined in the introduction, biblical theology is the method that traces or elaborates on an idea or theme through various passages of Scripture. Besides the abstraction ladder, biblical theology is also used by the Dalit biblical interpreters to make contextualized application of biblical texts to their readers.

This section will demonstrate how Dalit interpreters employ biblical theology. Consider the DBC's treatment of 2 Sam 5:24–25. The Dalit interpreter cites Exod 3:7–12 to explain the way God becomes directly involved in a human battle. Just as the Lord heard the cry of the Israelites and acted directly to save the people from the Egyptians in Exod 3:7–12, so in 2 Sam 5:24–25 the Lord heard David's petition and directly guided the king to save his people from the Philistines. From this, the interpreter draws the lesson that the Lord always supports righteous people. Thus, Dalits should always trust the Lord for their deliverance.[22]

---

19. Massey, "1 and 2 Samuel," 430.
20. Massey, "1 and 2 Samuel," 439.
21. Carson, "Biblical Theology," 35, 39.
22. Massey, "1 and 2 Samuel," 439.

Comparing the Chronicler's Reading and the Asian Contextual Reading

For another example, commenting on 2 Sam 11:1—12:31, the Dalit interpreter refers to 2 Sam 16:21-22; 13:23-29; 18:15; and 1 Kgs 2:25 to explain how God's punishment was fulfilled in David's family. The interpreter cites these passages to indicate that three more of David's sons were killed, fulfilling God's punishment as spoken through the prophet Nathan. From this, the interpreter draws out an application that Dalit leaders should not act unrighteously like David and that Dalit people should speak out against injustices done to them.[23]

For a third example, consider the DBC's commentary on 2 Sam 23:8—24:25. The Dalit interpreter quotes Josh 15:63, Judg 1:21, and 2 Sam 5:6 to provide background on the presence of Canaanites living among the Israelites, tracing back to their incomplete expulsion in the time of Joshua. The interpreter cites these passages to explain why David had to buy land in his own country from a non-Israelite and consecrate this piece of land for his son to build the temple later on. From this, the interpreter argues that the non-Israelites played a role in the plan for the Jerusalem temple building, as the land for the temple originally belonged to the Canaanites. After explaining what these biblical passages meant, the Dalit interpreter then makes these texts relevant to the Dalit context, noting that many temples in India today have been built on lands of indigenous Indians, but the landowners have been marginalized and referred to as Dalits.[24]

In summary, these examples demonstrate that the Dalit interpreters use biblical teachings from other biblical books or chapters of the same book to interpret a particular passage. In other words, Dalit biblical reading uses biblical theology to understand what the texts meant and make them relevant to the Dalit context.

Fusion of the Two Horizons

A hermeneutical concept foundational to the three methods of contextualization discussed above (i.e., seeking parallel situations between biblical contexts and Asian contexts, using the concept of the abstraction ladder, and incorporating biblical theology) is the fusion of two horizons. Put succinctly, contextualizing a biblical text is a fusion of two horizons in biblical interpretation. According to Gadamer, interpretation is a fusion of

---

23. Massey, "1 and 2 Samuel," 442.
24. Massey, "1 and 2 Samuel," 446.

horizons "between the text and its interpreter."[25] Thiselton, however, argues that there is no such fusion in reality. He contends, "In practice, because the interpreter cannot leap out of the historical tradition to which he belongs, the two horizons can never become totally identical; at best they remain separate but close."[26] Nevertheless, as we shall discuss below, Dalit biblical interpretation still attempts to make the two horizons identical and create a fusion.

Massey states that Samuel–Kings has relevant messages for Dalits because the term "dalit" occurs three times in the linguistic form of the Hebrew root דַּל (*dal*) in 1 Sam 2:8, 2 Sam 3:1, and 2 Sam 13:4.[27] The root דַּל (*dal*) in Hebrew means poor, weak and haggard.[28] The term "dalit" in Sanskrit has similar meanings, referring to poor (enslaved in terms of economic perspective), powerless (weak in terms of political perspective), and oppressed people in India.[29] The fusion here is that the Hebrew root דַּל (*dal*) of the term "dalit" occurs in Samuel–Kings.

Massey examines all occurrences of the root דַּל (*dal*) in the Hebrew Bible and finds that this root refers to the poor and weak in terms of survival (e.g., Exod 30:15; Job 5:16; Ps 82:34; etc.), physical condition (e.g., Gen 41:19; 2 Sam 13:4; etc.), economic status (e.g., Ruth 3:10; Prov 10:15; 19:4, 17; etc.), political standing (e.g., 2 Sam 3:1; Prov 28:15; etc.), legal status (e.g., Job 20:18–19; Prov 29:7, 14; Amos 2:4–8; etc.), and religious context (e.g., Isa 17:4, 25:4, etc.).[30] The entire community of Israelites in Judah is described as Dalits in the exilic period (e.g., Ps 79:8; 2 Kgs 24:13–14; 25:11–12; etc., with occurrences of the root דַּל [*dal*]).[31] The equivalent terms to the Hebrew root דַּל [*dal*] in the Greek language are found in the New Testament referring to the poor, as in Luke 21:1–2 (πενιχρός); 2 Cor 9:9 (πένης), 8:9 (πτωχεύω); Rev 2:9 (πτωχεία); etc.[32]

Moreover, messianic messages for delivering God's people referring to Dalits are clearly stated in the Hebrew Bible with occurrences of the root דַּל

---

25. Gadamer, *Truth and Method*, 370.
26. Thiselton, *Two Horizons*, xix.
27. Massey, *One Volume*, 51. Massey mistypes 1 Sam 1:8; the correct verse is 1 Sam 2:8.
28. Massey, "Relevance," 51.
29. Massey, "Dalits in India," 23.
30. Massey, *Towards Dalit Hermeneutics*, 6.
31. Massey, *Towards Dalit Hermeneutics*, 13, 19.
32. Massey, *Towards Dalit Hermeneutics*, 26.

Comparing the Chronicler's Reading and the Asian Contextual Reading

(*dal*) (e.g., Isa 11:1–5; Zeph 3:11–12; etc.)[33] Based on this biblical evidence, Massey concludes that the issues of the Dalits were addressed in the Bible.[34] He states, "The existence of Dalits and their problems were part and parcel of the life of the biblical people."[35] He concludes that the problems of Dalits existed throughout the history of humankind because ancient times and the messianic messages speaking of delivering God's people from the state of *dalitness* are not only for Dalits but also for common human society.[36] Massey further observes that Western interpreters have not yet recognized the root דַּל (*dal*) in the Bible relating to Dalits because they read through a Western lens and are not familiar with Dalit issues.[37]

In short, Dalit readers find Dalit issues and themselves in the Bible via the root דַּל (*dal*). This represents a fusion of the two horizons between the biblical text and Dalit readers. Massey argues that Dalit problems and solutions indeed existed in the Bible and were presented in the biblical record of how God dealt with his people through different periods. Solutions for the deliverance of God's "Dalit" people were demonstrated through patterns of deliverance and messianic messages, both of which offer hope for the present-day Dalits.

Using Deconstruction

Besides the aforementioned ways to read biblical passages faithfully and apply the biblical messages appropriately to readers' contexts, Dalit interpreters sometimes allow Dalits' interests to determine or even deconstruct the meaning of biblical passages.

Dalit biblical interpreters have asserted that modern Western scholars interpret the Bible from the perspective of those with power and those who oppress. Dalit biblical reading challenges any biblical interpretation that supports oppressive structures and values.[38] Dalit hermeneutics protests against oppression. Thus, Gnanavaram argues that Dalit hermeneutics is similar to prophetic hermeneutics and to Jesus' teachings, stating that "the prophetic hermeneutics of the Bible becomes the model for Dalit

---

33. Massey, *Towards Dalit Hermeneutics*, 23–24.
34. Massey, *Towards Dalit Hermeneutics*, 11.
35. Massey, *Towards Dalit Hermeneutics*, 7.
36. Massey, *Towards Dalit Hermeneutics*, 33–34.
37. Massey, *Towards Dalit Hermeneutics*, 27–28.
38. Gnanavaram, "Hermeneutical Issues," 123–24.

hermeneutics."[39] But Gnanavaram also admits that, while protesting oppression, Dalit interpretation is *biased* in its support for the oppressed. Nevertheless, he argues that this bias is biblical because the biblical God supports and takes care of the oppressed.[40] Jayachitra likewise asserts,

> The task of Dalit hermeneutics is to decode the meanings of the words of a given text and the social structures of the community that produced the text in order to make them relevant for the interpreter's accustomed social structures and cultural codes.[41]

Hence, when Dalit interpreters encounter any biblical passage supporting powerful people or oppressive structures, they reread the text through the lens of the oppressed Dalits to counterbalance those interpretations that support the oppressors. For example, commenting on 2 Sam 6:1–23, which recounts the death of Uzzah, the Dalit interpreter expresses suspicion as to whether YHWH actually punished Uzzah. The interpreter poses a rhetorical question: "How can He punish someone who did not belong to the priestly class only because he tried to save the Ark from falling?"[42] The interpreter reinterprets this passage, arguing that God could not have punished Uzzah because, throughout the Bible, God protects the oppressed people (2 Sam 6:6–9). With this conviction, the interpreter concludes that this passage was narrated by a priest and it tells a lie about God. Indeed, many similar lies are narrated in sacred books of other religions to humiliate the Dalits, coerce them into performing menial jobs, and forbid them from serving the Lord or entering the temple.[43] Here, the Dalit interpreter clearly allows his concern for the oppressed to subvert the meaning of 2 Sam 6:6–9.

Given this kind of biased perspective in biblical interpretation, it is not surprising to find Dalit interpreters using the deconstruction approach. In the introductions to the DBC volume, the editors identify deconstruction as an approach used by the DBC commentators. The introductions state that Dalit interpreters in the DBC volumes (Old Testament and New Testament) use this approach to deconstruct ideas of royal perception, hierarchy, purity, and pollution, and to present an alternate Dalit worldview

---

39. Gnanavaram, "Hermeneutical Issues," 124.
40. Gnanavaram, "Hermeneutical Issues," 124.
41. Jayachitra, "Jesus and Ambedkar," 127.
42. Massey, "1 and 2 Samuel," 440.
43. Massey, "1 and 2 Samuel," 440.

Comparing the Chronicler's Reading and the Asian Contextual Reading

in dialogue with the biblical worldview.[44] Jesurathnam also observes that deconstruction is frequently used by Dalit women in biblical interpretation, as many female interpreters who have received theological education introduce this approach to Dalit women to promote "deconstructing the patriarchal notions in the biblical text."[45]

The term "deconstruction" was introduced by Jacques Derrida and further developed by literary scholars.[46] Deconstruction identifies binary oppositions in a text, interprets implications behind the oppositions, reverses the oppositions, overturns previously and commonly accepted worldviews, and proposes alternative meanings based on the new binary converse.[47] In other words, using deconstruction creates a new meaning from a text, one which subverts what the text actually says.[48] As such, deconstruction serves the reader-response perspective because it opens the text "to a variety of interpretations that reflect the ideology of the reader."[49]

Consider the DBC's comments on 2 Sam 6:6–9. The Dalit interpreter identifies the binary oppositions, namely, the priests and non-priests, explaining that the priests are similar to people of Brahmanic caste in India, and the non-priests are like Dalits in India. Second Samuel 6:7 clearly states that YHWH's anger was against Uzzah when he put out his hand to the ark of YHWH, and YHWH smote Uzzah. Massey, however, asserts that God cannot punish Uzzah because God consistently supports the oppressed. He unambiguously states that 2 Sam 6:6–9, which narrates the divine punishment for Uzzah's touching the Ark, is "a lie about God."[50] Since Massey claims that 2 Sam 6:6–9 tells a lie about God, he implies that the reason for Uzzah's punishment is quite different from what the text explicitly says.[51] In this way, the Dalit interpreter deconstructs 2 Sam 6:6–9 and denies that Uzzah's death was caused by divine punishment, even though that is what the text plainly states.

---

44. Massey, *One Volume*, xix; John and Massey, *One Volume*, xvii.
45. Jesurathnam, "Contextual Reading," 163.
46. Tate, *Handbook for Biblical Interpretation*, 105.
47. Tate, *Handbook for Biblical Interpretation*, 109.
48. Tompkins, *Reader-Response Criticism*, 249.
49. Olson, "Literary and Rhetorical Criticism," 20.
50. Massey, "1 and 2 Samuel," 440.
51. The interpreter implies that God did not punish Uzzah and that the priestly author of this passage told a lie about God.

From our observations of the DBC's interpretation, we find that the instances of applying deconstruction are much fewer than the instances of relevant contextualization. For instance, the passage of 2 Sam 6:6–9 is the sole instance in which the DBC uses deconstruction in its interpretation of 1 and 2 Samuel. Although the use of deconstruction is low in the DBC, this practice contrasts strikingly with the more common use of relevant contextualization.

Conclusion of Dalit Biblical Reading Evaluation

Just as Jackson Wu demonstrates that reading the Bible with Eastern eyes does not mean reading into the Bible if interpreters use cultural contexts in Asia that are similar to biblical contexts,[52] Craig Keener and M. Daniel Carroll R. admit that Western readers sometimes cannot understand the Bible correctly if they do not read it through the lens of majority world Christians, which is closer to biblical situations than the Western lens.[53] Asian interpreters have tried to provide relevant contextualization to biblical interpretation by finding parallels between the biblical context and the Asian context, using the abstraction ladder, biblical theology, and fusing of the two horizons. Besides these avenues to obtain relevant contextualization, Dalit interpreters are also encouraged to use deconstruction to serve the Dalit readers' perspective. Such a deconstruction approach actually undermines the DBC's goal of contextualization because it denies the original meaning and context of the biblical text.

Evaluation of the Chronicler's Reading

Having examined the Asian contextual approach to Dalit biblical interpretation, we will now explore whether the Chronicler brought the postexilic contextual issues of his time to his reading of biblical sources in ways similar to Asian contextual reading. Although the names of modern techniques in biblical interpretation—such as biblical theology, the fusion of horizons in hermeneutics, or the abstraction ladder—did not exist in the Chronicler's time, we will demonstrate that the Chronicler indeed employed similar techniques in his reading of biblical sources.

52. Wu, *Reading Romans*, 13.
53. Keener and Carroll R., *Global Voices*, 1–2.

Comparing the Chronicler's Reading and the Asian Contextual Reading

Demonstrating Main Features of Contextual Biblical Reading

In the contextual approach, both the original context of a biblical passage and the present context of today's readers are important.[54] By correctly understanding a biblical text and appropriately addressing the questions of today's readers through the biblical text, "our theology, in turn, will be more relevant and responsive to the burning issues which we have to face in our concrete situation."[55] The examples below will demonstrate that the Chronicler's reading of his sources reflects these features. The following sections will first illustrate how the Chronicler's reading closely aligns with what the text meant, and then will show how the Chronicler's reading is relevant to his audience in the postexilic period.

The Chronicler's Reading of 2 Samuel 6:1–19

The Chronicler performs a contextual reading of 2 Sam 6:1–19, which is a narrative of David taking the ark to Jerusalem. The following table highlights several key details.

Table 7. The Chronicler's Reading of 2 Samuel 6:1–19

	1 Chronicles 13:1–5
	1 Chr 13:1–4 is the Chronicler's *Sondergut*[56]
2 Samuel 6:1–2	1 Chronicles 13:5–6
וַיֹּסֶף עוֹד דָּוִד אֶת־כָּל־בָּחוּר בְּיִשְׂרָאֵל שְׁלֹשִׁים אָלֶף	וַיַּקְהֵל דָּוִיד אֶת־כָּל־יִשְׂרָאֵל מִן־שִׁיחוֹר מִצְרַיִם וְעַד־לְבוֹא חֲמָת לְהָבִיא אֶת־אֲרוֹן הָאֱלֹהִים מִקִּרְיַת יְעָרִים
(David again gathered all the chosen men of Israel, thirty thousand.)	(So David assembled all Israel from the Shihor of Egypt to Lebo-hamath, to bring the ark of God from Kiriath-jearim.)
וַיֵּלֶךְ דָּוִד וְכָל־הָעָם אֲשֶׁר אִתּוֹ מִבַּעֲלֵי יְהוּדָה לְהַעֲלוֹת מִשָּׁם אֵת אֲרוֹן הָאֱלֹהִים	וַיַּעַל דָּוִיד וְכָל־יִשְׂרָאֵל בַּעֲלָתָה אֶל־קִרְיַת יְעָרִים אֲשֶׁר לִיהוּדָה לְהַעֲלוֹת מִשָּׁם אֵת אֲרוֹן הָאֱלֹהִים
(David and *all the people* with him set out and went from Baalah Judah, to bring up from there the ark of God.)	(And David and *all Israel* went up to Baalah, that is, to Kiriath-jearim, which belongs to Judah, to bring up from there the ark of God.)

---

54. Padilla, "Interpreted Word," 300, 302.

55. Padilla, "Interpreted Word," 307.

56. The Chronicler's *Sondergut* means the Chronicler's unique material.

2 Samuel 6:7	1 Chronicles 13:10
וַיִּחַר־אַף יְהוָה בְּעֻזָּה וַיַּכֵּהוּ שָׁם הָאֱלֹהִים עַל־הַשַּׁל וַיָּמָת שָׁם עִם אֲרוֹן הָאֱלֹהִים	וַיִּחַר־אַף יְהוָה בְּעֻזָּא וַיַּכֵּהוּ עַל אֲשֶׁר־שָׁלַח יָדוֹ עַל־הָאָרוֹן וַיָּמָת שָׁם לִפְנֵי אֱלֹהִים
(And the anger of the Lord was kindled against Uzzah and God struck him there *against the error*[57] and he died there beside the ark of God.)	(The anger of the Lord was kindled against Uzzah; he struck him down *because he put out his hand to the ark* and he died there before God.)
2 Samuel 6:13–14	1 Chronicles 15:26–27
וַיְהִי כִּי צָעֲדוּ נֹשְׂאֵי אֲרוֹן־יְהוָה שִׁשָּׁה צְעָדִים וַיִּזְבַּח שׁוֹר וּמְרִיא וְדָוִד מְכַרְכֵּר בְּכָל־עֹז לִפְנֵי יְהוָה וְדָוִד חָגוּר אֵפוֹד בָּד	וַיְהִי בֶּעְזֹר הָאֱלֹהִים אֶת־הַלְוִיִּם נֹשְׂאֵי אֲרוֹן בְּרִית־יְהוָה וַיִּזְבְּחוּ שִׁבְעָה־פָרִים וְשִׁבְעָה אֵילִים וְדָוִד מְכֻרְבָּל ׀ בִּמְעִיל בּוּץ וְכָל־הַלְוִיִּם הַנֹּשְׂאִים אֶת־הָאָרוֹן וְהַמְשֹׁרְרִים וּכְנַנְיָה הַשַּׂר הַמַּשָּׂא הַמְשֹׁרְרִים וְעַל־דָּוִיד אֵפוֹד בָּד
(And when those who bore the ark of the Lord had gone six paces, he sacrificed an ox and a fatling. David danced before the Lord with all his might; David was girded with a linen ephod.)	(And because God helped the Levites who were carrying the ark of the covenant of the Lord, they sacrificed seven bulls and seven rams. David was clothed with a robe of fine linen, as also were all the Levites who were carrying the ark, and the singers, and Chenaniah the leader of the music of the singers, and David wore a linen ephod.)

The Chronicler adds in the beginning of this passage an introduction (1 Chr 13:1–4) to the event described in 2 Sam 6:1–19. These four verses (1 Chr 13:1–4) help the Chronicler's readers understand the historical context and the reason for this event. The Chronicler describes David's house as being unlike Saul's house, which neglected the ark of YHWH (1 Chr 13:3). Moreover, although the Chronicler follows 2 Sam 6 in stating that David initiated this ark transfer, the Chronicler provides the additional information that David consulted his people and that the whole assembly of Israelites agreed to bring the ark to Jerusalem (1 Chr 13:1–4).[58] Here, the Chronicler shows his readers a difference between David and Saul.

For 2 Sam 6:1–2 (// 1 Chr 13:5–6), the Chronicler's source indicates the number of the chosen men and then states the phrase דָּוִד וְכָל־הָעָם אֲשֶׁר

---

57. Translation follows MT 2 Sam 6:7, which reads עַל־הַשַּׁל (against the error). LXX 2 Sam 6:7 does not have this phrase.

58. Japhet, *I and II Chronicles*, 274; Klein and Krüger, *1 Chronicles*, 330.

Comparing the Chronicler's Reading and the Asian Contextual Reading

אִתּוֹ מִבַּעֲלֵי יְהוּדָה ("David and *all the people* with him set out and went from Baalah Judah," 2 Sam 6:1–2). The Chronicler, instead of repeating the number, reads אֶת־כָּל־יִשְׂרָאֵל מִן־שִׁיחוֹר מִצְרַיִם וְעַד־לְבוֹא חֲמָת ("*all Israel* went up to Baalah, that is, to Kiriath-jearim, which belongs to Judah," 1 Chr 13:5) and וְכָל־יִשְׂרָאֵל בַּעֲלָתָה ("*all Israel* went up to Baalah," 1 Chr 13:6). Here, the Chronicler's reading does not subvert the plain meaning of his source when replacing "all the people" with "all Israel." Moreover, the Chronicler shows his readers the unity of "all Israel" in joining David in this event. The concept of "all Israel" is a major theme in Chronicles (e.g., 1 Chr 11:1, 4; 13:1–6; 28:1; 2 Chr 7:8; 11:16; 15:9–10; 30:11, 18, 21, 25).[59] Through this term, the Chronicler conveys a message of the unity of Israel in the postexilic era, as indicated in chapter 3, the section on the identity of the Chronicler's community.

For 2 Sam 6:7 (// 1 Chr 13:10), whether or not the phrase עַל־הַשַּׁל ("against the error"), which is lacking in LXX, was originally included in 2 Sam 6:7, the Chronicler adds the phrase אֲשֶׁר־שָׁלַח יָדוֹ עַל־הָאָרוֹן ("*he put out his hand to the ark*") to inform his readers of Uzzah's specific act which led to his death. For 2 Sam 6:13 (// 1 Chr 15:26), the Chronicler adds the phrase וַיְהִי בֶּעְזֹר הָאֱלֹהִים אֶת־הַלְוִיִּם נֹשְׂאֵי אֲרוֹן בְּרִית־יְהוָה ("and because God helped the Levites who were carrying the ark of the covenant of the Lord," 1 Chr 15:26). And for 2 Sam 6:14 (// 1 Chr 15:27), the Chronicler adds the phrase וְדָוִיד מְכֻרְבָּל בִּמְעִיל בּוּץ וְכָל־הַלְוִיִּם הַנֹּשְׂאִים אֶת־הָאָרוֹן וְהַמְשֹׁרְרִים וּכְנַנְיָה הַשַּׂר הַמַּשָּׂא הַמְשֹׁרְרִים ("David was clothed with a robe of fine linen, as also were all the Levites who were carrying the ark, and the singers, and Chenaniah the leader of the music of the singers," 1 Chr 15:27a). Here the Chronicler adds these two phrases to explain that on this occasion the task of carrying the ark was assigned to the Levites. In other words, the Chronicler shows his readers that this time David followed God's regulation concerning how the ark was to be transported.

The Chronicler makes the event of 2 Sam 6:1–19 clearer to his readers in terms of David's obedience to God's law. The Chronicler then supplements a theological comment (1 Chr 15:26) that YHWH helped the Levites, which implies that this time the transport of the ark was acceptable to YHWH.[60] For other details of 2 Sam 6:13–14 (// 1 Chr 15:26–27), the Chronicler does not subvert the meaning of his source. For example, where 2 Sam 6:13 states that David sacrificed an ox and a fatling when the ark had

---

59. Klein and Krüger, *1 Chronicles*, 46; Thompson, *1, 2 Chronicles*, 33–35.
60. Japhet, *I and II Chronicles*, 305–6; Klein and Krüger, *1 Chronicles*, 356.

marched six steps, the Chronicler reads this verse and specifies that seven bulls and seven rams were sacrificed (1 Chr 15:26) as David danced (1 Chr 15:29). Although the Chronicler does not repeat David's dancing activity in 2 Sam 6:14 (// 1 Chr 15:27), the Chronicler does describe it a verse later (2 Sam 6:16 // 1 Chr 15:29).

In short, the above analysis shows that the Chronicler's reading of this account explains what his source meant. The Chronicler provides additional information to explain the transport of the ark and helps his readers understand the story narrated in the biblical sources more clearly.

Moreover, the Chronicler's reading of 2 Sam 6:1–19 also serves his ideology, which is relevant to his postexilic community. Regarding the relevance of the Chronicler's reading to postexilic concerns, we note that the author of 1 Esdras[61] reminds his readers that the duty of carrying the ark of YHWH should be performed by the Levites (1 Esd 1:3). When the book of Kings narrates the story of King Josiah without mentioning that Josiah asked the Levites to carry the ark of YHWH (2 Kgs 22:1—23:30), the author of 1 Esdras retells this story to make clear that Josiah asked the Levites to carry the ark of YHWH (1 Esd 1:3). This demonstrates that the information about the Levites' duty in carrying the ark was important to the postexilic community because it conforms to God's law (Deut 10:8). The postexilic community acknowledged that their fathers were exiled because they did not obey God's law, and thus, the postexilic community should remember and keep God's law seriously (Neh 9:28–36). The term לֵוִי (Levites) is frequently used in the book of Chronicles (113 times), while the Chronicler's source (Samuel–Kings) uses it only four times. This is further evidence that the Levites' role was indeed important in the postexilic period since it reflects the Chronicler's audience's concern about obeying God's law. Therefore, the Chronicler adds that the ark of YHWH was carried by the Levites with God's help (1 Chr 15:26), and this concern is reinforced again by 1 Esdras.

In conclusion, while the Chronicler reads 2 Sam 6:1–19, he also provides additional explanation or clarification on the events narrated in 2 Sam 6:1–19 for his readers. The Chronicler makes this passage relevant to his postexilic concerns by emphasizing the expectation of a unified Israel and highlighting the Levites' duty of carrying the ark according to God's desire.

---

61. Although the book of 1 Esdras narrates events from Josiah's reform to the return of the exiled Jews, the book was composed around 165 BCE because its linguistic features and writing style are similar to those of the book of Esther (see Goodman, "Esdras," 610).

Comparing the Chronicler's Reading and the Asian Contextual Reading

The Chronicler's Reading of 2 Samuel 10:1–2

The Chronicler also performs a contextual reading when he reads 2 Sam 10:1–2 (// 1 Chr 19:1–2) and conveys a message relevant to the concerns of his postexilic community by adding another phrase לְנַחֲמוֹ ("to comfort him," 1 Chr 19:2) at the end of the verse. The table below presents this reading of the Chronicler.

Table 8. The Chronicler's Reading of 2 Samuel 10:1–2

2 Samuel 10:1–2	1 Chronicles 19:1–2
וַיְהִי אַחֲרֵי־כֵן וַיָּמָת מֶלֶךְ בְּנֵי עַמּוֹן וַיִּמְלֹךְ חָנוּן בְּנוֹ תַּחְתָּיו׃	וַיְהִי אַחֲרֵי־כֵן וַיָּמָת נָחָשׁ מֶלֶךְ בְּנֵי־עַמּוֹן וַיִּמְלֹךְ בְּנוֹ תַּחְתָּיו׃
וַיֹּאמֶר דָּוִד אֶעֱשֶׂה־חֶסֶד עִם־חָנוּן בֶּן־נָחָשׁ כַּאֲשֶׁר עָשָׂה אָבִיו עִמָּדִי חֶסֶד	וַיֹּאמֶר דָּוִיד אֶעֱשֶׂה־חֶסֶד עִם־חָנוּן בֶּן־נָחָשׁ כִּי־עָשָׂה אָבִיו עִמִּי חֶסֶד
וַיִּשְׁלַח דָּוִד לְנַחֲמוֹ בְּיַד־עֲבָדָיו אֶל־אָבִיו	וַיִּשְׁלַח דָּוִיד מַלְאָכִים לְנַחֲמוֹ עַל־אָבִיו
וַיָּבֹאוּ עַבְדֵי דָוִד אֶרֶץ בְּנֵי עַמּוֹן׃	וַיָּבֹאוּ עַבְדֵי דָוִיד אֶל־אֶרֶץ בְּנֵי־עַמּוֹן אֶל־חָנוּן לְנַחֲמוֹ׃
(Some time afterward, the king of the Ammonites died, and his son Hanun succeeded him. David said, "I will deal loyally with Hanun son of Nahash, just as his father dealt loyally with me." So David sent envoys to *console* him concerning his father. When David's envoys came into the land of the Ammonites. . . .)	(Some time afterward, King Nahash of the Ammonites died, and his son succeeded him. David said, "I will deal loyally with Hanun son of Nahash, for his father dealt loyally with me." So David sent messengers to *console* him concerning his father. When David's servants came to Hanun in the land of the Ammonites, to *console* him. . . .)

Although 2 Sam 10:2 explains that David sent his servants to console Hanun, the Chronicler uses the same phrase לְנַחֲמוֹ ("to console him" or "to comfort him") twice to emphasize David's good intentions in sending his servants to the Ammonites.[62] Comfort was a need of the people in postexilic time. Zechariah 1:12–17 states that Zion and Jerusalem in the postexilic period needed the Lord's comfort, which he promised (Zech 1:17; cf. Isa 40:1) due to their severe affliction by the gentiles. God's people needed to seek YHWH instead of diviners who comfort in vain (Zech 10:1–2). Moreover, Sirach[63] advises his postexilic community to take comfort and stay far from

---

62. Kalimi, *Reshaping of Ancient Israelite History*, 348.
63. The book of Sirach (also called the Wisdom of Ben Sira) is an Old Testament

sorrow (Sir 30:23). Writing before the end of the Second Temple period, the author of 4 Esdras[64] narrates that Ezra was commanded to comfort people in lowly situations (4 Esd 4:13). Ezra himself also needed comfort from God (4 Esd 12:8) when he could not understand the purposes of the Most High for this world through the vision that YHWH revealed to Ezra, which made him frightened (4 Esd 12:3–8). In short, the Chronicler uses the postexilic concern of comfort to read 2 Sam 10:2, emphasizing the act of comfort (לְנַחֲמוֹ).

In summary, the examples above have demonstrated that the Chronicler's reading of his sources reflects the main features of the contextual approach to biblical interpretation. On the one hand, the Chronicler deals with the biblical world of events narrated in his sources by supplementing information to explain or clarify what his sources meant. On the other hand, the Chronicler also provides commentaries that relate to the concerns of his postexilic community.

Reflecting the So-Called Abstraction Ladder

Just as Asian contextual interpreters use the abstraction ladder, the Chronicler's reading also demonstrates this technique. The abstraction ladder is used when a reader cannot find an analogy between the biblical situation and the reader's situation for application to the reader's context. In such cases, the reader seeks general principles, lessons, or teachings from biblical texts about God or about the God-human relationship to apply to the reader's audience. The following examples will demonstrate that the Chronicler's reading indeed employs the abstraction ladder.

---

apocryphal book written in Hebrew by Yeshua ben Eleazar ben Sira (Ben Sira is the short name in Hebrew), who considered himself a scribe or wisdom teacher around 200–170 BCE. The book then was translated into Greek by Ben Sira's grandson around 132–16 BCE. See VanderKam, *Introduction to Early Judaism*, 115–19.

64. Michael E. Stone and Frank Moore Cross review studies on the date of 4 Esdras and point out that, although scholars do not agree on a certain date for the book's composition, internal evidence and external evidence of the book's citations indicate that the date of 4 Esdras should be close to the collapse of the Second Temple. This book belongs to the postexilic period. See Stone and Cross, *Fourth Ezra*, 10.

Comparing the Chronicler's Reading and the Asian Contextual Reading

The Chronicler's Reading of 1 Samuel 31:1–13

The Chronicler reads in detail the account of Saul's final battle and death (1 Sam 31:1–13 // 1 Chr 10:1–12) and then presents his own conclusion concerning the theological reasons for Saul's death and the kingdom's transfer to David's house (1 Chr 10:13–14). Saul's death took place in the preexilic period, not in the postexilic era. Thus, there is no similarity between the Chronicler's biblical source (1 Sam 31:1–13) and his postexilic context. Even so, the Chronicler finds a general principle concerning the God-human relationship from his biblical source. The Chronicler indicates that Saul's unfaithful relationship with YHWH was the reason for his death. Here the Chronicler reads the account of Saul's death (1 Sam 31:1–13//1 Chr 10:1–12) and shares the lesson concerning one's relationship with God from the reading (1 Chr 10:13–14). In modern terms of interpretation, this is an instance of the abstraction ladder. Unfaithfulness is one of the main characteristics of the postexilic community. Ackroyd observes that the word מָעַל (unfaithful act), which occurs twice in 1 Chr 10:13, is also found in Neh 1:8; 13:27; and Ezra 9–10.[65] The people of God have been exiled because of their unfaithfulness to YHWH (Neh 1:8). Ezra repeatedly calls out the people's many acts of unfaithfulness toward YHWH and his law (Ezra 9:2, 4, 6; 10:2, 6, and 10). Writing before the end of the Second Temple period, the author of 4 Esdras similarly explained that the Israelites did not receive the inheritance which the Lord reserved for them (4 Esd 7:9–14) because they had been unfaithful to God's statutes (4 Esd 7:24). Thus, we see how the Chronicler, through his commentary on the theological reasons for Saul's downfall (1 Chr 10:13–14), gives to his postexilic community a relevant lesson concerning the consequences of unfaithfulness to YHWH. In this way, the Chronicler employs the abstraction ladder to obtain a relevant message from 1 Sam 31:1–13 for his postexilic audience.

The Chronicler's Reading of 2 Samuel 7:14–15

For another example, the Chronicler uses the abstraction ladder when he reads 2 Sam 7:14–15 as follows.

---

65. Ackroyd, *Chronicler in His Age*, 318–19.

Reading the Bible as a Postexilic Biblical Author Read

Table 9. The Chronicler's Reading of 2 Samuel 7:14–15

2 Samuel 7:14–15	1 Chronicles 17:13
אֲנִי אֶהְיֶה־לּוֹ לְאָב וְהוּא יִהְיֶה־לִּי לְבֵן אֲשֶׁר בְּהַעֲוֺתוֹ וְהֹכַחְתִּיו בְּשֵׁבֶט אֲנָשִׁים וּבְנִגְעֵי בְּנֵי אָדָם וְחַסְדִּי לֹא־יָסוּר מִמֶּנּוּ כַּאֲשֶׁר הֲסִרֹתִי מֵעִם שָׁאוּל אֲשֶׁר הֲסִרֹתִי מִלְּפָנֶיךָ	אֲנִי אֶהְיֶה־לּוֹ לְאָב וְהוּא יִהְיֶה־לִּי לְבֵן וְחַסְדִּי לֹא־אָסִיר מֵעִמּוֹ כַּאֲשֶׁר הֲסִירוֹתִי מֵאֲשֶׁר הָיָה לְפָנֶיךָ
(I will be a father to him, and he shall be a son to me. When he commits iniquity, I will punish him with a rod such as mortals use, with blows inflicted by human beings. But I will not take my steadfast love from him, as I took it from Saul, whom I put away from before you.)	(I will be a father to him, and he shall be a son to me. I will not take my steadfast love from him, as I took it from him who was before you.)

In 2 Sam 7, YHWH revealed to David that although he was not permitted to build the temple, his son would be the one to construct a house for YHWH. The context of this biblical source was preexilic and, as such, was not analogous to the Chronicler's postexilic context. Reading 2 Sam 7:14–15, the Chronicler presents a general principle concerning God's character, namely, faithfulness in keeping his promise. However, the Chronicler omits reading the clause אֲשֶׁר בְּהַעֲוֺתוֹ וְהֹכַחְתִּיו בְּשֵׁבֶט אֲנָשִׁים וּבְנִגְעֵי בְּנֵי אָדָם ("When he commits iniquity, I will punish him with a rod such as mortals use, with blows inflicted by human beings") in 2 Sam 7:14 (// 1 Chr 17:13), thereby making the Lord's promise to David and his descendants unambiguously unconditional and uninfluenced by the sins of David's son.[66] Here, the Chronicler is using the abstraction ladder to highlight God's faithfulness in keeping his promise. This would engender hope in the Chronicler's postexilic community because the sins of David's sons would never affect God's promise and steadfast love to David's house (1 Chr 17:13–14). This message of hope is also affirmed in Sir 47–51. The author of Sirach narrates God's promise to David concerning the permanence of the Davidic throne (Sir 47:11). He also recounts the sins of David's son Solomon (Sir 47:19–21), while emphasizing that Solomon's failures would not affect God's covenant of kingship with David (Sir 47:22). The book continues to narrate the sins of the leaders of the two kingdoms, including

---

66. Japhet, *I and II Chronicles*, 334.

David's sons (Sir 47:23—48:15a; 49:4b), except for Hezekiah and Josiah (Sir 49:4a). Those sins led to the exile of both the northern kingdom (Sir 48:15b) and the southern kingdom (Sir 49:4c). Nevertheless, the author of Sirach still gives thanks to the Lord for his endless steadfast love and for gathering the people of God from exile. He affirms that God could make a horn to sprout for the Davidic house, and so he praises God for that (Sir 51:12). Thus, God's promise and steadfast love are the foundation of hope for the Chronicler's postexilic readers.

In summary, the examples above have demonstrated that the Chronicler uses the abstraction ladder to derive relevant messages for his contemporary readers, especially as he highlights the human-God relationship and God's faithful character in that relationship.

Using the So-Called Biblical Theology

As defined above, biblical theology is the tracing or elaborating of an idea or theme through various passages of Scripture. In other words, an interpreter uses the teachings of other biblical passages to shed light on an issue encountered in the passage being interpreted. As such, biblical theology is one of the tools employed by the Chronicler as he reads his sources. In particular, the Chronicler often uses the teachings of the Pentateuch for interpreting Samuel. For example, the Chronicler explains that the Lord put Saul to death because he consulted a medium (1 Chr 10:13–14). Klein and Krüger indicate that this commentary by the Chronicler conforms to the teaching of the Pentateuch. The Torah (Lev 20:6, 27; Deut 18:11) states that people who consult a medium shall be put to death.[67]

The following examples illustrate how the Chronicler uses biblical theology in his reading of biblical sources.

---

67. Klein and Krüger, *1 Chronicles*, 291.

Reading the Bible as a Postexilic Biblical Author Read

Table 10. The Chronicler's Reading of 2 Samuel 5:21

2 Samuel 5:21	1 Chronicles 14:12
וַיַּעַזְבוּ־שָׁם אֶת־עֲצַבֵּיהֶם וַיִּשָּׂאֵם דָּוִד וַאֲנָשָׁיו	וַיַּעַזְבוּ־שָׁם אֶת־אֱלֹהֵיהֶם וַיֹּאמֶר דָּוִד וַיִּשָּׂרְפוּ בָּאֵשׁ
(They[68] abandoned their idols there, and David and his men *carried* them *away*.)	(They abandoned their gods there and David *gave the order and they were burned in the fire*.[69])

Second Samuel 5:21 is part of the narrative describing David's victory over the Philistines. This verse states that David and his men carried (וַיִּשָּׂאֵם) the Philistines' idols away. In contrast, the Chronicler writes וַיֹּאמֶר דָּוִד וַיִּשָּׂרְפוּ בָּאֵשׁ ("David gave the order and they were burnt there," 1 Chr 14:12). The Chronicler's source (2 Sam 5:21) does not clearly state what David and his men did to the idols after carrying them away, but the Chronicler clarifies that David commanded them to burn the idols. Deuteronomy 7:25 prohibits the Israelites from coveting gold and silver on idols and requires the people to burn the idols of the Canaanites. The Chronicler further expounds that David's actions in this event complied with the Torah's requirement.[70] In this manner, the Chronicler uses biblical theology as he interprets his source.

Table 11. The Chronicler's Reading of 2 Samuel 8:18

2 Samuel 8:18	1 Chronicles 18:17
וּבְנָיָהוּ בֶּן־יְהוֹיָדָע וְהַכְּרֵתִי וְהַפְּלֵתִי וּבְנֵי דָוִד כֹּהֲנִים הָיוּ	וּבְנָיָהוּ בֶּן־יְהוֹיָדָע עַל־הַכְּרֵתִי וְהַפְּלֵתִי וּבְנֵי־דָוִיד הָרִאשֹׁנִים לְיַד הַמֶּלֶךְ
(Benaiah son of Jehoiada was over the Cherethites and the Pelethites; and David's sons *were priests*.)	(Benaiah son of Jehoiada was over the Cherethites and the Pelethites; and David's sons *were chiefs at the king's side*.[71])

---

68. Translation follows MT 2 Sam 5:21, which reads וַיַּעַזְבוּ־שָׁם (*they abandoned*).

69. Translation follows MT 1 Chr 14:12, which reads וַיֹּאמֶר דָּוִד וַיִּשָּׂרְפוּ בָּאֵשׁ (*and David gave the order and they were burned in the fire*).

70. Japhet, *I and II Chronicles*, 289. Scholars indicate that the Chronicler makes a harmonization of 2 Sam 5:21 with Deut 7:25. See Curtis and Madsen, *Books of Chronicles*, 209; Kalimi, *Reshaping of Ancient Israelite*, 155; Klein and Krüger, *1 Chronicles*, 342.

71. Translation follows MT 1 Chr 18:17, which reads הָרִאשֹׁנִים לְיַד הַמֶּלֶךְ (*were chiefs at the king's side*).

Comparing the Chronicler's Reading and the Asian Contextual Reading

For the phrase וּבְנֵי דָוִד כֹּהֲנִים הָיוּ ("and the sons of David were priests") in 2 Sam 8:18 (// 1 Chr 18:17), the Chronicler reads וּבְנֵי־דָוִיד הָרִאשֹׁנִים לְיַד הַמֶּלֶךְ ("and David's sons *were chiefs at the king's side*," 1 Chr 18:17). David was from the tribe of Judah (Ruth 4:18–22). Thus, David's sons did not belong to the priestly descendants nor to the Levite tribe, and they could not be priests according to the Law of Moses (Lev 7:35–36). The Chronicler's reading (chiefs) does not subvert the plain meaning of his source (the priests) because the term chiefs (הָרִאשֹׁנִים) has broad implications. Many kinds of people, including priests, may become chiefs. Scholars indicate that the Chronicler paraphrases the role of David's sons to harmonize with the law.[72] For David, the role of the priests at his side was very important. The Chronicler reads that the sons of David were chiefs at the king's side, which shows that David's sons were in an important position to the king just as the priests were important to the king. This reading of the Chronicler follows his source and also complied with Lev 7:35–36.[73]

In summary, the examples above have demonstrated that the Chronicler draws on the Pentateuch to present his interpretation and commentary. This feature reflects the so-called biblical theology that modern Bible interpreters often use.

Fusion of the Two Horizons

As indicated above, contextualizing a biblical text is a fusion of two horizons, namely, the fusion of horizons "between the text and its interpreter."[74] Like Dalit interpreters who find themselves (by connecting the term *dalit* to the Bible through the Hebrew word דַּל [*dal*]) and their issues in biblical texts, the Chronicler has also seen himself and his contemporary readers, as well as their contextual issues, in his biblical sources and then applies his biblical sources directly to the postexilic context. The following examples will demonstrate that the Chronicler indeed employs the fusion of two horizons in his reading of biblical sources.

---

72. Curtis and Madsen, *Books of Chronicles*, 237; Kalimi, *Reshaping of Ancient Israelite History*, 153–54.

73. For 2 Sam 8:18, which narrates that David's sons were priests, a possible reason is that kings could take cultic functions in the ancient Near East. See Auld, *I and II Samuel*, 431. Thus, David occasionally performed cultic duties, such as wearing an ephod before the ark (2 Sam 6:14). Consequently, David's sons might have taken on the priesthood, but the office is just a temporary arrangement. See Anderson, *2 Samuel*, 137–38.

74. Gadamer, *Truth and Method*, 370.

Reading the Bible as a Postexilic Biblical Author Read

The Chronicler reads 1 Kgs 8:34 (// 2 Chr 6:25) as follows.

Table 12. The Chronicler's Reading of 1 Kings 8:34

1 Kings 8:34	2 Chronicles 6:25
וְאַתָּה תִּשְׁמַע הַשָּׁמַיִם וְסָלַחְתָּ לְחַטַּאת עַמְּךָ יִשְׂרָאֵל וַהֲשֵׁבֹתָם אֶל־הָאֲדָמָה אֲשֶׁר נָתַתָּ לַאֲבוֹתָם׃	וְאַתָּה תִּשְׁמַע מִן־הַשָּׁמַיִם וְסָלַחְתָּ לְחַטַּאת עַמְּךָ יִשְׂרָאֵל וַהֲשֵׁיבוֹתָם אֶל־הָאֲדָמָה אֲשֶׁר־נָתַתָּה לָהֶם וְלַאֲבֹתֵיהֶם׃
(Then you[75] hear in heaven, forgive the sin of your people Israel, and bring them again to the land that you gave to their ancestors.)	(May you hear from heaven, and forgive the sin of your people Israel, and bring them again to the land that you gave *to them* and to their ancestors.)

This reading by the Chronicler makes the biblical passage more directly applicable to the Chronicler's postexilic readers than his source text. Scholars indicate that, with the additional phrase לָהֶם (*"to them"*) placed before וְלַאֲבֹתֵיהֶם ("and to their fathers"), the Chronicler is indicating that YHWH has indeed forgiven the sin of his people and brought them back to the land. This land was not only given to their fathers in the past but is *now* being given to *them* (לָהֶם), namely, the Chronicler himself and his readers presently residing in the land.[76] Here, the Chronicler's reading finds himself and his contemporary readers in the biblical passage (1 Kgs 8:33–34 // 2 Chr 6:24–25) as he makes the fusion of the two horizons.

In like manner, the Chronicler contextually reads Solomon's prayer in 1 Kgs 8:23–53 and Ps 132:8–10. For the last words of Solomon's prayer (Ps 132:8–10 // 2 Chr 6:41–42), the Chronicler changes the singular word מְשִׁיחֶךָ ("your anointed one," Ps 132:10) to the plural מְשִׁיחֶיךָ ("your anointed ones," 2 Chr 6:42).

---

75. Translation follows MT 1 Kgs 8:34, which reads וְאַתָּה תִּשְׁמַע (you hear).
76. Beentjes, "Psalms and Prayers," 27; Japhet, *Ideology*, 303.

Comparing the Chronicler's Reading and the Asian Contextual Reading

Table 13. The Chronicler's Reading of Psalm 132:10

Psalm 132:10	2 Chronicles 6:42
בַּעֲבוּר דָּוִד עַבְדֶּךָ אַל־תָּשֵׁב פְּנֵי מְשִׁיחֶךָ	יְהוָה אֱלֹהִים אַל־תָּשֵׁב פְּנֵי מְשִׁיחֶיךָ זָכְרָה לְחַסְדֵי דָּוִיד עַבְדֶּךָ
(For your servant David's sake do not turn away the face of *your anointed one*.)	(O LORD God, do not reject *your anointed ones*,[77]
	Remember your steadfast love for/to[78] your servant David.")

According to the literary context of Psalm 132, מְשִׁיחֶךָ ("your anointed one," Ps 132:10) indicates the king in the past. For the Chronicler's source in 1 Kgs 8:46–53, its literary context indicates a future king. On the one hand, the reading of the Chronicler ("*your anointed ones*") is faithful to what both of his sources meant (Ps 132:10 and 1 Kgs 8:46–53). Klein and Hanson also assert that the reading of the Chronicler ("*your anointed ones*") refers to both the king in the past and a future king whom the postexilic community expected to come to restore the monarchy.[79] On the other hand, the Chronicler's reading hopes to see in his postexilic community the fulfillment of Solomon's supplication on the basis of YHWH's steadfast love to David (2 Chr 6:42 // Ps 132:10a). In this respect, the Chronicler's reading demonstrates the fusion of his source and his postexilic reader's expectation.

Faithful to Sources Even with Supplemental Information

While Dalit interpreters sometimes do not read the Bible faithfully when they use deconstruction and subvert what the texts meant, this study holds that the Chronicler's reading is faithful to his sources. But that does not mean that the Chronicler only repeats the same words as his sources, though he often does so. Rather, it means that although the Chronicler's reading sometimes alters the original words of his biblical sources to serve his purposes, the Chronicler's reading does not subvert what his sources meant and is correct in terms of theology according to the Torah and the teachings of other biblical passages.

---

77. Translation follows MT 2 Chr 6:42, which reads מְשִׁיחֶיךָ (your anointed ones).

78. Scholars indicate that this preposition should be understood both ways. See Curtis and Madsen, *Books of Chronicles*, 345; Klein and Hanson, *2 Chronicles*, 100; Sakenfeld, *Meaning of Hesed*, 158.

79. Klein and Hanson, *2 Chronicles*, 99.

Reading the Bible as a Postexilic Biblical Author Read

Faithful Even with Additional Information

The Chronicler occasionally provides additional information while reading his sources, but the Chronicler still reads his sources faithfully. For instance, the Chronicler's reading of 1 Kgs 15:9–24 (// 2 Chr 14:2—17:1) is three times as long as his biblical source (sixteen verses in 1 Kgs 15:9–24 and forty-seven verses in 2 Chr 14:2—17:1). However, the Chronicler's reading does not subvert what 1 Kgs 15:9–24 meant. Scholars generally concur that the Chronicler's reading closely relies on his sources.[80] While the Chronicler's source describes Asa as a faithful king, the Chronicler's additional information elaborates on the details of Asa's faithfulness. While 1 Kgs 15:9–24 presents the length of Asa's reign in the beginning of the account (1 Kgs 15:10), the Chronicler puts it at the end of the narrative in Chronicles (2 Chr 16:13) after providing supplementary information about Asa's life (2 Chr 14:2—16:12). The Chronicler's source begins with Asa's religious reform as evidence that Asa did what was right before YHWH (1 Kgs 15:9–12). The expansion of the Chronicler's Asa account consists of a fuller description and explanation of Asa's religious reform. The table below summarizes the Chronicler's reading vis-à-vis the book of Kings.

Table 14. The Chronicler's Reading of 1 Kings 15:9–24

1 Kings 15:9–24	2 Chronicles 14:2—17:1
1 Kgs 15:9–10—Asa's total number of years on the throne (forty-one years).	
1 Kgs 15:11–12—What Asa did was right in the eyes of YHWH. Asa performed religious reform.	2 Chr 14:3–5—What Asa did was good and right in the eyes of YHWH. Asa performed religious reform and his country had rest.
	2 Chr 14:6—15:15 describes the outcome (blessings) of Asa's religious reform and what happened during this reform.
	Asa fortified many cities and his army became stronger. When the Ethiopian army of a million soldiers attacked, YHWH helped Asa to defeat the Ethiopians when Asa sought YHWH for help. Asa then continued to execute religious reform after YHWH encouraged him through the words of Azariah.

---

80. Japhet, *I and II Chronicles*, 702; Levin, *Chronicles*, 57; Lowry, *Reforming Kings*, 97; Schnittjer, *Old Testament*, 782.

Comparing the Chronicler's Reading and the Asian Contextual Reading

1 Kings 15:9–24	2 Chronicles 14:2—17:1
1 Kgs 15:13–15—Asa demoted his mother from her position as queen because she worshiped idols. Asa brought votive gifts to the Jerusalem temple.	2 Chr 15:16–19—Asa demoted his mother from her position as queen because she worshiped idols. Asa brought votive gifts to the Jerusalem temple.
Asa did not execute a complete religious reform since he did not take away the high places, but Asa's heart was true to YHWH.	Asa did not execute a complete religious reform since he did not take away the high places, but Asa's heart was true to YHWH.
1 Kgs 15:16–24—Asa engaged in a war against Baasha, the king of Israel. Asa took all the treasures from the temple and from his house to pay to Ben-hadad, the king of Syria, to secure his assistance. Consequently, Asa took back some of his cities taken by Baasha.	2 Chr 16:1–6—Asa engaged in a war against Baasha, the king of Israel. Asa took all the treasures from the temple and from his house to pay Ben-hadad, the king of Syria, to secure his assistance. Consequently, Asa took back some of his cities taken by Baasha.
	2 Chr 16:7–10 describes the tragic outcome of Asa's abuse of the treasures in the temple to seek help from the Syrians instead of seeking YHWH's help. Hanani the seer declared that Asa would have wars from then on. Asa's reign then became brutally oppressive.
1 Kgs 15:23–24—Conclusion of Asa's life. All Asa's activities were written in the annals of the kings of Judah. Asa was diseased in his feet, then died and was buried.	2 Chr 16:11—17:1—Conclusion of Asa's life. All Asa's activities were written in the book of the kings of Judah and Israel.
	Asa was severely diseased in his feet and he sought help from physicians instead of seeking YHWH.
	Asa died after forty-one years on the throne and then he was buried.

In current scholarship, the main dispute over the Chronicler's account of Asa's reign is the historicity and reliability of the Chronicler's *Sondergut* (2 Chr 14:6—15:15).[81] Some scholars hold that the biblical narratives by themselves are reliable historical records, but others (the minimalists) argue that a biblical story should not be accepted as historical unless it has archeological evidence supporting its historical claims.[82] In the case of the Chronicler's *Sondergut* relating to the Asa account, archeological evidence has not yet been discovered.[83] Even so, Philip Davies, a prominent mini-

---

81. Williamson, *1 and 2 Chronicles*, 255–58; Lowry, *Reforming Kings*, 97.
82. Knauth, "Israel," 514; Hill, "History of Israel 3," 445.
83. On the discrepancy in the chronology of Asa's life (2 Chr 16:1 and 1 Kgs 16:8), Levin summarizes four views concerning this issue (see Levin, *Chronicles*, 75–77), but

malist, argues that although a biblical story by itself cannot demonstrate its historicity, it does reflect the ideology of its author. Davies states,

> Unless we have evidence other than a biblical story, we cannot accept any claim for historicity, because in themselves, the narratives do not prove anything about their content; what they do constitute is evidence of themselves, as stories once told, and the historian's first question is: why was this story told, and what does this story tell us about its writers and hearers or readers?[84]

In this case, the Chronicler's Asa account includes two sections. First, the Chronicler reads close to his sources (1 Kgs 15:9–24 // 2 Chr 14:3–5; 15:16—16:6, 16:11—17:1) and does not subvert what his source meant. Second, the Chronicler's *Sondergut* (2 Chr 14:6—15:15; 16:7–10) reflects the Chronicler's ideologies in the postexilic context. The Chronicler's additional information for further elaboration of the Asa account makes the biblical reading relevant to the Chronicler's postexilic audience. For example, the Chronicler repeatedly states that Asa did the right things (activities of religious reform) before YHWH's eyes and thus the Lord gave his land rest (נוח) from wars for years (2 Chr 14:5–6 [MT], 15:15). During the Hellenistic age in the postexilic context, the Greek idea of *homonoia* (concord) circulated widely in the empire in response to the need to prevent frequent internal wars among Greek forces.[85] While reading the Asa account (1 Kgs 15:9–24), the Chronicler conveys the message to his postexilic audience that YHWH would give rest from wars to people who did right in YHWH's eyes, just as Asa did in breaking down the altars of foreign idols, seeking the Lord, and keeping YHWH's laws. However, the Chronicler also alerts his postexilic audience that to maintain a peaceful life and rest from wars, the people must constantly rely on YHWH. The Chronicler's last stage of Asa's life conveys the message that trusting in humans instead of relying on YHWH for military success and health will result in God's punishment of political unrest (2 Chr 16:7–14). In short, the Chronicler's supplementary reading of his source's Asa account does not subvert what his source meant (1 Kgs 15:9–24) and contextually conveys theological messages (2 Chr 14:6—15:15; 16:7–10) that are relevant to the concerns of his postexilic audience.

---

there is no conclusive answer. One of the views is that there is a textual error. This is the simplest answer, and the numbers in 2 Chr 15:19 and 16:1 might be twenty-five and twenty-six respectively.

84. Davies, *History of Ancient Israel*, 141.
85. Mitchell and Edelman, "Chronicles," 244.

Comparing the Chronicler's Reading and the Asian Contextual Reading

Faithful as Confirmed by the Postexilic Community

The Chronicler's reading of 2 Kgs 21:1–18 (// 2 Chr 33:1–20) has been criticized for changing the portrait of Manasseh from that of a *sinful* king (2 Chr 33:1–9 // 2 Kgs 21:1–9) to that of a *repentant* king (2 Chr 33:10–20). If the account of the repentant Manasseh is proved to be reliable, then the Chronicler's reading is faithful and vice versa. This study argues that the Chronicler's contextual reading of the Manasseh account (2 Kgs 21:1–18 // 2 Chr 33:1–20) is faithful to his sources, as confirmed by the postexilic community.

While 2 Kgs 21:1–18 describes Manasseh as arguably the most wicked king in the history of the southern kingdom, 2 Chr 33:1–20 depicts Manasseh's life in two stages: the wicked Manasseh and then the repentant Manasseh. For the stage of the wicked Manasseh, scholars have carefully examined the Chronicler's reading of 2 Kgs 21:1–9 (// 2 Chr 33:1–9) and concluded that the Chronicler's reading is faithful to what his sources meant.[86] Knoppers summarizes the close parallels between the Chronicler's source and his reading as demonstrated in the table below.[87]

Table 15. Parallels between 2 Chronicles 33:1–9 and 2 Kings 21:1–9

King Manasseh	2 Kings 21	2 Chronicles 33
Opening Notice	2 Kgs 21:1	2 Chr 33:1
Negative Evaluation	2 Kgs 21:2	2 Chr 33:2
Enumeration of Sins	2 Kgs 21:3–6	2 Chr 33:3–6
Conditional Promise	2 Kgs 21:7–8	2 Chr 33:7–8
Unprecedented Iniquity	2 Kgs 21:9	2 Chr 33:9

For the remaining verses of his sources (2 Kgs 21:10–18) which elaborate the sins of Manasseh through the words of the prophets, the Chronicler's reading does not repeat this detailed description. Rather, the Chronicler summarizes this section in 2 Chr 33:10 by saying that Manasseh ignored the words of the prophets.[88] The Chronicler then provides supplementary information concerning the second stage of King Manasseh's life (2 Chr 33:11–20), portraying him as repentant. There are three main views concerning the Chronicler's depiction of the repentant Manasseh.

---

86. Abadie, "From the Impious Manasseh," 95; Evans, "Manasseh," 496.
87. Knoppers, "1 Chronicles 16," 214.
88. Japhet, *I and II Chronicles*, 1008.

Reading the Bible as a Postexilic Biblical Author Read

Some scholars argue that there is no archeological evidence to support the historicity of the Chronicler's reading in 2 Chr 33:11–20.[89] Some even claim that the Chronicler distorted the history depicted in Samuel–Kings,[90] but this claim is a huge assumption because it assumes the entire historicity of the Chronicler's source, Samuel–Kings, and then supposes that the Chronicler distorted the history with the Chronicler's ideological or theological agenda. In scholarship, historicity of biblical texts should be justified via extrabiblical supporting evidence and archeological evidence. No one can prove the historicity of Samuel–Kings as well as Chronicles.

Others think that the Chronicler's additional information is reliable, although archeological evidence in support of it has not yet been found. For example, Dillard suggests several occasions on which Manasseh may have revolted against the Assyrian rulers, i.e., during the times of Asshurbanipal or Esarhaddon, when there were internal wars among Assyrian forces. Manasseh may have joined a rebel faction to fight against the Assyrian rulers. The Assyrian rulers were able defeat the rebel forces.[91] Having been defeated, Manasseh was then captured and exiled to Babylon as indicated by the Chronicler's account (2 Chr 33:11). In terms of archeological records, an inscription of Esarhaddon lists twenty-two kings who joined rebel forces and were defeated by Esarhaddon. Unfortunately, this tablet is damaged in the place where the names of the rebellious kings are supposed to appear. Therefore, we do not have the list of names which might have included Manasseh.[92] On the other hand, Dillard observes that there is no archeological evidence that contradicts the Chronicler's Manasseh account and there are multiple fitting historical occasions for Manasseh's rebellion against the Assyrians, his exile, and return.[93] Sara Japhet holds the middle position that although the historicity of Chronicler's Manasseh account is not certain, it is also difficult to believe that the Chronicler has no evidence at all for his portrait of the repentant Manasseh and that he simply fabricated the story of Manasseh's repentance out of thin air.[94]

Our position is that the Chronicler reads the account of the wicked Manasseh faithfully to what his source meant (2 Kgs 21:1–9 // 2 Chr

---

89. Ackroyd, *I and II Chronicles*, 198; Klein and Hanson, *2 Chronicles*, 477.
90. Curtis and Madsen, *Books of Chronicles*, 14.
91. Dillard, *2 Chronicles*, 265.
92. Evans, "Manasseh," 499.
93. Dillard, *2 Chronicles*, 265.
94. Japhet, *I and II Chronicles*, 1009.

33:1–9) as mentioned above. The historicity of the Chronicler's repentant Manasseh has not yet been proven, but it has not been disproven either. The Chronicler may have additional sources for his portrait of the repentant Manasseh, which the Deuteronomist did not have.[95] When the postexilic community recognized that the Chronicler's Manasseh was different from the Deuteronomist's Manasseh, the Chronicler should have been able to cite reliable sources for the repentant Manasseh to convince his audience.[96] Indeed, the Chronicler explicitly cites two sources, namely, the book of the Kings of Israel and the book of Hozai (2 Chr 33:18–19). Therefore, instead of questioning the historicity of the Chronicler's repentant Manasseh, one can choose to consider the Deuteronomist's sinful Manasseh as an incomplete portrait. Schnittjer rightly suggests that the Deuteronomist may have had access to the sources of the repentant Manasseh but did not incorporate this source into his presentation in order to highlight Manasseh as the one king most culpable for the fall of Jerusalem.[97] Indeed, Manasseh had shed so much innocent blood, and this grave sin is linked to the fall of Jerusalem by the prophet Jeremiah (Jer 19:4; 2 Kgs 21:16).

The Chronicler chose to include the second stage of Manasseh's life to present to the postexilic audience an amazing paradigm of exile–repentance–restoration–religious reform, as his readers continue to wait for YHWH to deliver them completely from the imperial rulers.[98] The case of Manasseh shows the postexilic community that no matter how wicked a person is, YHWH still accepts true repentance as demonstrated in sincere prayers and appropriate actions. Although some scholars reject the historicity of the repentant Manasseh due to the lack archeological evidence, the postexilic community likely accepted the portrait of the reformed Manasseh as reliable because the repentant Manasseh is also reflected in LXX Chr 33, the Prayer of Manasseh (LXX), and a Qumran psalm (4Q381) containing the superscription "The Prayer of Manasseh." No matter when those documents were composed, either before or after the Chronicler's portrait of Manasseh, those writings are clear evidence that the tradition of Manasseh's repentance circulated among the postexilic community during the Second Temple period. Therefore, we conclude that the Chronicler's reading of the Manasseh account is faithful to his source (2 Kgs 21:1–18 // 2 Chr 33:1–20)

---

95. Levin, *Chronicles*, 381.
96. Schnittjer, *Old Testament*, 821.
97. Schnittjer, *Old Testament*, 821.
98. Knoppers, "1 Chronicles 16," 226.

Reading the Bible as a Postexilic Biblical Author Read

even when his presentation includes supplementary information not found in his extant sources, for the reliability of his account is confirmed by his broader postexilic community.[99]

Faithful Even with Alternative Wording

Regarding the Chronicler's reading of 1 Sam 31:1–13 (// 1 Chr 10:1–14), the above section has shown that the Chronicler reads this passage and makes it relevant to his postexilic audience through his commentary regarding unfaithfulness to YHWH, which led to disastrous consequences (1 Chr 10:13–14). This section will demonstrate that the Chronicler's reading is faithful to what his sources meant, even though his wording sometimes deviates from his sources.

Table 16. The Chronicler's Reading of 1 Samuel 31:10

1 Samuel 31:10	1 Chronicles 10:10
וַיָּשִׂמוּ אֶת־כֵּלָיו בֵּית עַשְׁתָּרוֹת וְאֶת־גְּוִיָּתוֹ תָּקְעוּ בְּחוֹמַת בֵּית שָׁן	וַיָּשִׂימוּ אֶת־כֵּלָיו בֵּית אֱלֹהֵיהֶם וְאֶת־גֻּלְגָּלְתּוֹ תָקְעוּ בֵּית דָּגוֹן
(They put his armor in the temple of *Astarte*; and they fastened *his body to the wall of Beth-shan*.)	(They put his armor in the temple of *their gods*, and fastened *his head in the temple of Dagon*.)

The Chronicler interprets this verse in the following way. The word עַשְׁתֹּרֶת (Astoreth) refers to the Canaanite god (Judg 2:13, 10:6; 1 Sam 7:3–4; 12:10). The house of Astoreth belonged to the Philistines where Saul's weapons were put. Thus, the Chronicler's reading בֵּית אֱלֹהֵיהֶם ("the house of their gods") is a correct interpretation. Similarly, the Chronicler's reading of Saul's corpse is a further explanation of his source. For the phrase וְאֶת־גְּוִיָּתוֹ תָּקְעוּ בְּחוֹמַת בֵּית שָׁן ("and they fastened *his body to the wall of Beth-shan*," 1 Sam 31:10), the Chronicler reads וְאֶת־גֻּלְגָּלְתּוֹ תָקְעוּ בֵּית דָּגוֹן ("and [they] fastened *his head in the temple of Dagon*," 1 Chr 10:10). The Chronicler focuses

---

99. The section above demonstrates that no one can prove whether Samuel–Kings is true and the Chronicler distorted Samuel–Kings or vice versa. An Old Testament historical book reflects the ideologies and theologies of its writer and its first readers in terms of why it was written. The focus of the study is not the Chronicler's faithful interpretation of *history* since no one can prove the historicity of the Chronicler's sources. The study demonstrates that the Chronicler read his sources faithfully as the textual sources appeared in the MT Hebrew Bible.

Comparing the Chronicler's Reading and the Asian Contextual Reading

on explaining the fate of Saul's head instead of his body. While the Chronicler's source presents the fate of Saul's *body*, which was hung on the wall of Beth-shan, the Chronicler's reading provides an explanation pertaining to Saul's *head*, which was cut off from the body and brought to the Philistines' temple of Dagon. Saul's body would have been rotten and not be convenient for being placed in the Dagon temple. Here, the Chronicler's reading does not subvert what his source meant and helps his readers understand more clearly how the Philistines treated Saul's weapons and corpse.

The Chronicler sometimes alters the wording of his biblical source to align not only with the Pentateuch but also with the Chronicler's understanding in terms of the literary context of the passage and accurately according to other biblical passages. Despite of the wording alteration, the Chronicler's reading is faithful to what his source meant according to the source's literary and historical contexts. For example, while reading 2 Sam 7–8 (// 1 Chr 17–18), the Chronicler does not include the phrase וַיהוָה הֵנִיחַ־לוֹ מִסָּבִיב מִכָּל־אֹיְבָיו ("and YHWH gave him rest from all his enemies around") in 2 Sam 7:1 and reads 2 Sam 7:11 differently as follows.

Table 17. The Chronicler's Reading of 2 Samuel 7:1–11

2 Samuel 7:1–11	1 Chronicles 17:1a–10
Verse 1:	Verse 1a:
וַיְהִי כִּי־יָשַׁב הַמֶּלֶךְ בְּבֵיתוֹ וַיהוָה הֵנִיחַ־לוֹ מִסָּבִיב מִכָּל־אֹיְבָיו	וַיְהִי כַּאֲשֶׁר יָשַׁב דָּוִיד בְּבֵיתוֹ
(Now when the king was settled in his house, *and the* LORD *had given him rest from all his enemies around him*. . .)	(Now when David settled in his house. . .)
Verse 11:	Verse 10:
וּלְמִן־הַיּוֹם אֲשֶׁר צִוִּיתִי שֹׁפְטִים עַל־עַמִּי יִשְׂרָאֵל וַהֲנִיחֹתִי לְךָ מִכָּל־אֹיְבֶיךָ וְהִגִּיד לְךָ יְהוָה כִּי־בַיִת יַעֲשֶׂה־לְּךָ יְהוָה	וּלְמִיָּמִים אֲשֶׁר צִוִּיתִי שֹׁפְטִים עַל־עַמִּי יִשְׂרָאֵל וְהִכְנַעְתִּי אֶת־כָּל־אוֹיְבֶיךָ וָאַגִּד לָךְ וּבַיִת יִבְנֶה־לְּךָ יְהוָה
(from the time that I appointed judges over my people Israel;	(from the time that I appointed judges over my people Israel;
and I will give you rest from all your enemies.	and I will subdue all your enemies.
Moreover the LORD declares to you that the LORD will make you a house.)	Moreover I declare to you that the LORD will build you a house.)

Reading the Bible as a Postexilic Biblical Author Read

Regarding the literary context of 2 Sam 7, the Chronicler omits the phrase וַיהוָה הֵנִיחַ־לוֹ מִסָּבִיב מִכָּל־אֹיְבָיו ("and the Lord had given him rest from all his enemies around him") in 2 Sam 7:1 to prevent an ambiguity with YHWH's promise to David in 2 Sam 7:11 (//1 Chr 17:10) that the Lord would give David rest from all his enemies.[100] It is obvious from 2 Sam 8, 10–11, 20, and 1 Kgs 4:24–25 that the king was not at rest from war against Israel's enemies in David's time until the time of Solomon's reign. Thus, for the phrase וַהֲנִיחֹתִי לְךָ מִכָּל־אֹיְבֶיךָ ("and I will give you rest from all your enemies," 2 Sam 7:11) in his source, the Chronicler's reading וְהִכְנַעְתִּי אֶת־כָּל־אוֹיְבֶיךָ ("and I will subdue all your enemies," 1 Chr 17:10) expounds what YHWH will do to David's enemies to give him rest. This reading of the Chronicler is faithful to not only what 2 Sam 7:11 meant but also to what 2 Sam 7–8 (// 1 Chr 17–18) meant. The king and his people will have rest when YHWH subdues all their enemies. Here, the Chronicler's reading of 2 Sam 7 is correct according to both the literary and historical contexts of his sources. Moreover, this reading of the Chronicler is also relevant to his postexilic context when the Chronicler's postexilic community was still under imperial dominion. Their enemies had not been subdued yet, and they were expecting God to deliver them from their enemies. In short, the Chronicler's contextual reading of 2 Sam 7:1–11 (// 1 Chr 17:1a–10) is faithful to his source although he altered the wording of his source.

Conclusion

If Western biblical scholarship reads the Bible primarily to discover the biblical text's original historical meaning according to its authorial intent,[101] the Chronicler's reading of biblical sources not only achieves that aim but also finds messages relevant to the Chronicler's postexilic audience. In a similar manner, practitioners of Asian contextual biblical interpretation seek to

---

100. Kalimi, *Reshaping of Ancient Israelite History*, 38–39. For a possible solution for the tension between 2 Sam 7:11 and the historical fact that God didn't give David rest from all his enemies in his lifetime, 2 Sam 7:11, read in the larger literary and historical context, was not intended to be taken *literalistically*. The Chronicler eliminated the possibility of that literalistic understanding.

101. Osborne, *Hermeneutical Spiral*, 24; Yong, *Future of Evangelical Theology*, 94–110. Dietrich and Luz refer to Western biblical scholarship in general. They observe that "Western biblical scholarship ... [is] concerned only with the reconstruction of a past with all its problems ... disconnected from the real concerns of present-day readers." Dietrich and Luz, *Bible in a World Context*, ix–x.

explain biblical passages in their original contexts and then apply the texts with relevance to present-day readers. Although the modern names of the techniques in biblical interpretation, such as the fusion of the two horizons, the abstraction ladder, or biblical theology, did not exist during the Chronicler's time, we have demonstrated in this chapter that the Chronicler did use similar techniques in his reading of biblical sources. Although the Chronicler sometimes alters the wording of his sources, his reading is still faithful to his sources and is also sound in terms of theology according to the teachings of the Torah and other biblical passages.

Comparison and Suggestions

Comparison Between the Two Biblical Readings

There are similarities and differences between Dalit biblical reading and the Chronicler's reading of biblical sources. Unlike the DBC, which is a work of biblical commentary, the Chronicler's use of biblical sources is not a commentary in the modern sense. Chapter 1 has already discussed that scholars have proposed different terms for the Chronicler's use of biblical sources, such as midrash (exegesis), interpretation, redaction, rewriting, or historiography. Despite the different terms, the Chronicler's main purpose is to actualize them appropriately and contextually for his postexilic readers. Both the Chronicler's reading and Dalit biblical reading aim to provide relevant contextualization in their readings through biblical theology, the abstraction ladder, and the fusion of the two horizons.

Although there are similarities between Dalit biblical reading and the Chronicler's reading, some different principles, methods, or techniques of interpretation have been detected. First, the method of seeking parallel situations between the original contexts of biblical passages and the present contexts of contemporary readers is frequently used by Dalit interpreters. Second, although both the Dalit interpreters and the Chronicler read biblical passages to serve their interests, the outcomes of their practices are different. To serve the interest of the Dalits, Dalit interpreters sometimes use deconstruction to negate what the Bible meant. For the Chronicler's reading, although the Chronicler sometimes alters the wording of his biblical sources, the Chronicler's interpretation remains faithful to what his biblical sources meant and is correct in terms of theology according to the Torah and the teachings of other biblical passages.

In summary, Dalit biblical interpreters and the Chronicler read biblical passages to serve their audience's concerns and interests. Dalit interpreters, however, are encouraged to use deconstruction to read the Bible to serve Dalit concerns.[102] This practice subverts and negates the meaning of the Bible. In contrast, the Chronicler's reading is faithful to his sources, though he does not always reproduce his sources verbatim. According to this viewpoint, when the Chronicler deviates from the mere reproduction of his sources, his interpretive approach would fall into the reader-centered category. Since the Chronicler's work as a whole is far from a mere reproduction, one should conclude that the Chronicler's reading largely belongs to the reader-centered category of interpretation that prioritizes contextualization. Although the Chronicler's reading sometimes alters the wording of his sources to serve his interest, his reading remains faithful to what his sources meant in accordance with their literary and historical contexts and is correct in terms of biblical theology. In this respect, the Chronicler indeed employs authored-centered interpretation and lets the Scriptures control his reading of biblical sources. Thus, it is also appropriate to claim that the Chronicler's reading falls in between the two categories of contextualization.[103]

Suggestions for Dalit Biblical Reading

Since Massey, the general editor of the DBC, calls Dalit biblical readers to imitate the Chronicler's reading method,[104] let us now suggest ways to improve the Dalit interpretive method so that it more closely imitates the Chronicler's approach. Above all, Dalit interpreters should not use deconstruction to undermine or even subvert the original meaning of a biblical passage. As we have already noted, the DBC interpreter uses deconstruction to read 2 Sam 6:6–9 and concludes that it tells a lie about God. Massey states, "All throughout the Bible we know that God is on the side of the oppressed and the weak; then how can He punish someone who did not belong to the priestly class only because he tried to save the Ark?"[105] But

---

102. John and Massey, *One Volume*, xvii; Massey, "Jeremiah," xix.

103. Carson, "Church and Mission," 220. The two categories of readings of the Bible as aforementioned: The first lets the readers' contexts determine the meaning of the Bible. The second lets the Bible be in control and attempts to address the Bible's meaning in terms of its relevance to a certain context.

104. Massey, "History," 65.

105. Massey, "1 and 2 Samuel," 440.

the Bible never states that God always supports oppressed and low-status people even if they violate God's teachings. Indeed, YHWH affirmed that the exiled and afflicted Judeans living in Egypt would be punished by the Lord because they committed sins against YHWH and followed their forefathers' sinful ways (Jer 44:1–14). Moreover, even Massey himself reads Jer 44:1–14 and admits that those Judean refugees were condemned for committing sins against the Lord.[106] In other words, the Dalit interpretation of 2 Sam 6:6–9 contradicts the teaching of the whole Bible and presents an erroneous theological message.

Rather than using deconstruction, Dalit interpreters could have used other techniques such as the abstraction ladder, biblical theology, or sought parallels between the biblical and contemporary context to achieve relevant contextualization without rejecting what the text actually meant. Using the abstraction ladder, the Dalit interpreter could point out that David, though he was a king with good intentions, committed a serious mistake in transporting the ark of YHWH on a cart and thereby failed to meet the Torah's requirements (Num 4:15, 7:9). Similarly, powerful individuals or leaders in Indian communities, even in Christian communities, despite their good intentions, sometimes make decisions that violate God's teachings. We do not know whether Uzzah acknowledged David's mistake in the mode of transportation, but we do know that Uzzah was punished by YHWH when he touched the ark, as 2 Sam 6:6–9 clearly states. Even sincere leaders can err and violate God's commandments, leading to disastrous consequences for those who follow them. Dalit Christians must not follow their leaders' decisions when such decisions are contrary to God's word. Even for the noble goal of relevant contextualization, Dalit Christians must not accept the interpretive technique of their Bible teachers when that technique undermines the authority and integrity of God's word.

Furthermore, regarding the reader-response perspective of the contextual model, Dalit interpreters could learn from the Chronicler's use of this perspective. Like the Chronicler's reading, which often alters the wording of his biblical sources but does not subvert nor distort what the sources meant, Dalit interpreters should learn from the Chronicler's way of reading biblical passages close to what the texts meant in accordance with their literary and historical contexts. Moreover, we should interpret biblical texts correctly in accordance with the Pentateuch and biblical teachings in other passages as the Chronicler did.

---

106. Massey, "Jeremiah," 838.

6

Concluding Chapter

Summary of Findings

OUR STUDY HAS DEMONSTRATED that each of the two modern reading approaches to the Bible reflects certain aspects of the Chronicler's interpretive approach as evidenced in the book of Chronicles. The following table summarizes the common and differing features of each reading approach vis-à-vis the Chronicler's reading.

Table 18. Summary of the Chronicler's Reading and the Two Modern Biblical Readings

	The Chronicler's Reading	The Postcolonial Reading	The Asian Contextual Reading (Dalit Biblical Interpretation)
Continuity with Western reading approaches	Not Applicable	Yes	Yes
Faithful to what the text meant	No and Yes[1]	No	Yes and No (when using deconstruction)
Seeking parallel situations or themes	Yes	Yes	Yes
Use of abstraction ladder	Yes	No	Yes

1. No, if we insisted that the Chronicler must read exactly all words of his sources. But the study demonstrates the answer is "Yes."

Concluding Chapter

	The Chronicler's Reading	The Postcolonial Reading	The Asian Contextual Reading (Dalit Biblical Interpretation)
Use of biblical theology	Yes	Yes[2]	Yes
Fusion of the two horizons	Yes	No	Yes

This present study finds that the Chronicler's reading of biblical sources serves as a precedent for the postcolonial reading and the Asian contextual reading of the Bible. Broadly speaking, the Chronicler reads biblical materials in ways similar to the two modern reading approaches because they all share the twofold aim of biblical reading: studying the Bible for both what the text meant and what the text means.

To study the Bible for what the text meant to its first readers, the two modern reading approaches employ Western reading strategies such as the historical-critical method and literary approaches.[3] Although practitioners of the two modern reading approaches use such strategies to investigate what the text meant, not all of them read the Bible faithfully according to what the text meant. For Dalit biblical interpretation, the general editor of the Dalit Bible Commentary series encourages Dalit interpreters to use deconstruction in reading the Bible.[4] For postcolonial biblical interpretation, its main founder holds that authority of the Christian Bible and that of the other Asian sacred texts are equal,[5] because the Bible does not contain the exclusive truth.[6] Thus, practitioners of the postcolonial approach often do not interpret the Bible faithfully according to what the text meant.

As for the Chronicler's method, one should not insist that repeating the sources exactly word for word is requisite for a faithful reading of the Chronicler's biblical sources, for such an insistence would require that the Chronicler's work could be nothing other than a patchwork of copying-and-pasting. However, the book of Chronicles is obviously a product of higher theological, hermeneutical, and literary merit than that. Although

---

2. This feature has been discussed in chapters 3 and 4. For example, Kim uses biblical theology to study uncircumcised people throughout the Old Testament. See Kim, *Decolonizing Josiah*, 230–31.

3. This feature has been discussed in chapter 3.

4. Massey, *One Volume*, xix.

5. Sugirtharajah, "From Orientalist to Post-Colonial," 25–26.

6. Sugirtharajah, "Bible and Its Asian Readers," 65; Sugirtharajah, *Exploring Postcolonial Biblical Criticism*, 123, 127.

the Chronicler's reading sometimes alters the wording of his sources, it remains faithful to his sources in accordance with their historical and literary contexts. Moreover, the Chronicler's reading is always in agreement with the teachings of the Pentateuch and other biblical texts.

In studying the Bible for what the text means to contemporary readers, Asian interpreters use strategies such as seeking parallel situations and themes between biblical and contemporary contexts, biblical theology, the abstraction ladder, and the fusion of the two horizons. The first two strategies have been employed by both modern reading approaches and the Chronicler's reading. The abstraction ladder, however, has not been used by the postcolonial reading because this approach only selects portions of the Bible that are deemed relevant to comment on. This is not surprising, as chapter 5 has demonstrated that the abstraction ladder is used when readers cannot find a biblical passage relevant and similar to the readers' context. Practitioners of the postcolonial approach do not need the abstraction ladder because they choose not to comment on biblical texts that are not relevant to their audience. The postcolonial Bible commentary series focuses on demonstrating colonial perspectives embedded in selected biblical texts to pave the way for other Bible interpreters to employ the postcolonial reading and produce more postcolonial readings of the Bible in the future.[7] Although the Chronicler's reading is also a selective reading, chapter 5 has indicated that the Chronicler also used the abstraction ladder because the Chronicler read some passages which could not be applied directly to the Chronicler's postexilic context. Regarding the fusion of the two horizons, this strategy is used by both the Chronicler and Dalit biblical readers, as they find issues relevant to their contemporary audiences within biblical texts.

Generally, the two modern reading approaches reflect closely the Chronicler's reading approach. The main difference between the Chronicler's reading and these approaches is that the Dalit biblical reading and the postcolonial reading fall into the first category of Carson's because they let contemporary readers' contexts control and determine the meaning of the Bible.[8] Concerning the Chronicler's reading, this study concludes that the Chronicler's reading falls in between the two categories. This is why the

---

7. Gossai, "Introduction," 7; Segovia, "Introduction," 68.

8. Carson discerns two kinds of readings of the Bible. The first lets the readers' contexts determine the meaning of the Bible. The second lets the Bible be in control and attempts to address the Bible's meaning in terms of its relevance to a certain context of readers. See Carson, "Church and Mission," 220.

table above indicates "No and Yes" in the box on "faithful to what the text meant" for the Chronicler's reading. The Chronicler's reading would align with Carson's first category if we insisted that the Chronicler must read exactly all words of his sources.[9] Chapters 4 and 5 have presented many instances of the Chronicler letting his contemporary contextual concerns shape how he alters the wording of his sources. On the whole, however, the Chronicler's reading actually belongs to Carson's second category, as this present work has demonstrated that the Chronicler's reading does not subvert what his biblical sources meant and is always consistent with the teachings of the Pentateuch and other biblical books.

Suggestions on How to Read the Bible to Achieve the Dual Aim

Having examined the two modern approaches to biblical interpretation, we now present suggestions on how Asian biblical interpretation can be enhanced to follow the Chronicler's reading more closely and achieve the dual aim of biblical interpretation: to read the Bible faithfully according to what the texts meant and appropriately for contemporary significance and application for readers.

Regarding Asian contextual approaches to the Bible, James Massey, the chief editor of the Dalit Bible Commentary, states that the Chronicler's reading is a good model for Dalit biblical reading and that the Chronicler's reading approach "can be fruitfully imitated to the benefit of the Dalit community."[10] However, when Massey urges Dalit biblical interpreters to use deconstruction in reading the Bible,[11] he causes Dalit biblical reading to diverge from the Chronicler's reading approach. While the Chronicler's reading is faithful to his biblical sources, Dalit biblical interpreters, in contrast, sometimes use deconstruction, which negates and subverts what the texts meant, thereby preventing them from reading biblical texts faithfully according to what the texts meant. Consequently, Dalit biblical interpretation becomes self-contradictory when its practitioners are urged both to follow the Chronicler's reading as the normative model and to use

---

9. Putting the Chronicler's reading into the first classification also applies to other instances where the Chronicler's readings seem different from what his sources meant.
10. Massey, "History," 65.
11. Massey, *One Volume*, xix.

deconstruction as a reading strategy. To be faithful to the biblical text, Dalit biblical interpreters should not practice deconstruction.

Why are Dalit interpreters urged to use deconstruction in biblical reading? The purpose is to serve the Dalit need for liberation from all kinds of oppression.[12] To achieve this purpose and follow the Chronicler's approach, Dalit biblical readers can use parallel situations between the biblical contexts and the Dalit contexts, the abstraction ladder, biblical theology, and the fusion of the two horizons, instead of deconstruction. For example, in the case of the Dalit interpreter using deconstruction to read 2 Sam 6:6–9 concerning Uzzah's death, chapter 5 has presented an illustration on how Dalit readers could have used biblical theology, the abstraction ladder, and parallel situations to read this passage both faithfully according to what the text meant and appropriately to serve the benefit of the Dalit community.[13] Let us present another illustration of using these techniques to attain a faithful and relevant reading of this passage. David's wrong action in carrying YHWH's ark on a cart is the root cause of Uzzah's death. God allowed Uzzah's death to stop David's wrongdoing. David was afraid of YHWH and thus stopped doing this wrongdoing when the punishment happened (2 Sam 6:9–10). Like King David doing wrong, Indian church leaders have erred when discriminating against Dalit church members.[14] Uzzah was certainly not an outcaste person such as a Dalit or untouchable person. Although Uzzah was not a priest, as a son of Abinadab (1 Sam 7:1; 2 Sam 6:3), he was probably a Levite.[15] Since Uzzah was allowed to accompany King David and the king's officials, if Uzzah were an Indian, he would have belonged to a high caste. God's punishment of Uzzah alerted the king and stopped his wrong action. Similarly, Dalit Christians can pray for God to intervene in any wrongdoing by their church leaders and to stop them from continuing their wrongful deeds. Dalit Christians may even beseech God to discipline the erring church people, whether they are of high or low caste, so that they will fear the Lord and cease their wrongdoing. In this way, parallel situations between biblical contexts and Dalit contexts can be used to read this passage faithfully to the text and appropriately to Dalit contexts and interests.

---

12. Massey, *One Volume*, xix.

13. See detail of the illustration in chapter 5's conclusion.

14. See details of how Dalit Christians suffer discrimination among Christian communities in chapter 3.

15. MacLeod, "Uzza."

Concluding Chapter

As for postcolonial biblical interpretation, the Chronicler's approach shares with this modern approach the feature of reading biblical texts through the lens of colonial perspectives in order to resist any kind of dominion and colonialism. However, while the Chronicler's reading is both faithful to his biblical sources and appropriate for his postexilic community's colonial context, practitioners of the postcolonial approach do not often read the Bible faithfully when they ignore the world of biblical texts.

As discussed in chapter 4, while one of the main purposes of postcolonial biblical reading is to resist all oppression, practitioners of the postcolonial approach let their postcolonial interests do violence to the biblical texts when they ignore the literary context, structure, and genre of biblical texts to serve their postcolonial ideology. To avoid this self-defeating outcome and achieve the twofold aim of biblical reading, postcolonial biblical interpreters should take the Chronicler's reading as a model. This present study proposes that practitioners of postcolonial reading must not ignore the world of the Bible and can use biblical theology and the abstraction ladder to achieve the twofold aim of reading the Bible.

For instance, while reading the book of Ruth, the postcolonial reader interprets Orpah as the central character instead of Ruth because Orpah returned to her mother's house and resisted assimilation into the Israelites.[16] Chapter 4 has demonstrated that this reading ignores the literary context of the Ruth narrative, which shows that Ruth is the central character and that Orpah is only a foil for Ruth. To achieve the twofold aim of sound biblical interpretation, the postcolonial interpreter may use biblical theology to make the point that Ruth ultimately became an ancestor of Jesus Christ (Matt 1:5). Besides Ruth, several other gentiles (non-Israelites) also became ancestors of Jesus Christ (Matt 1:1–17). Ruth and these other gentiles foreshadow God's eventual redemptive plan to incorporate gentiles as gentiles into the people of God. God's salvation is for all peoples and all nations, not only the Israelites (John 3:16; Rom 1:16–17; 11:25–26). In God's overall plan of salvation, Israelites make up only a small fraction of the people of God. In fact, gentiles comprise the majority of God's people under the new covenant. The overall population of the Jewish people throughout the world is currently around fifteen million people,[17] while the number of gentile Christians reaches into the billions. Even if one day all the Jewish people accept Jesus Christ as the Lord, the number of gentiles in the body of Christ

---

16. Donaldson, "Sign of Orpah," 142.
17. "Jewish Population Rises"; "Jewish Population By Country."

will remain the majority. In short, postcolonial interpreters can use biblical theology to see God's overall plan of redemption through the story of Ruth. This will help postcolonial readers discover that, although Ruth assimilated into the Israelites, this was only an initial step, suited for the particular historical and theological context of that ancient Israelite world. But even as such, it foreshadowed the far greater inclusion of the gentiles under the new covenant, for the New Testament clearly presents the further step in God's plan to include gentiles as gentiles into the community of God's people, namely, the church. The above redemptive-historical reading is faithful to what the Ruth narrative meant and also avoids the hegemony of the Israelites over gentiles in the Christian community as insisted by postcolonial readers. This reading uses biblical theology and the abstraction ladder, as the relationship between God and human beings is drawn from a faithful reading the book of Ruth to serve postcolonial concerns.

To sum up, this present study finds that the two modern reading approaches, aiming to achieve the twofold goal of biblical interpretation, generally reflect the Chronicler's reading as summarized in the table above. One important thing to keep in mind is that any given reading approach must not be self-contradictory. In particular, when the practitioners of Dalit biblical reading and postcolonial reading let contemporary readers' contexts determine the meaning of the Bible, their reading becomes self-conflicting (their interpretative practice conflicts with their reading purposes).

With that in mind, this study proposes a reading model that synthesizes the strengths of the Chronicler's approach and those of the two modern reading approaches as follows. Asian readers should subscribe to the foundational criterion of interpretation, namely, to read the Bible faithfully according to what the texts meant. With that original meaning of the biblical text as the foundation, interpreters may then use other tools such as biblical theology, the abstraction ladder, seeking parallels between the biblical contexts and the contemporary readers' contexts, and the fusion of the two horizons to apply the biblical texts in ways that are relevant to their contemporary contexts and interests.

To meet the foundational criterion, Asian readers may use historical-critical and literary methods, which are initial steps in the two modern reading approaches, as they have been inherited from the West. In reality, it is not easy to reconstruct authorial intent with complete accuracy since readers inevitably bring their own perspectives to their reading. As an illustration, Jerry Hwang shows that, although Robert Thomas and Walter

Kaiser both employ the same approach (grammatical-historical approach), they arrive at different interpretative outcomes on the same issue of Old Testament prophetic fulfillment.[18] The reason for this is that, although the two scholars try to read faithfully the authorial intent of biblical texts, they implicitly and inevitably bring their own information and points of view into interpretative practice.[19] But if interpreters do not try to study what biblical texts meant, they will fall into an entirely subjective reading of the Bible that is controlled by their own modern perspectives. Hence, the foundational criterion prevents contemporary readers from the entirely subjective reading of the Bible. Since Kevin Vanhoozer states that studying the original meaning of the text is "to confine the text to its own time,"[20] this present study holds that faithful readings of what the text(s) meant try to read the Bible in its historical and literary contexts, though interpretative outcomes may not be exactly the same. The attempt to meet the foundational criterion, as mentioned above, is, in the words of Jerry Hwang, an attempt to gain access to the mind of God, the ultimate author of the Bible.[21] Conversely, unfaithful readings of what the text(s) meant ignore reading the Bible in its historical and literary contexts of the text(s) or deconstructing the meaning of God's Word. Distinguishing clearly the foundational criterion of reading, i.e., being faithful to what the text meant, on the one hand, and the various purposes of reading to serve diverse Bible readers, on the other hand, is essential.

Implications of the Study

A general consensus in the publishing industry is that the Bible is the best-selling book of all time.[22] The need for reading the Bible remains great. In particular, the need for sound and relevant Asian biblical interpretation is quite significant. As Andrew Spurgeon observes, "Christianity has shifted from being a Western majority religion to a South, South-Eastern, and Eastern majority religion."[23] This present research proposes a biblical foundation for Asian biblical interpretation for the following reasons.

18. Hwang, "Authorial Intent," 24–26.
19. Hwang, "Authorial Intent," 27–28.
20. Vanhoozer, *Is There a Meaning*, 421.
21. Hwang, "Authorial Intent," 28.
22. Strauss, *How to Read the Bible*, 2.
23. Spurgeon, *Romans*, xi.

First, while Asian biblical interpreters study the Bible both for what the text meant and for what the text means, Western biblical scholars, in contrast, usually undervalue the aspect of reading for what the text means to readers today.[24] Amos Yong observes that Western biblical scholars emphasize exegetical issues related to "what the text meant" as *historical* investigation, but view considerations of "what the text means" as *theological* study.[25] Consequently, this has caused tensions for many Asian biblical interpreters who are influenced by Western scholarship but are seeking to read the Bible both for what the text meant and for what the text means.[26] A key goal of this present work is to encourage biblical interpreters and ordinary Christians to read the Bible with the twofold aim because this interpretive approach is biblically based, as demonstrated in the book of Chronicles. Moreover, this present work has identified specific reading strategies that Asian biblical interpreters can employ to produce commentaries and other publications that achieve the twofold aim of biblical interpretation without reading into the texts (eisegesis).

Second, this present research has demonstrated a continuity between the Western and the Asian ways of biblical interpretation because both prevailing Asian interpretive approaches actually employ Western reading methods in the initial and foundational steps of a holistic interpretation. As the general editor of the Asia Bible commentary series has stated, the Asia Bible Commentary series is not an attempt to reject Western biblical studies or to spurn Western influences since "a house divided cannot stand."[27] Likewise, this present work supports the complementary partnership between Western biblical interpretation and Asian biblical reading.

For Further Research

The Chronicler's use and reading of biblical sources belongs to the field of inner-biblical interpretation.[28] Besides the Chronicler's use and reading of biblical sources as demonstrated in his work, there are other

---

24. DeSilva, *Introduction*, xix.
25. Yong, *Future of Evangelical Theology*, 94.
26. Yong, *Future of Evangelical Theology*, 110.
27. Spurgeon, *Romans*, xi.
28. For more details on this field, see Zakovitch, "Inner-Biblical Interpretation," 27–63; Menn, "Inner-Biblical Exegesis," 55–79.

Concluding Chapter

instances of inner-biblical interpretation such as Ezra-Nehemiah's use of the Pentateuch,[29] Joel's use of other Scriptures,[30] Paul's use of the Old Testament,[31] and so on. This study has compared and contrasted the Chronicler's reading with the two Asian biblical interpretive models. Other questions worthy of further study remain. They include: To what extent is the use of Scripture by other biblical authors similar to or different from the Chronicler's approach in terms of reading Scripture for both what the text meant and what the text means? How does the use of Scripture by other biblical authors compare to the two modern approaches of biblical interpretation? Further research on these questions can produce significant contributions to advance the fields of inner-biblical exegesis, biblical intertextuality, and biblical hermeneutics. This present investigation is but an initial step and hopefully also a helpful step forward for those disciplines.

---

29. Pakkala, "Quotations and References."
30. Strazicich, *Joel's Use of Scripture*.
31. Porter and Stanley, *As It Is Written*.

Bibliography

Abadie, Philippe. "From the Impious Manasseh (2 Kings 21) to the Convert Manasseh (2 Chronicles 33): Theological Rewriting by the Chronicler." In *The Chronicler as Theologian: Essays in Honor of Ralph W. Klein*, edited by M. Patrick Graham et al., 89–104. Journal for the Study of the Old Testament Supplement Series 371. New York: T&T Clark, 2003.

Ackroyd, Peter R. *I and II Chronicles, Ezra, Nehemiah: Introduction and Commentary*. London: SCM, 1973.

———. "The Chronicler as Exegete." *Journal for the Study of the Old Testament* 2 (Apr. 1977) 2–32.

———. *The Chronicler in His Age*. Journal for the Study of the Old Testament Supplement Series 101. Sheffield: Sheffield Academic, 1991.

Agosto, Efraín. "The Letter to the Philippians." In *A Postcolonial Commentary on the New Testament Writings*, edited by Fernando F. Segovia and R. S. Sugirtharajah, 281–93. The Bible and Postcolonialism. New York: T&T Clark, 2009.

Aleaz, K. P. "Some Features of a Dalit Theology." *The Asia Journal of Theology* 18:1 (Apr. 2004) 146–67.

Alexander, Philip S. "Retelling the Old Testament." In *It Is Written: Scripture Citing Scripture*, edited by Barnabas Lindars et al., 99–121. Cambridge: Cambridge University Press, 1988.

Anderson, Arnold A. *2 Samuel*. Word Biblical Commentary 11. Waco, TX: Word, 1989.

———. *Psalms 73–150*. Repr. The New Century Bible Commentary. Grand Rapids: Eerdmans, 1992.

Arnold, Bill T. *1 and 2 Samuel: The NIV Application Commentary*. The NIV Application Commentary. Grand Rapids: Zondervan, 2003.

Auld, A. Graeme. *Kings Without Privilege: David and Moses in the Story of the Bible's Kings*. Edinburgh: T&T Clark, 1994.

———. *Life in Kings: Reshaping the Royal Story in the Hebrew Bible*. Ancient Israel and Its Literature 30. Atlanta: SBL, 2017.

———. "What Was the Main Source of the Books of Chronicles?" In *The Chronicler as Author: Studies in Text and Texture*, edited by Matt Patrick Graham and Steven Linn McKenzie, 91–99. Journal for the Study of the Old Testament Supplement Series 263. Sheffield: Sheffield Academic, 1999.

Bibliography

Aune, David E. *Greco-Roman Literature and the New Testament: Selected Forms and Genres*. Sources for Biblical Study 21. Atlanta: Scholars, 1988.

Balentine, Samuel E. "Foreword." In *Postcolonial Commentary and the Old Testament*, edited by Hemchand Gossai, 8–9. New York: T&T Clark, 2018.

Barbiero, Gianni. "Psalm 132: A Prayer of 'Solomon.'" *The Catholic Biblical Quarterly* 75:2 (Apr. 2013) 239–58.

Beentjes, Pancratius C. "Psalms and Prayers in the Book of Chronicles." In *Psalms and Prayers: Papers Read at the Joint Meeting of the Society of Old Testament Study and Het Oudtestamentische Werkgezelschap in Nederland en België, Apeldoorn August 2006*, edited by Bob Brecking and Eric Peels, 9–44. Leiden: Brill, 2007.

———. *Tradition and Transformation in the Book of Chronicles*. Studia Semitica Neerlandica 52. Leiden: Brill, 2008.

Ben Zvi, Ehud. "When the Foreign Monarch Speaks." In *The Chronicler as Author: Studies in Text and Texture*, edited by Matt Patrick Graham and Steven Linn McKenzie, 209–28. Journal for the Study of the Old Testament Supplement Series 263. Sheffield: Sheffield Academic, 1999.

Berlin, Adele. *Poetics and Interpretation of Biblical Narrative*. Repr. Winona Lake, IN: Eisenbrauns, 1999.

———. "Psalms in the Book of Chronicles." In *Shai Le-Sarah Japhet: Studies in the Bible, Its Exegesis, and Its Languages*, edited by Moshe Bar-Asher et al., 21–36. Jerusalem: Bialik Institute, 2007.

Berquist, Jon L. "Constructions of Identity in Postcolonial Yehud." In *Judah and the Judeans in the Persian Period*, edited by Oded Lipschitz and Manfred Oeming, 53–66. Winona Lake, IN: Eisenbrauns, 2006.

Boda, Mark J. *1–2 Chronicles*. Edited by Philip Wesley Comfort. Cornerstone Biblical Commentary 5a. Carol Stream, IL: Tyndale, 2005.

———. "Identity and Empire, Reality and Hope in the Chronicler's Perspective." In *Community Identity in Judean Historiography: Biblical and Comparative Perspectives*, edited by Gary N Knoppers and Kenneth A Ristau, 249–72. Winona Lake, IN: Eisenbrauns, 2009.

Boer, Roland, ed. *Postcolonialism and the Hebrew Bible: The Next Step*. Society of Biblical Literature. Semeia Studies 70. Atlanta: SBL, 2013.

Booij, Th. "Psalm 132: Zion's Well-Being." *Biblica* 90:1 (2009) 75–83.

Braun, Roddy. *1 Chronicles*. Word Biblical Commentary 14. Waco, TX: Word, 1986.

Brenner-Idan, Athalya, and Archie C. C. Lee, eds. *Samuel, Kings and Chronicles*. Texts @ Contexts. London: T&T Clark, 2017.

Brenner-Idan, Athalya, and Gale A. Yee, eds. *Joshua and Judges*. Texts @ Contexts. Minneapolis: Fortress, 2013.

Brenner-Idan, Athalya, et al., eds. *The Five Scrolls*. Texts @ Contexts. London: Bloomsbury T&T Clark, 2019.

———. *Genesis*. Texts @ Contexts. Minneapolis: Fortress, 2010.

Broadbent, Ralph. "One Step Beyond or One Step Too Far? Towards a Postcolonial Future for European Biblical and Theological Scholarship." In *Postcolonial Interventions: Essays in Honor of R. S. Sugirtharajah*, edited by Tat-siong Benny Liew, 296–309. Sheffield: Sheffield Phoenix, 2009.

Brooke, George J. "Psalms 105 and 106 at Qumran." *Revue de Qumran* 14:2 (Dec. 1989) 267–92.

Bibliography

———. "Rewritten Bible." In *Encyclopedia of the Dead Sea Scrolls*, edited by Lawrence H. Schiffman and James C. VanderKam, 2:777–81. New York: Oxford University Press, 2000.

Bubash, Paul. "Dalit Theology and Spiritual Oppression: A Call to Holiness in a Universal Church." *Journal of Theta Alpha Kappa* 38:2 (2014) 36–51.

Butler, Trent C. "A Forgotten Passage from a Forgotten Era (1 Chr 16:8–36)." *Vetus Testamentum* 28:2 (Apr. 1978) 142–50.

Campbell, Antony F. "Martin Noth and the Deuteronomistic History." In *The History of Israel's Traditions: The Heritage of Martin Noth*, edited by Steven L. McKenzie and M. Patrick Graham, 31–62. Journal for the Study of the Old Testament Supplement Series 182. Sheffield: Sheffield Academic, 1994.

Carson, D. A. "Biblical Theology." In *Dictionary of Biblical Criticism and Interpretation*, edited by Stanley E. Porter, 35–41. New York: Routledge, 2007.

———. "Church and Mission: Reflections on Contextualization and the Third Horizon." In *The Church in the Bible and the World: An International Study*, edited by D. A. Carson, 213–57. Eugene, OR: Wipf & Stock, 2002.

Carter, Warren. "The Gospel of Matthew." In *A Postcolonial Commentary on the New Testament Writings*, edited by Fernando F. Segovia and R. S. Sugirtharajah, 69–104. The Bible and Postcolonialism. New York: T&T Clark, 2009.

Carvalho, Corrine L. "Psalm 132: A Methodological Inquiry." *The Catholic Biblical Quarterly* 57:4 (Oct. 1995) 643–54.

Chia, Philip P. "Biblical Studies in a Rising Asia." In *The Future of the Biblical Past: Envisioning Biblical Studies on a Global Key*, edited by Roland Boer and Fernando F. Segovia, 81–96. Society of Biblical Literature Semeia Studies. Atlanta: SBL, 2012.

———. "Differences and Difficulties: Biblical Interpretation in the Southeast Asian Context." In *Ways of Being, Ways of Reading: Asian American Biblical Interpretation*, edited by Mary F. Foskett and Jeffrey K. Kuan, 45–59. St. Louis: Chalice, 2006.

———. "On Naming the Subject: Postcolonial Reading of Daniel 1." In *The Postcolonial Biblical Reader*, edited by R. S. Sugirtharajah, 171–85. Malden, MA: Blackwell, 2006.

Ching, Wong Wai. "Postcolonialism." In *Dictionary of Third World Theologies*, edited by Virginia Fabella and R. S. Sugirtharajah, 169–70. Maryknoll, NY: Orbis, 2000.

Cho, E. S. "Josianic Reform in the Deuteronomistic History Reconstructed in the Light of Factionalism and Use of Royal Apology." PhD diss., The Graduate Theological Union, 2002.

Clarke, Sathianathan. "Dalit Theology." In *Dictionary of Third World Theologies*, edited by Virginia Fabella and R. S. Sugirtharajah, 64–65. Maryknoll, NY: Orbis, 2000.

———. "Viewing the Bible Through the Eyes and Ears of Subalterns in India." *Biblical Interpretation* 10:3 (2002) 245–66.

Coote, Robert B., and Mary P. Coote. *Power, Politics, and the Making of the Bible: An Introduction*. Minneapolis: Fortress, 1990.

Cross, Frank Moore. *Canaanite Myth and Hebrew Epic: Essays in the History of the Religion of Israel*. Cambridge: Harvard University Press, 1973.

Crowell, Bradley L. "Postcolonial Studies and the Hebrew Bible." *Currents in Biblical Research* 7:2 (Feb. 2009) 217–44.

Curtis, Edward Lewis, and Albert Alonzo Madsen. *A Critical and Exegetical Commentary on the Books of Chronicles*. International Critical Commentary. Edinburgh: T&T Clark, 1976.

Bibliography

Davies, Philip R. *The History of Ancient Israel: A Guide for the Perplexed*. London: Bloomsbury T&T Clark, 2015.

———. *In Search of "Ancient Israel": A Study in Biblical Origins*. London: Bloomsbury T&T Clark, 2015.

———. *Rethinking Biblical Scholarship: Changing Perspectives 4*. Copenhagen International Seminar. London: Routledge, 2014.

DeSilva, David Arthur. *An Introduction to the New Testament: Contexts, Methods, and Ministry Formation*. 2nd ed. Downers Grove, IL: InterVarsity, 2018.

Dharamraj, Havilah. "On the Doctrine of Scripture: An Asian Conversation." In *Asian Christian Theology: Evangelical Perspectives*, edited by Timoteo D. Gener and Stephen T. Pardue, 39–60. Carlisle, UK: Langham Global Library, 2019.

Dietrich, Walter, and Ulrich Luz, eds. *The Bible in a World Context: An Experiment in Contextual Hermeneutics*. Grand Rapids: Eerdmans, 2002.

Dillard, Raymond B. *2 Chronicles*. Word Biblical Commentary 15. Waco, TX: Word, 1987.

Dirksen, Peter B. *1 Chronicles*. Edited by Cornelis Houtman. Historical Commentary on the Old Testament. Leuven: Peeters, 2005.

Donaldson, Laura E. "The Sign of Orpah: Reading Ruth through Native Eyes." In *Ruth and Esther: A Feminist Companion to the Bible*, edited by Athalya Brenner, 130–44. Sheffield: Sheffield Academic, 1999.

Duke, Rodney K. "Chronicles, Books Of." In *Dictionary of the Old Testament: Historical Books*, edited by Bill T. Arnold and H. G. M. Williamson, 161–81. Downers Grove, IL: IVP Academic, 2005.

———. "Recent Research in Chronicles." *Currents in Biblical Research* 8:1 (Oct. 2009) 10–50.

Erickson, Diandra Chretain. "Judges." In *Postcolonial Commentary and the Old Testament*, edited by Hemchand Gossai, 122–41. New York: T&T Clark, 2018.

Evans, Carl D. "Manasseh, King of Judah." In *The Anchor Bible Dictionary*, edited by David Noel Freedman, 4:496–99. New York: Doubleday, 1992.

Fetalsana-Apura, Lily. *A Filipino Resistance Reading of Joshua 1:1–9*. International Voices in Biblical Studies 9. Atlanta: SBL, 2019.

Foskett, Mary F., and Jeffrey K. Kuan, eds. *Ways of Being, Ways of Reading: Asian American Biblical Interpretation*. St. Louis: Chalice, 2006.

Fowl, Stephen E. *Theological Interpretation of Scripture*. Cascade Companions. Eugene, OR: Cascade, 2009.

Gadamer, Hans-Georg. *Truth and Method*. Translated by Joel Weinsheimer and Donald G. Marshall. 2nd rev. ed. London: Continuum, 2004.

García-Alfonso, Cristina. "Judges: Subaltern Women." In *Postcolonial Commentary and the Old Testament*, edited by Hemchand Gossai, 106–21. New York: T&T Clark, 2018.

Garland, David E. *Mark: The NIV Application Commentary*. The NIV Application Commentary. Grand Rapids: Zondervan, 1996.

Giffone, Benjamin D. "Sit at My Right Hand: The Chronicler's Portrait of the Tribe of Benjamin in the Social Context of Yehud." PhD diss., University of Stellenbosch, 2014.

Gnanadason, Aruna. "We Dare to Be Pregnant and Give Birth to Our Dreams Again: Searching Our Faith and Rediscovering Our Power—and Our History of Resistance and of Struggle." *Church & Society* 86:5 (May 1996) 62–68.

Bibliography

Gnanavaram, M. "Hermeneutical Issues in Dalit Theology." *Arasaradi Journal of Theological Reflection* 11:1–2 (Dec. 1998) 118–28.

Goodman, William R. "Esdras, First Book of." In *The Anchor Bible Dictionary*, edited by David Noel Freedman, 2:609–11. New York: Doubleday, 1992.

Gossai, Hemchand. "Introduction." In *Postcolonial Commentary and the Old Testament*, edited by Hemchand Gossai, 1–7. New York: T&T Clark, 2018.

———, ed. *Postcolonial Commentary and the Old Testament*. New York: T&T Clark, 2018.

Grabbe, Lester L., ed. *A History of the Jews and Judaism in the Second Temple Period*. Vol. 1. Library of Second Temple Studies 47. New York: T&T Clark, 2004.

———. "The 'Persian Documents' in the Book of Ezra: Are They Authentic?" In *Judah and the Judeans in the Persian Period*, edited by Oded Lipschitz and Manfred Oeming, 531–70. Winona Lake, IN: Eisenbrauns, 2006.

Grayson, Albert Kirk. *Assyrian and Babylonian Chronicles*. Texts from Cuneiform Sources. Winona Lake, IN: Eisenbrauns, 2000.

Grol, Harm van. "1 Chronicles 16: The Chronicler's Psalm and Its View of History." In *Rewriting Biblical History*, edited by Jeremy Corley and Harm van Grol, 97–121. Berlin: de Gruyter, 2011.

Hatcher, Mark J. "Biblical Interpretation and the Shaping of Religious Worlds: A Study of Bible Study for Critical Contextualization." PhD diss., Asbury Theological Seminary, 2004.

Hebden, Keith. *Dalit Theology and Christian Anarchism*. Ashgate New Critical Thinking in Religion, Theology, and Biblical Studies. Farnham, Surrey, UK: Routledge, 2011.

Hill, A. E. "History of Israel 3: United Monarchy." In *Dictionary of the Old Testament: Historical Books*, edited by Bill T. Arnold and H. G. M. Williamson, 442–52. Downers Grove, IL: IVP Academic, 2005.

Ho, Craig Y. S. "Conjectures and Refutations: Is 1 Samuel xxxi 1–13 Really the Source of 1 Chronicles x 1–12?" *Vetus Testamentum* 45:1 (Jan. 1995) 82–106.

Ho, Huang Po. "Micah." In *Global Bible Commentary*, edited by Daniel Patte, 295–300. Nashville: Abingdon, 2004.

Hoekema, Alle G. "Genesis 1–11 from an Indonesian Perspective: A New Commentary by Gerrit Singgih." *Exchange* 42:3 (2013) 215–31.

Hoglund, Kenneth G. "The Material Culture of the Persian Period and the Sociology of the Second Temple Period." In *Second Temple Studies III: Studies in Politics, Class, and Material Culture*, edited by Philip R. Davies and John M. Halligan, 14–18. Journal for the Study of the Old Testament Supplement Series 340. London: Sheffield Academic, 2002.

Hordern, Richard. "Systematic Theology and Biblical Interpretation: Hermeneutical Questions in Light of Liberation Theology." PhD diss., Union Theological Seminary, 1983.

Hossfeld, Frank-Lothar, and Erich Zenger. *Psalms 3: A Commentary on Psalms 101–150*. Edited by Klaus Baltzer. Translated by Linda M. Maloney. Hermeneia. Minneapolis: Fortress, 2011.

Hwang, Jerry. "Authorial Intent and Reader Response: A Journey in Evangelical Hermeneutics with E. D. Hirsch, Jr." *Journal of Asian Evangelical Theology* 18:1 (Mar. 2014) 19–31.

"India's Dalits Still Fighting Untouchability." *BBC News*, June 27, 2012. https://www.bbc.com/news/world-asia-india-18394914.

Bibliography

Jaffrelot, Christophe. "Dalits Still Left Out." *The Indian Express* (blog), Feb. 18, 2016. https://indianexpress.com/article/opinion/columns/rohith-vemula-discrimination-against-dalits-still-left-out/.

Janzen, David. *Chronicles and the Politics of Davidic Restoration: A Quiet Revolution*. Library of Hebrew Bible/Old Testament Studies 655. New York: Bloomsbury T&T Clark, 2017.

Japhet, Sara. *I and II Chronicles: A Commentary*. The Old Testament Library. Louisville: Westminster John Knox, 1993.

———. *From the Rivers of Babylon to the Highlands of Judah: Collected Studies on the Restoration Period*. Winona Lake, IN: Eisenbrauns, 2006.

———. *The Ideology of the Book of Chronicles and Its Place in Biblical Thought*. Winona Lake, IN: Eisenbrauns, 2009.

Jayachitra, L. "Jesus and Ambedkar: Exploring Common Loci for Dalit Theology and Dalit Movements." In *Dalit Theology in the Twenty-First Century: Discordant Voices, Discerning Pathways*, edited by Sathianathan Clarke et al., 121–36. New Delhi: Oxford University Press, 2010.

Jesurathnam, J. "Contextual Reading of Psalm 22: With Special Reference to Indian Christian Dalit Interpretations." PhD diss., University of Edinburgh, 2006.

"Jewish Population By Country 2021." World Population Review. https://worldpopulationreview.com/country-rankings/jewish-population-by-country.

"Jewish Population Rises to 15.2 Million Worldwide." The Jewish Agency for Israel, Sept. 5, 2021. https://www.jewishagency.org/jewish-population-5782.

John, T. K., and James Massey, eds. *One Volume Dalit Bible Commentary: New Testament*. New Delhi: Center for Dalit/Subaltern Studies, 2010.

Johnson, Ben J. M. Review of *The Deuteronomic History and the Book of Chronicles: Scribal Works in an Oral World* by Raymond F. Person. *Journal of the Evangelical Theological Society* 54:1 (Mar. 2011) 137–39.

Johnstone, William. *1 Chronicles 1–2 Chronicles 9: Israel's Place Among the Nations*. Journal for the Study of the Old Testament Supplement Series 253. Sheffield: Sheffield Academic, 1997.

———. *Chronicles and Exodus: An Analogy and Its Application*. Journal for the Study of the Old Testament Supplement Series 275. Sheffield: Sheffield Academic, 1998.

Jonker, Louis C. "'My Wife Must Not Live in King David's Palace' (2 Chr 8:11): A Contribution to the Diachronic Study of Intermarriage Traditions in the Hebrew Bible." *Journal of Biblical Literature* 135:1 (2016) 35–47.

Kaiser, Walter C. *Toward Rediscovering the Old Testament*. Grand Rapids: Zondervan, 1991.

Kalimi, Isaac. *An Ancient Israelite Historian: Studies in the Chronicler, His Time, Place, and Writing*. Studia Semitica Neerlandica 46. Assen: Royal Van Gorcum, 2005.

———. *The Reshaping of Ancient Israelite History in Chronicles*. Winona Lake, IN: Eisenbrauns, 2005.

Kalimi, Isaac, and James D. Purvis. "King Jehoiachin and the Vessels of the Lord's House in Biblical Literature." *The Catholic Biblical Quarterly* 56:3 (July 1994) 449–57.

Keener, Craig S., and M. Daniel Carroll R., eds. *Global Voices: Reading the Bible in the Majority World*. Peabody, MA: Hendrickson, 2013.

Keil, Carl Friedrich, and Franz Delitzsch. *1 and 2 Kings, 1 and 2 Chronicles*. Peabody, MA: Hendrickson, 1996.

Bibliography

Keiter, Sheila Tuller. "The Jewish Understanding of the Scriptural Solomon Narrative: Examining Biblical, Classical Rabbinic, and Major Medieval Responses." PhD diss., UCLA, 2018.

Kessler, John. "Persia's Loyal Yahwists: Power Identity and Ethnicity in Achaemenid Yehud." In *Judah and the Judeans in the Persian Period*, edited by Oded Lipschitz and Manfred Oeming, 91–122. Winona Lake, IN: Eisenbrauns, 2006.

Kim, Daniel Eunseung. "From Rest to Rest: A Comparative Study of the Concept of Rest in Mesopotamian and Israelite Literature." PhD diss., University of Aberdeen, 2015.

Kim, Uriah Y. *Decolonizing Josiah: Toward a Postcolonial Reading of the Deuteronomistic History*. The Bible in the Modern World 5. Sheffield: Sheffield Phoenix, 2005.

———. *Identity and Loyalty in the David Story: A Postcolonial Reading*. Hebrew Bible Monographs 22. Sheffield: Sheffield Phoenix, 2008.

Kim, Uriah Y., and Seung Ai Yang, eds. *T&T Clark Handbook of Asian American Biblical Hermeneutics*. T&T Clark Handbooks. New York: T&T Clark, 2019.

Kinukawa, Hisako. "Mark." In *Global Bible Commentary*, edited by Daniel Patte, 367–78. Nashville: Abingdon, 2004.

Klein, Ralph W. "Psalms in Chronicles." *Currents in Theology and Mission* 32:4 (Aug. 2005) 264–75.

Klein, Ralph W., and Paul D. Hanson. *2 Chronicles: A Commentary*. Hermeneia. Philadelphia: Fortress, 2012.

Klein, Ralph W., and Thomas Krüger. *1 Chronicles: A Commentary*. Hermeneia. Minneapolis: Fortress, 2006.

Klein, William W., et al. *Introduction to Biblical Interpretation*. 3rd ed. Grand Rapids: Zondervan, 2017.

Kleinig, John W. *The Lord's Song: The Basis, Function, and Significance of Choral Music in Chronicles*. Journal for the Study of the Old Testament Supplement Series 156. Sheffield: JSOT, 1993.

Klink, Edward W., and Darian R. Lockett. *Understanding Biblical Theology: A Comparison of Theory and Practice*. Grand Rapids: Zondervan, 2012.

Knauth, R. J. D. "Israel." In *Dictionary of the Old Testament: Historical Books*, edited by Bill T. Arnold and H. G. M. Williamson, 514–20. Downers Grove, IL: IVP Academic, 2005.

Knoppers, Gary N. *I Chronicles 1–9: A New Translation with Introduction and Commentary*. The Anchor Bible. New York: Doubleday, 2003.

———. *I Chronicles 10–29: A New Translation with Introduction and Commentary*. Anchor Yale Bible Commentaries 12B. New York: Doubleday, 2004.

———. "Nehemiah and Sanballat: The Enemy Without or Within?" In *Judah and the Judeans in the Fourth Century B.C.E*, edited by Oded Lipschitz, Gary N. Knoppers, and Rainer Albertz, 305–31. Winona Lake, IN: Eisenbrauns, 2007.

———. *Two Nations Under God: The Deuteronomistic History of Solomon and the Dual Monarchies*. Vol. 2: *The Reign of Jeroboam, the Fall of Israel, and the Reign of Josiah*. Harvard Semitic Monographs 53. Atlanta: Scholars, 1994.

Kuan, Jeffrey K. "Asian Biblical Interpretation." In *Dictionary of Biblical Interpretation*, edited by John H. Hayes, 1:70–77. Nashville: Abingdon, 1999.

Kumari, B. M. Leela. "The Untouchable 'Dalits' of India and Their Spiritual Destiny." In *Another World Is Possible: Spiritualities and Religions of Global Darker Peoples*, edited by Dwight N. Hopkins and Marjorie Lewis, 9–19. Cross Cultural Theologies. London: Routledge, 2009.

Kwok Pui-lan. *Introducing Asian Feminist Theology*. Introductions in Feminist Theology. Sheffield: Sheffield Academic, 2000.

———. "Making the Connections: Postcolonial Studies and Feminist Biblical Interpretation." In *The Postcolonial Biblical Reader*, edited by R. S. Sugirtharajah, 45–64. Malden, MA: Blackwell, 2006.

Laato, Antti. "Psalm 132: A Case Study in Methodology." *The Catholic Biblical Quarterly* 61:1 (Jan. 1999) 24–33.

———. "Psalm 132 and the Development of the Jerusalemite/Israelite Royal Ideology." *The Catholic Biblical Quarterly* 54:1 (Jan. 1992) 49–66.

Laffey, Alice. "Leviticus." In *Postcolonial Commentary and the Old Testament*, edited by Hemchand Gossai, 27–56. New York: T&T Clark, 2018.

Lallawmzuala, K. "Issues in Biblical Interpretation: Towards a Tribal Biblical Hermeneutics." In *Bible Readings from the Northeast India Context*, edited by Takatemjen, 1–16. Nagaland, India: North East India Society for Biblical Studies, 2014.

Lau, Peter H. W. "Back Under Authority: Towards an Evangelical Postcolonial Hermeneutic." *Tyndale Bulletin* 63:1 (2012) 131–44.

Law, David R. *Historical Critical Method: A Guide for the Perplexed*. T&T Clark Guides for the Perplexed. London: Continuum, 2012.

Lee, Archie C. C. "Cross-Textual Hermeneutics and Identity in Multi-Scriptural Asia." In *Christian Theology in Asia*, edited by Sebastian C. H. Kim, 179–204. Cambridge: Cambridge University Press, 2008.

———. "Lamentations." In *Global Bible Commentary*, edited by Daniel Patte, 226–33. Nashville: Abingdon, 2004.

Lee, Moonjang. "Asian Biblical Interpretation." In *Dictionary for Theological Interpretation of the Bible*, edited by Kevin J. Vanhoozer et al., 68–72. Grand Rapids: Baker Academic, 2005.

———. "A Post Critical Reading of the Bible as a Religious Text." *The Asia Journal of Theology* 14:2 (Oct. 2000) 272–85.

Levin, Yigal. *The Chronicles of the Kings of Judah: 2 Chronicles 10–36; A New Translation and Commentary*. London: T&T Clark, 2018.

Liew, Tat-Siong Benny. *What Is Asian American Biblical Hermeneutics? Reading the New Testament*. Intersections. Asian and Pacific American Transcultural Studies. Honolulu: University of Hawaii Press, 2008.

Lim Chin Ming Stephen. "Asian Biblical Hermeneutics as Multicentric Dialogue: Towards a Singaporean Way of Reading." PhD diss., King's College London, 2016.

Loader, J. A. "Redaction and Function of the Chronistic 'Psalm of David.'" *Old Testament Society of South Africa* 19 (1976) 69–75.

Lowry, Rich. *The Reforming Kings: Cult and Society in First Temple Judah*. Edited by David J. A. Clines and Philip R. Davies. Journal for the Study of the Old Testament Supplement Series 120. Sheffield: JSOT, 1991.

MacLeod, M. A. "Uzza." In *New Bible Dictionary*, edited by D. R. W. Wood and I. Howard Marshall, 1220. Downers Grove, IL: InterVarsity, 1996.

Marbury, Herbert R. "Reading Persian Dominion in Nehemiah: Multivalent Language, Co-option, Resistance, and Cultural Survival." In *Focusing Biblical Studies: The Crucial Nature of the Persian and Hellenistic Periods*, edited by Jon L. Berquist and Alice Hunt, 158–76. New York: T&T Clark, 2014.

Bibliography

Massey, James. "1 and 2 Samuel." In *One Volume Dalit Bible Commentary: Old Testament*, edited by James Massey, 420–50. New Delhi: Centre for Dalit/Subaltern Studies, 2015.

———. "Dalits in India: Key Problems/Issues and Role of Religion." In *Another World Is Possible: Spiritualities and Religions of Global Darker Peoples*, edited by Dwight N. Hopkins and Marjorie Lewis, 20–32. Cross Cultural Theologies. London: Routledge, 2009.

———. *Down Trodden: The Struggles of India's Dalits for Identity, Solidarity, and Liberation*. The Risk Book Series 79. Geneva: WCC Publications, 1997.

———. "History and Community Formation: A Model for Dalits." In *One Volume Dalit Bible Commentary: Old Testament*, edited by James Massey, 65–67. New Delhi: Centre for Dalit/Subaltern Studies, 2015.

———. "Jeremiah." In *One Volume Dalit Bible Commentary: Old Testament*, edited by James Massey, 815–40. New Delhi: Centre for Dalit/Subaltern Studies, 2015.

———, ed. *One Volume Dalit Bible Commentary: Old Testament*. New Delhi: Centre for Dalit/Subaltern Studies, 2015.

———. "Relevance of 1 and 2 Samuel for Dalits." In *One Volume Dalit Bible Commentary: Old Testament*, 51–55. New Delhi: Centre for Dalit/Subaltern Studies, 2015.

———. *Towards Dalit Hermeneutics: Rereading the Text, the History, and the Literature*. Delhi: ISPCK, 1994.

McConville, J. G. *I and II Chronicles*. The Daily Study Bible-Old Testament. Philadelphia: Westminster, 1984.

McKenzie, Steven L. *1–2 Chronicles*. Abingdon Old Testament Commentaries 13–14. Nashville: Abingdon, 2004.

———. "The Chronicler as Redactor." In *The Chronicler as Author: Studies in Text and Texture*, edited by Matt Patrick Graham and Steven Linn McKenzie, 70–90. Journal for the Study of the Old Testament Supplement Series 263. Sheffield: Sheffield Academic, 1999.

McKnight, Edgar V. "Reader-Response Criticism." In *To Each Its Own Meaning: An Introduction to Biblical Criticisms and Their Application*, edited by Steven L. McKenzie and Stephen R. Haynes, 230–52. Revised and expanded. Louisville: Westminster John Knox, 1999.

Melanchthon, Monica J. "Dalits, Bible, and Method." SBL Forum, Oct. 2005. https://www.sbl-site.org/publications/article.aspx?ArticleId=459.

———. "Song of Songs." In *Global Bible Commentary*, edited by Daniel Patte, 180–85. Nashville: Abingdon, 2004.

———. "Unleashing the Power Within: The Bible and Dalits." In *The Future of the Biblical Past: Envisioning Biblical Studies on a Global Key*, edited by Fernando F. Segovia and Roland Boer, 49–65. Society of Biblical Literature Semeia Studies. Atlanta: SBL, 2012.

Mendels, Doron. "Palestine Among the Empires from the 4th to the 1st Century BCE: Impact and Reaction." In *Symbiosis, Symbolism, and the Power of the Past: Canaan, Ancient Israel, and Their Neighbors from the Late Bronze Age Through Roman Palaestina*, edited by William G. Dever and Seymour Gitin, 145–52. Winona Lake, IN: Eisenbrauns, 2003.

Menn, Esther. "Inner-Biblical Exegesis in the Tanak." In *A History of Biblical Interpretation*, edited by Alan J. Hauser and Duane Frederick Watson, 1:55–79. Grand Rapids: Eerdmans, 2003.

Bibliography

Milner, Murray. *Status and Sacredness: A General Theory of Status Relations and an Analysis of Indian Culture*. New York: Oxford University Press, 1994.

Mitchell, Christine. "The Testament of Darius (DNa/DNb) and Constructions of Kings and Kingship in 1–2 Chronicles." In *Political Memory in and After the Persian Empire*, edited by Jason M. Silverman and Caroline Waerzeggers, 363–80. Ancient Near East Monographs 13. Atlanta: SBL, 2015.

Mitchell, Lynette, and Diana Edelman. "Chronicles and Local Greek Histories." In *What Was Authoritative for Chronicles?*, edited by Ehud Ben Zvi and Diana Vikander Edelman, 229–52. Winona Lake, IN: Eisenbrauns, 2011.

Moon, Cyris Hee-Suk. "Culture in the Bible and the Culture of the Minjung." *Ecumenical Review* 39:2 (Apr. 1987) 180–86.

Moore, Stephen D. "The Revelation to John." In *A Postcolonial Commentary on the New Testament Writings*, edited by Fernando F. Segovia and R. S. Sugirtharajah, 436–54. The Bible and Postcolonialism. New York: T&T Clark, 2009.

Moore, Stephen D., and Fernando F. Segovia. "Postcolonial Biblical Criticism: Beginnings, Trajectories, Intersections." In *Postcolonial Biblical Criticism: Interdisciplinary Intersections*, edited by Fernando F. Segovia and Stephen D. Moore, 1–22. The Bible and Postcolonialism. New York: T&T Clark, 2007.

Murphy, Frederick J. "Second Temple Judaism." In *The Blackwell Companion to Judaism*, edited by Jacob Neusner and Alan Avery-Peck, 58–77. Chichester: Blackwell, 2000.

Nakanose, Shigeyuki. *Josiah's Passover: Sociology and the Liberating Bible*. The Bible & Liberation Series. Maryknoll, NY: Orbis, 1993.

Nelavala, Surekha. "Smart Syrophoenician Woman: A Dalit Feminist Reading of Mark 7:24–31." *The Expository Times* 118:2 (Nov. 2006) 64–69.

Noth, Martin. *The Chronicler's History*. Journal for the Study of the Old Testament Supplement Series 50. Sheffield: JSOT, 1987.

Olson, Dennis T. "Literary and Rhetorical Criticism." In *Methods for Exodus*, edited by Thomas B. Dozeman, 13–54. Methods in Biblical Interpretation. Cambridge: Cambridge University Press, 2010.

Oommen, George. "The Emerging Dalit Theology: A Historical Appraisal." *Religion Online*. https://www.religion-online.org/article/the-emerging-dalit-theology-a-historical-appraisal/.

Osborne, Grant R. *Hermeneutical Spiral: A Comprehensive Introduction to Biblical Interpretation*. Downers Grove, IL: InterVarsity, 2006.

Padilla, C. Rene. "The Interpreted Word: Reflections on Contextual Hermeneutics." In *A Guide to Contemporary Hermeneutics: Major Trends in Biblical Interpretation*, edited by Donald K. McKim, 297–308. Eugene, OR: Wipf & Stock, 1999.

Pagolu, Augustine. "Reading the Bible in an Asian Context." *Journal of Asian Evangelical Theology* 17:1 (Mar. 2013) 5–21.

Pakkala, Juha. "The Quotations and References of the Pentateuchal Laws in Ezra-Nehemiah." In *Changes in Scripture: Rewriting and Interpreting Authoritative Traditions in the Second Temple Period*, edited by Hanne von Weissenberg et al., 193–222. Beihefte zur Zeitschrift für die Alttestamentliche Wissenschaft 419. Berlin: de Gruyter, 2011.

Patte, Daniel, ed. *Global Bible Commentary*. Nashville: Abingdon, 2004.

Payne, J. Barton. "1 and 2 Chronicles." In *The Expositor's Bible Commentary*, edited by Frank E. Gaebelein, 4:303-564. Grand Rapids: Zondervan, 1990.

Bibliography

Perdue, Leo G., and Warren Carter. *Israel and Empire: A Postcolonial History of Israel and Early Judaism*. Edited by Coleman A Baker. London: Bloomsbury T&T Clark, 2015.

Person, Raymond F. *The Deuteronomic History and the Book of Chronicles: Scribal Works in an Oral World*. Ancient Israel and Its Literature 6. Atlanta: SBL, 2010.

———. "The Problem of 'Literary Unity' from the Perspective of the Study of Oral Traditions." In *Empirical Models Challenging Biblical Criticism*, edited by Raymond F. Person and Robert Rezetko, 217–38. Ancient Israel and Its Literature 25. Atlanta: SBL, 2016.

Po Ho, Huang. *Embracing the Household of God: A Paradigm Shift from Anthropocentric Tradition to Creation Responsibility in Doing Theology*. PTCA Study Series 7. Tainan, Taiwan: Programme for Theology and Cultures in Asia, 2014.

Porter Stanley E., and Christopher D. Stanley. *As it Is Written: Studying Paul's Use of Scripture*. Society of Biblical Literature Symposium Series 50. Atlanta: SBL, 2008.

Premnath, Devadasan N. "Biblical Interpretation in India: History and Issues." In *Ways of Being, Ways of Reading: Asian American Biblical Interpretation*, edited by Mary F. Foskett and Jeffrey K. Kuan, 1–16. St. Louis: Chalice, 2006.

Prior, John. "Ecclesiastes." In *Global Bible Commentary*, edited by Daniel Patte, 175–79. Nashville: Abingdon, 2004.

Ragui, Taimaya. "Mapping Hermeneutical Trends in North East India." *Journal of Asian Evangelical Theology* 20:1 (Mar. 2016) 45–59.

Raja, A. Maria Arul. "Creating Caste-Free Humanity in Dialogue with Genesis." In *One Volume Dalit Bible Commentary: Old Testament*, edited by James Massey, 3–14. New Delhi: Centre for Dalit/Subaltern Studies, 2015.

———. "A Dialogue Between Dalits and the Bible." *Journal of Dharma: Dharmaram Journal of Religions and Philosophies* 24:1 (Mar. 1999) 40–50.

———. "Genesis." In *One Volume Dalit Bible Commentary: Old Testament*, edited by James Massey, 150–88. New Delhi: Centre for Dalit/Subaltern Studies, 2015.

———. "Reading the Bible from a Dalit Location: Some Points for Interpretation." *Voices from the Third World* 23:1 (June 2000) 77–91.

Rajkumar, Peniel. *Dalit Theology and Dalit Liberation: Problems, Paradigms and Possibilities*. Ashgate New Critical Thinking in Religion, Theology, and Biblical Studies. Farnham, Surrey, UK: Ashgate, 2010.

———. "'How' Does the Bible Mean? The Bible and Dalit Liberation in India." *Political Theology* 11:3 (July 2010) 410–30.

Rawat, Ramnarayan S., and K. Satyanarayana, eds. *Dalit Studies*. Durham: Duke University Press, 2016.

Reimer, Reg. *Vietnam's Christians: A Century of Growth in Adversity*. Pasadena, CA: William Carey Library, 2011.

Rezetko, Robert. "Dating Biblical Hebrew: Evidence from Samuel-Kings and Chronicles." In *Biblical Hebrew: Studies in Chronology and Typology*, edited by Ian Young, 215–50. Journal for the Study of the Old Testament Supplement Series 369. New York: T&T Clark, 2003.

———. "'Late' Common Nouns in the Book of Chronicles." In *Reflection and Refraction: Studies in Biblical Historiography in Honour of A. Graeme Auld*, edited by Robert Rezetko et al., 379–418. Supplements to Vetus Testamentum 113. Leiden: Brill, 2007.

Richter, Sandra L. Review of *The Deuteronomic History and the Book of Chronicles: Scribal Works in an Oral World*, by Raymond F. Person, Jr. *Biblical Interpretation* 21:3 (2013) 421–23.

Bibliography

Ristau, Kenneth A. "Reading and Rereading Josiah." In *Community Identity in Judean Historiography: Biblical and Comparative Perspectives*, edited by Gary N. Knoppers and Kenneth A. Ristau, 219–48. Winona Lake, IN: Eisenbrauns, 2009.

Robinson, Haddon. "The Heresy of Application." *Christianity Today*, 1997. https://www.christianitytoday.com/pastors/1997/fall/7l4020.html.

Sakenfeld, Katharine D. *The Meaning of Hesed in the Hebrew Bible: A New Inquiry*. Repr. Eugene, OR: Wipf & Stock, 2002.

Sano, Roy I. "Shifts in Reading the Bible: Hermeneutical Moves among Asian Americans." *Semeia* 90 (2002) 105–18.

Schniedewind, William M. "The Chronicler as an Interpreter of Scripture." In *The Chronicler as Author: Studies in Text and Texture*, edited by Matt Patrick Graham and Steven Linn McKenzie. Journal for the Study of the Old Testament Supplement Series 263. Sheffield: Sheffield Academic, 1999.

———. *The Word of God in Transition: From Prophet to Exegete in the Second Temple Period*. Journal for the Study of the Old Testament Supplement Series 197. Sheffield: Sheffield Academic, 1995.

Schnittjer, Gary Edward. *Old Testament Use of Old Testament: A Book-by-Book Guide*. Grand Rapids: HarperCollins Christian, 2021.

Schreiner, David B. "Double Entendre, Disguised Verbal Resistance, and the Composition of Psalm 132." *Bulletin for Biblical Research* 28:1 (2018) 20–33.

Segovia, Fernando F. "Introduction: Configurations, Approaches, Findings, Stances." In *A Postcolonial Commentary on the New Testament Writings*, edited by Fernando F. Segovia and R. S. Sugirtharajah, 1–68. The Bible and Postcolonialism. London: T&T Clark, 2009.

Segovia, Fernando F., and R. S. Sugirtharajah, eds. *A Postcolonial Commentary on the New Testament Writings*. The Bible and Postcolonialism. New York: T&T Clark, 2009.

Shipp, R. Mark. "'Remember His Covenant Forever': A Study of the Chronicler's Use of the Psalms." *Restoration Quarterly* 35 (1993) 29–39.

Smend, Rudolf. "The Law and the Nations: A Contribution to Deuteronomistic Tradition History." In *Reconsidering Israel and Judah: Recent Studies on the Deuteronomistic History*, edited by Gary N. Knoppers and J. G. McConville, 95–111. Sources for Biblical and Theological Study 8. Winona Lake, IN: Eisenbrauns, 2000.

Snyman, Gerrie. "The Chronicler's Narrative on Saul (1 Chron. 10:1–14): A Decolonial Reading of Chronicles." In *Postcolonial Commentary and the Old Testament*, edited by Hemchand Gossai, 157–94. New York: T&T Clark, 2018.

Soares-Prabhu, George M. "Two Mission Commands: An Interpretation of Matthew 28:16–20 in the Light of a Buddhist Text." *Biblical Interpretation* 2:3 (Nov. 1994) 264–82.

Spurgeon, Andrew B. *Romans: A Pastoral and Contextual Commentary*. Asia Bible Commentary. Carlisle, UK: Langham Global Library, 2020.

———. *Twin Cultures Separated by Centuries: An Indian Reading of 1 Corinthians*. Carlisle, UK: Langham Global Library, 2016.

Stendahl, Krister. "Biblical Theology, Contemporary." In *The Interpreter's Dictionary of the Bible*, edited by George Arthur Buttrick, 1:418–32. Nashville: Abingdon, 1962.

Stern, Ephraim. "The Religious Revolution in Persian-Period Judah." In *Judah and the Judeans in the Persian Period*, edited by Oded Lipschitz and Manfred Oeming, 199–208. Winona Lake, IN: Eisenbrauns, 2006.

Bibliography

Stone, Michael Edward, and Frank Moore Cross. *Fourth Ezra: A Commentary on the Book of Fourth Ezra*. Hermeneia. Minneapolis: Fortress, 1994.
Strauss, Mark L. *How to Read the Bible in Changing Times: Understanding and Applying God's Word Today*. Grand Rapids: Baker, 2011.
Strazicich, John. *Joel's Use of Scripture and the Scripture's Use of Joel: Appropriation and Resignification in Second Temple Judaism and Early Christianity*. Biblical Interpretation Series 82. Leiden: Brill, 2007.
Sugirtharajah, R. S. *Asian Biblical Hermeneutics and Postcolonialism: Contesting the Interpretations*. The Biblical Seminar 64. Sheffield: Sheffield Academic, 1999.
———. *The Bible and Asia*. Cambridge: Harvard University Press, 2013.
———. *The Bible and Empire: Postcolonial Explorations*. Cambridge: Cambridge University Press, 2005.
———. "The Bible and Its Asian Readers." *Biblical Interpretation* 1:1 (Feb. 1993) 54–66.
———. *The Bible and the Third World: Precolonial, Colonial, and Postcolonial Encounters*. Cambridge: Cambridge University Press, 2001.
———. *Exploring Postcolonial Biblical Criticism: History, Method, Practice*. Malden, MA: Wiley-Blackwell, 2012.
———. "From Orientalist to Post-Colonial: Notes on Reading Practices." *The Asia Journal of Theology* 10:1 (Apr. 1996) 20–27.
———. "Introduction, and Some Thoughts on Asian Biblical Hermeneutics." *Biblical Interpretation* 2:3 (1994) 251–63.
———. "The Master Copy: Postcolonial Notes on the King James Bible." In *The King James Version at 400: Assessing Its Genius as Bible Translation and Its Literary Influence*, edited by David G. Burke et al., 499–518. Atlanta: SBL, 2013.
———. "Matthew 5–7: The Sermon on the Mount and India." In *Global Bible Commentary*, edited by Daniel Patte, 361–66. Nashville: Abingdon, 2004.
———, ed. *The Postcolonial Bible*. The Bible and Postcolonialism 1. Sheffield: Sheffield Academic, 1998.
———. "Postcolonial Biblical Interpretation." In *Voices from the Margin: Interpreting the Bible in the Third World*, edited by R. S. Sugirtharajah, 64–84. 3rd ed. Maryknoll, NY: Orbis, 2006.
———, ed. *The Postcolonial Biblical Reader*. Malden, MA: Blackwell, 2006.
———. *Postcolonial Criticism and Biblical Interpretation*. Oxford: Oxford University Press, 2002.
———. *Postcolonial Reconfigurations: An Alternative Way of Reading the Bible and Doing Theology*. London: SCM, 2003.
———. *Troublesome Texts: The Bible in Colonial and Contemporary Culture*. Bible in the Modern World 17. Sheffield: Sheffield Phoenix, 2008.
———. "Tsunami, Text, and Trauma: Hermeneutics after the Asian Tsunami." *Biblical Interpretation* 15:2 (2007) 117–34.
———, ed. *Voices from the Margin: Interpreting the Bible in the Third World*. 3rd ed. Maryknoll, NY: Orbis, 2006.
Swarup, Paul. "Zechariah." In *Global Bible Commentary*, edited by Daniel Patte, 318–24. Nashville: Abingdon, 2004.
Taehang Ohm, Andrew. "Two Faces of Manasseh: A Comparative Reading of 2 Kings 21:1–18 and 2 Chronicles 33:1–20." PhD diss., University of Aberdeen, 2008.

Bibliography

Talshir, Zipora. "The Three Deaths of Josiah and the Strata of Biblical Historiography (2 Kings xxiii 29-30, 2 Chronicles xxxv 20-25, 1 Esdras i 23-31)." *Vetus Testamentum* 46:2 (Apr. 1996) 213-36.

Tate, Marvin E. *Psalms 51-100*. Word Biblical Commentary 20. Waco, TX: Word, 2000.

Tate, W. Randolph. *Handbook for Biblical Interpretation: An Essential Guide to Methods, Terms, and Concepts*. Grand Rapids: Baker Academic, 2012.

Thiselton, Anthony C. *New Horizons in Hermeneutics: The Theory and Practice of Transforming Biblical Reading*. Grand Rapids: Zondervan, 1998.

———. *The Two Horizons: New Testament Hermeneutics and Philosophical Description with Special Reference to Heidegger, Bultmann, Gadamer, and Wittgenstein*. Grand Rapids: Eerdmans, 1980.

Thompson, John Arthur. *1, 2 Chronicles*. The New American Commentary 9. Nashville: Broadman & Holman, 1994.

Tompkins, Jane P., ed. *Reader-Response Criticism: From Formalism to Post-Structuralism*. Baltimore: Johns Hopkins University Press, 1980.

Tov, Emanuel. *Textual Criticism of the Hebrew Bible*. 2nd rev. ed. Minneapolis: Fortress, 2001.

Van Seters, John. *In Search of History: Historiography in the Ancient World and the Origins of Biblical History*. New Haven: Yale University Press, 1983. Repr., Winona Lake, IN: Eisenbrauns, 1997.

VanderKam, James C. *An Introduction to Early Judaism*. Grand Rapids: Eerdmans, 2001.

Vanhoozer, Kevin J. *Is There a Meaning in This Text? The Bible, the Reader, and the Morality of Literary Knowledge*. Grand Rapids: Zondervan, 1998.

———, ed. *Theological Interpretation of the Old Testament: A Book by Book Survey*. Grand Rapids: Baker Academic, 2008.

Villanueva, Federico G. "The Challenge of Asian Biblical Interpretation Today." *Journal of Asian Evangelical Theology* 18:1 (Mar. 2014) 5-18.

———. *Psalms 1-72: A Pastoral and Contextual Commentary*. Asia Bible Commentary. Carlisle, UK: Langham Global Library, 2016.

Wallace, Howard N. "What Chronicles Has to Say About Psalms." In *The Chronicler as Author: Studies in Text and Texture*, edited by Matt Patrick Graham and Steven Linn McKenzie, 267-91. Journal for the Study of the Old Testament Supplement Series 263. Sheffield: Sheffield Academic, 1999.

Warhurst, Amber. "Merging and Diverging: The Chronicler's Integration of Material from Kings, Isaiah, and Jeremiah in the Narratives of Hezekiah and the Fall of Judah." PhD diss., University of St Andrews, 2011.

Watts, James W. *Psalm and Story: Inset Hymns in Hebrew Narrative*. Journal for the Study of the Old Testament Supplement Series 139. Sheffield: JSOT, 1992.

Weingart, K. "What Makes an Israelite an Israelite? Judean Perspectives on the Samarians in the Persian Period." *Journal for the Study of the Old Testament* 42:2 (2017) 155-75.

Welch, Adam Cleghorn. *The Work of the Chronicler: Its Purpose and Its Date*. London: Oxford University Press, 1939.

Wellhausen, Julius. *Prolegomena to the History of Ancient Israel*. Repr. Eugene, OR: Wipf & Stock, 2003.

Westphal, Merold. "The Philosophical/Theological Response." In *Biblical Hermeneutics: Five Views*, edited by Stanley E. Porter and Beth M. Stovell, 160-73. Spectrum Multiview Book. Downers Grove, IL: IVP Academic, 2012.

Bibliography

Williams, Joshua E. Review of *The Deuteronomic History and the Book of Chronicles: Scribal Works in an Oral World*, by Raymond F. Person, Jr. *Southwestern Journal of Theology* 55:2 (2013) 316–17.
Williamson, H. G. M. *1 and 2 Chronicles*. Repr. New Century Bible Commentary. Grand Rapids: Eerdmans, 1987.
———. *Israel in the Books of Chronicles*. Cambridge: Cambridge University Press, 1977.
Wilson, Gerald H. *The Editing of the Hebrew Psalter*. Society of Biblical Literature Dissertation Series 76. Chico, CA: Scholars, 1985.
Wilson, Ian Douglas. "Yahweh's Anointed: Cyrus, Deuteronomy's Law of the King, and Yehudite Identity." In *Political Memory in and After the Persian Empire*, edited by Jason M. Silverman and Caroline Waerzeggers, 325–61. Ancient Near East Monographs 13. Atlanta: SBL, 2015.
Wintle, Brian, ed. *South Asia Bible Commentary: A One-Volume Commentary on the Whole Bible*. Grand Rapids: Zondervan, 2015.
Wong, Angela Wai Ching. "Esther." In *Global Bible Commentary*, edited by Daniel Patte, 135–40. Nashville: Abingdon, 2004.
Wood, D. R. W., and I. Howard Marshall, eds. *New Bible Dictionary*. 3rd ed. Downers Grove, IL: InterVarsity, 1996.
Wright, Christopher J. H. *The Mission of God: Unlocking the Bible's Grand Narrative*. Westmont: InterVarsity, 2013.
Wu, Jackson. *Reading Romans with Eastern Eyes: Honor and Shame in Paul's Message and Mission*. Downers Grove, IL: IVP Academic, 2019.
Yee, Gale A. "Postcolonial Biblical Criticism." In *Methods for Exodus*, edited by Thomas B. Dozeman, 193–234. Methods in Biblical Interpretation. Cambridge: Cambridge University Press, 2010.
Yeo, Khiok-Khng. "1 Thessalonians." In *Global Bible Commentary*, edited by Daniel Patte, 500–503. Nashville: Abingdon, 2004.
———. "Culture and Intersubjectivity as Criteria for Negotiating Meanings in Cross-Cultural Interpretations." In *The Meanings We Choose: Hermeneutical Ethics, Indeterminacy and the Conflict of Interpretations*, edited by Charles H. Cosgrove, 81–100. The Bible in the Twenty-First Century Series 5. New York: T&T Clark, 2004.
———. "On Confucian Xin and Pauline Pistis." *Sino-Christian Studies* 2 (Dec. 2006) 25–51.
———. *What Has Jerusalem to Do with Beijing? Biblical Interpretation from a Chinese Perspective*. Harrisburg, PA: Trinity Press International, 1998.
Yim, TaeSoo. "Reading the Bible from an Asian Perspective." *Madang: Journal of Contextual Theology in East Asia* 1:1 (June 2004) 25–48.
Yong, Amos. *The Future of Evangelical Theology: Soundings from the Asian American Diaspora*. Downers Grove, IL: IVP Academic, 2014.
Young, Ian, et al. *Linguistic Dating of Biblical Texts*. 2 vols. London: Equinox, 2008.
Zakovitch, Yair. "Inner-Biblical Interpretation." In *A Companion to Biblical Interpretation in Early Judaism*, edited by Matthias Henze, 27–63. Grand Rapids: Eerdmans, 2012.
Zerbe, Gordon, and Muriel Orevillo-Montenegro. "The Letter to the Colossians." In *A Postcolonial Commentary on the New Testament Writings*, edited by Fernando F. Segovia and R. S. Sugirtharajah, 294–303. The Bible and Postcolonialism. New York: T&T Clark, 2009.

www.ingramcontent.com/pod-product-compliance
Lightning Source LLC
Chambersburg PA
CBHW071452150426
43191CB00008B/1322